A Gardener Touched with Genius

The Life of Luther Burbank

Also by Peter Dreyer

THE FUTURE OF TREASON

A BEAST IN VIEW

A GARDENER TOUCHED WITH GENIUS

The Life of Luther Burbank

by Peter Dreyer

Coward, McCann & Geoghegan, Inc. New York

36559

In memory of
Walter Lafayette Howard (1872–1949)
and
George Harrison Shull (1874–1954),
who have in large part made this book possible

My measure for all subjects of science as of events is their impression on the soul. That mind is best which is most impressionable . . . But sensibility does not exhaust our idea of it. That is only half. Genius is not a lazy angel contemplating itself and things. It is insatiable for expression. Thought must take the stupendous step of passing into realization.

—Ralph Waldo Emerson,
The Natural History of Intellect

Contents

Illustrations follow page 130

Preface

. . . I, on my side, require of every writer, first or last, a simple account of his own life, and not merely what he has heard of other men's lives; some such account as he would send to his kindred from a distant land; for if he has lived sincerely it must have been in a distant land to me.

—Henry David Thoreau, *Walden*

"That is good," Burbank noted in his autobiography. "I will write of this Harvest of the Years of mine to you, my kindred, as though from a distant land!" It was of the utmost importance to him to have lived sincerely. He sought unremittingly to prove, not so much to others as to himself, that he had done so. In the end he had probably not quite succeeded, and Thoreau's irony (to which he was very likely blind) is no more than appropriate.

Despite the facade of simplicity that deceived critics and customers alike, he was an immensely intricate character. It was his

11

great misfortune that he was compelled to pursue the seedsman's trade to support the experimental work to which he by
choice devoted his life. It was his misfortune, too, that he possessed a mysterious charisma that drew sycophants and eulo-
gists like bees to nectar, and was never able to resist playing to
their adulation.

Burbank should be seen both in the long perspective of horticultural history and against the backdrop of his own times.
The science of genetics was born and grew to maturity during
his working career, and it was ultimately by geneticists that he
was unfairly judged. In a sense this book is in the nature of a
vindication. We can afford to be kinder to him than he was to
himself, and kinder, certainly, than the contemporary scientists
who dismissed him in silence.

In his own lifetime millions of words were written about him,
hardly any of them critical. To this day there has been only one
book published that assesses him in terms of his real merits and
real faults, Walter L. Howard's monograph *Luther Burbank: A
Victim of Hero Worship*. Appearing as a double number of the
periodical *Chronica Botanica* in the winter of 1945, it never
reached the general public, and is now hard to come by. It was
written, says Howard's son, Professor Walter E. Howard, "to
keep Burbank from becoming a victim of hero worship, with
the scientific community discrediting his contributions."[1] Its author, then Emeritus Professor of Pomology and late Director of
the College of Agriculture of the University of California at
Davis, had spent ten years privately researching Burbank's
plant contributions (these results were separately published as
Bulletin Number 691 of the University of California Agricultural Experiment Station at Berkeley) and had come to realize
the degree to which his genuine achievements had been
eclipsed by his overinflated popular reputation. The legend ob-
scured the man. Horticultural scientists, the only ones in a position to judge his work, came to dismiss him as no more than a
commercial breeder with a talent for publicity and something
of a fraud into the bargain. As the geneticist Donald F. Jones
observed, reviewing Howard's study:

Any writer about Burbank and his work has the difficult task of sifting the exaggerated claims and misstatements arising both from Burbank's uncritical estimate of his work and the publications of writers who knew little or nothing about the scientific aspects of the subject. On the other hand, there is the overly-critical attitude of specialists in the seed and nursery trade and professional geneticists and biologists, who properly resent and distrust the nonsense about Burbank that has been too prevalent in the popular press. The background and setting of the conflicting interests that swirled about Burbank during the latter part of his life make the real accomplishments of a long life of hard work begin to stand out.[2]

Now curiously enough, Jones (for many years head of the Department of Genetics at the Connecticut Agricultural Experiment Station) had himself written a book about Burbank during the latter's lifetime. Although giving him his due—uniquely so in acknowledging his priority in reporting true-breeding species hybrids—it seemed excessively critical to lay readers and failed to find a publisher (according to Howard, who had the manuscript before him when *he* wrote) because Jones, although trying

> to be fair and honest in his criticisms as he would in reviewing the work of a colleague . . . made the mistake—unconsciously, no doubt—of instilling into his otherwise impeccable statements slight traces of institutional venom. One publisher . . . offered to hold the manuscript and use it *after* Burbank's death. The author naturally refused this proposal as it would have defeated his purpose in writing . . . which was to dethrone a popular idol.[3]

Such was the atmosphere of controversy—by now so long dissipated that few people have any clear idea of who and what he was, let alone critical opinions—that surrounded the name Burbank during the twenties.

He remains a difficult subject for the biographer. Notwithstanding Howard's labors, even the list of his plant introductions—numbering somewhere between eight hundred and a thousand over a working life of some fifty years—remains inconclusive. The work of the horticulturist may extend over decades, experiments taking many years to complete. Dates are frequently obscure or contradictory. And in any case, as Thoreau—a writer always close to Burbank's heart—observed in his *Journal:*

> In a true history or biography, of how little consequence those events of which so much is commonly made! For example, how difficult for a man to remember in what towns or houses he has lived, or when! Yet one of the first steps of his biographer will be to establish these facts, and he will thus give an undue importance to many of them. I find in my Journal that the most important events in my life, if recorded at all, are not dated.

In writing Burbank's biography I have been fortunate enough to be able to refer to two primary sources not available to Jones and Howard. These are the correspondence of Professor Edward J. Wickson, for many years his friend and best promoter, and the papers of George H. Shull, one of the outstanding American plant geneticists of the day, who observed him at work on behalf of the Carnegie Institution of Washington from 1906 to 1911. Shull, too, had planned to write a book about Burbank, and no one was ever better qualified to do so, but it was never completed.

I have also, of course, had the use of Jones's manuscript (its author is, interestingly enough, linked with Shull as cooriginator of the pure line method of corn breeding which revolutionized American agriculture) and of Walter L. Howard's very extensive collection of what he called "Burbankia," much of which he was himself able to use only indirectly. Howard does not seem to have known of the existence of the Wickson papers. He was denied access to Shull's notes because the latter, though his project had been shelved, never entirely gave up the idea of bringing out a book of his own on the subject. "Shull," Howard says despondently, "could give us more information about Burbank than any man living, but he will not talk."

Since that time there has been only one other biography: Ken and Pat Kraft's *Luther Burbank: The Wizard and the Man* (Meredith Press, 1967). The Krafts painstakingly researched anecdotal and other material in Burbank's hometown of Santa Rosa, but they do not appear to have been aware of any of the aforementioned sources. Though informative on many points, their account is therefore largely without a critical base, and relies too heavily on the careless eulogies published during the first quarter of the century.

So I believe that the essential elements of the Burbank story are here brought together for the first time, almost fifty years after his death. That it can be told at all is substantially due to the work of Walter L. Howard, who was as indefatigable in researching Burbank's life as he was in cataloging his plant introductions, and of George Shull, an impartial and penetrating observer in the best scientific tradition: this book is accordingly dedicated to their memory. In writing it I have come to appreciate them both as men and as scientists: it has been a privilege to work in their company.

I am indebted to the Director of the Bancroft Library of the University of California at Berkeley, and to the Howard family, for permission to make use of the materials assembled by Professor Walter L. Howard; to the Library of the University of California at Davis for access to the correspondence of Professor E. J. Wickson; to the Carnegie Institution of Washington, the American Philosophical Society, Philadelphia, and the Shull family for their assistance and the use of the papers of George Harrison Shull; and to the Connecticut Agricultural Experiment Station for permission to quote from Donald F. Jones's manuscript "The Life and Work of Luther Burbank." Extracts from Burbank's autobiography, written with Wilbur Hall, are quoted by permission of the Houghton Mifflin Company.

Robert Ornduff, Professor of Botany and Director of the Botanical Garden at the University of California, Berkeley; Dr. Peter R. Day, head of the Department of Genetics at the Connecticut Agricultural Experiment Station; the National Program Staff of the U.S. Department of Agriculture, Agricultural

Research Service at Beltsville, Maryland; Leroy C. Johnson, manager of the Institute of Forest Genetics at Placerville, California; Dr. Peter Green of the University of Texas at Austin; Messrs. Stark Brothers Nurseries & Orchards Company, Louisiana, Missouri; the California Historical Society; Tim Huston of the Santa Rosa-Sonoma County Free Public Library; Earle E. Coleman of the University Archives, Princeton, and many others, including my mother, Greta E. Dreyer, have provided invaluable help. Needless to say, none of them is in any way responsible for such errors as may appear here.

Finally, my deepest thanks are due to Robert Briggs, Peggy Brooks, and Peter H. Matson for their continuing support, moral and otherwise, in writing this book, as well as to Roberta Phillips, who besides providing assistance in innumerable shapes and forms has argued convincingly against a preface any longer than this one.

ONE

The Sage of Santa Rosa

ONE JULY AFTERNOON, early this century, a remarkable expedition, including in its number three world-renowned scientists, made its way to the modest Santa Rosa home of Luther Burbank. The local people were not in the least surprised. Burbank was, after all, one of the best-known men in California—perhaps even in America—and curious folk, scientists included, often came to visit him. There was always someone wanting to talk about his work, to shake him by the hand and tell him of their admiration, or simply to catch a glimpse of him in his famous experimental gardens. The reputation of the great "plant wizard" had spread far and wide. That was easy enough to understand. Here, apparently, was a man who turned out wonderful new fruits, vegetables and flowers in a seemingly unending stream. There were Burbank potatoes in every pot, Burbank plums at every table. And this, they said, was just the beginning, with rumor now of miracles like the white blackberry,

17

the stoneless prune and a spineless cactus that would open up the deserts to stock raising. Farfetched gossip even told of oddities like coreless apples, seedless tomatoes and melons, huskless corn, green carnations and a black—or perhaps it was blue?—rose. No telling how he did it either. He was one of a kind. Most Santa Rosans were secretly a little in awe of him, though proud to be his neighbors. Singlehandedly he had put their little town on the map. And for all that he was such a down-to-earth, regular sort of fellow. He had the common touch and genius besides. It was a combination that was hard to beat.

There was in him, too, more than a little of the "prophet of the soul" Emerson had spoken of. And, like Emerson, the public loved a prophet of the soul. Behind his back (despite his ready sense of humor, it did not amuse him) they probably repeated the old joke: "Luther Burbank crossed the milkweed with the eggplant and produced an omelet." Joking aside, though, they were impressed. He was not without honor in his own country. Small wonder, then, that even foreigners—and important foreigners at that—came all the way here to see him.

The leader of the visiting group, a big, heavily built man, a full head taller than Burbank, with graying hair and beard, was the great Dutch botanist, Hugo de Vries, one of the three researchers who in 1900 had independently rediscovered and confirmed the laws of heredity so painstakingly worked out more than thirty years before by the Austrian monk, Gregor Mendel (1822–1884). On the basis of these laws the whole science of genetics was to arise, with all its multifarious and continuing implications for mankind. Ten years before Mendel's long-forgotten papers came to his attention, De Vries had published his own theory of "intracellular pangenesis," in which he proposed the idea that hereditary particles corresponding to the different adult characters must exist in all the cells of the organism—a remarkable foreshadowing of the modern concept of the gene. "These factors are the units which the science of heredity has to investigate," he insisted. "Just as physics and chemistry are based on molecules and atoms, even so the biological sciences must penetrate to these units in order to explain by their combinations the phenomena of the living world."[1] In his latest book, titled *Die Mutationstheorie,* he developed a new conception of the nature of species—which he viewed as complexes of discontinuous, independent and independently inheritable traits, subject to variations which took place by leaps and bounds. These variations he called "mutations," adding a significant new concept to the vocabulary of science and supplying the Darwinian theory of evolution with an element it had hitherto lacked. De Vries' view of mutation was inevitably subject to considerable modification in later years, but when that happened, it was as a result of a line of inquiry he himself had proposed, when, in a speech delivered at the opening of the Station for Experimental Evolution at Cold Spring Harbor, Long Island, he suggested using X-rays and radium to alter the hereditary particles in the germ cells. His was a mind much in advance of its time. "If the stature of de Vries has steadily increased as genetics has developed," writes L. C. Dunn, Emeritus Professor of Zoology at Columbia University, "it is perhaps in part because genetics grew to resemble the view he entertained in the 1880s—that the variety of the organic world was maintained through the properties and activities of material units which were the prime operators in the transmission of heredity, in evolution, and in development."[2]

With De Vries, the most important member of the group from Burbank's point of view, were two other prominent scientists. Svante Arrhenius of Sweden was one of the founders of modern physical chemistry. The previous year he had been awarded a Nobel Prize for his theory of electrolytic dissociation—which was based in part on De Vries' experimental observations. Jacques Loeb, a German-born biologist who was now a professor at Berkeley, was famous for his controversial experiments in artificial parthenogenesis. Loeb's work was also of considerable significance to the question of the inheritance of characters. In 1899 he had successfully caused sea urchin larvae to develop from unfertilized eggs by controlled changes in their environment, later going on to produce and raise parthenogenetic frogs to sexual maturity. Guiding the party were E., J. Wickson and W. J. V. Osterhout, two other professors from the University of California, both of them friends of Burbank's.

In addition to participating in the dedication of the Station for Experimental Evolution and giving a course of lectures at the University of California, De Vries had come to the United States to observe the evening primrose *Oenothera lamarckiana* in its native habitat. This was the plant which had led him to the concept of independent factors in heredity and ultimately to Mendel and the theory of mutations.

But he was also intensely interested in the new varieties of fruit being produced in California. "One reason which, more than others, made me accept an invitation to visit California," he admitted, "was the prospect of making the personal acquaintance of Luther Burbank." If any man living could shed light on the manner in which new traits came about, it would, he felt, be Burbank. He had hoped to meet him at a congress of hybridologists in London a few years before, but the American had as usual advanced the demands of his work as an excuse for not attending. Now, at the busiest time of the year for the experimental hybridizer, De Vries feared that he might have no time for visitors.

When it suited him, however, Burbank was prepared to make time. It was being dragged off his own ground, to congresses, conventions and lecture halls, where he might—heaven forfend!—be called upon to speak, that he hated. And if the importunities of the ill-informed and interfering bored and irritated him, he was more than flattered by the attentions of so select a company as this. Here in Santa Rosa, surrounded by the visible achievements of almost thirty years' labor, he felt none of the diffidence that had plagued him all his life. Loeb, Arrhenius and De Vries were names to conjure with, luminaries of the scientific firmament by any standard. His secret ambition was to be considered one of them—to be accepted into that great fraternity which had inherited the mantle of his boyhood hero, Darwin. With this meeting it seemed as though the long-delayed approbation of the hierarchy of science was finally being granted. He was fifty-five. In his own field—the development and introduction of new varieties of useful plant—he was second to no one. He must have thought it none too soon.

For their part the visitors found in their host an outwardly unassuming sort of man, short, spare, a little stoop-shouldered, but with sparkling blue eyes and a lively sense of fun. The house, where he lived with his mother, sister and one servant, was small and unpretentious. Burbank talked eagerly, regaling them with anecdotes that kept them laughing and taking down the photographs of his triumphs that covered the walls of his room to explain them. He had more of the gardener about him than the savant, De Vries thought. Perhaps the Hollander even wondered, as others before him had done, if this could actually be *the* Luther Burbank who had accomplished so many wonderful things, and earned himself such a reputation.

They spoke of Burbank's continuing work in crossing the wild beach plum—a scrubby tree able to grow and fruit under the most adverse conditions—with other American and Japanese plums. By this means hybrids had been created that combined the vitality of the beach plum (the fruit of which was almost worthless except for making preserves) with size, flavor and overall market quality. This involved not merely crossing six or eight types with each other, but using as many subspecies and varieties as possible, on a mass scale. And the only proof of the worth of each crossing, from which new combinations were indicated, was the fruit itself. "It can easily be seen what an immense amount of work, patience and capacity of judgement and choice is required to reach the ultimate aim," De Vries observed. "Yet Burbank told us on that remarkable evening of many such instances."[3]

The three Europeans were eager, above all, to discuss the theoretical implications of their host's work: De Vries and Loeb, whose own efforts had been directed at pinning down the nature and origin of new evolutionary traits, were particularly anxious to know whether Burbank could cast any light on this subject.

Darwin had envisaged two possible mechanisms of evolution as preceding the process of natural selection, which could in itself account for the survival of traits and species but not for their origin. The first of these was a sudden, spontaneous development of new types from the old stock, "approaching to the nature of monster." The second, which he thought to be the decisive one, was the gradual accumulation of the fluctuating variations always present within a species (evident in that no two individuals, plant or animal, are ever quite alike). In the early 1900s battle raged among biologists over the question of whether mutations were the prime instrument of evolution, or whether gradual individual variation, slowly cumulative in effect, was the important factor. The neo-Lamarckians who espoused the accumulation of fluctuations theory assumed that environment had a directly modifying influence. Conversely De Vries, William Bateson and other Mendelians favored the former's mutation theory and tended to minimize the effects of selection in the production of new characters. Surely Burbank, whose practical experience of hybridization and selection was greater than that of any man living, must be able to cast some light on this central problem in evolutionary thought?

De Vries took the first opportunity to bring the conversation around to the subject. One of the marvels they had seen at Burbank's Sebastopol experiment grounds near Santa Rosa was the so-called "stoneless prune." This was a small, blue-colored plum, with a seed something like an almond (it even tasted like an almond), surrounded by a pale, jelly-like integument, with only a few remnants of stony material, which could easily be bitten into. ("To take up a plum and bite through it without hesitation requires education," noted Professor Wickson, "so strong is the conception of the danger involved; but to bite freely and find the flavor enhanced by the nutty savor of the kernel brings reward in the new sensation which the palate experiences . . . To combine the flavors of pulp and kernel, to gain the nutritive properties of the latter and to escape the tedium and awkwardness of ejecting the stone, constitute an advance in prune character and motive which it is difficult to overvalue."[4]) In some of the hybrids more of the stony material survived, in others less. Burbank's plan was to cross the latter with superior varieties of prune in order to transmit the stoneless quality to them. Was this fruit evidence that a major trait like stoneless-ness could be arrived at by crossing ordinary varieties?

No, said Burbank. He had heard of a *prune sans noyau* (seed-less plum) known as a curiosity in France since at least the six-teenth century, and to be found there now as a worthless wild fruit of the hedgerows. Seeing the potential use of this oddity in hybridization, he had sent to a French nurseryman for the seed. This was grown at the Sebastopol grounds, and eventually produced a fruit about the size of a small cherrry, with a Dam-son color and flavor and a stone partially covering the pit, growing on an unproductive, rambling, thorny bush. After re-peated crossings with the standard French prune and other plums the quality of the fruit was slowly improved, while the remnant of stone was kept as small as possible. After about ten years' work, sweet and sour Damson-like fruit of various sizes resulted. There was, therefore, no exception to the rule: no re-ally new character.

The visitors were a little disappointed. They had hoped for some novel revelation. Even they (and for De Vries and Loeb, we should remember, this problem was "the fundamental idea, if not ultimate aim" of their studies) seem to that extent to have succumbed to his almost mystical reputation. Like so many of Burbank's lay admirers, they expected too much, experts of in-ternational stature though they were.

The other extraordinary things he had to show them, im-pressive though they might be, also failed to clarify the funda-mental theoretical question. There was the white blackberry, for example, a hybrid that produced an abundance of perfectly white fruit. (Delicious, De Vries noted). How could such a basic feature as the black color of the berry be eliminated merely by crossing? Again, there was no magical solution, merely the native ingenuity of the breeder. In Europe a white variety of the raspberry was known to occur from time to time, he reminded them, and in the Eastern states an insignificant variety of cultivated bramble with pale yellow berries was sometimes found. He had crossed this last with a variety known as Lawton's blackberry, and the end result was the white color of one parent with the eating qualities of the other.

The same was true of the "spineless" cactus by which Burbank set so much store; he had assiduously collected varieties of cactus from Mexico, South Africa and other countries* until one finally turned up that was without the usual spines on the stalks, and another that lacked spicules on the leaves. These characteristics were combined in a single plant by hybridization after an extensive series of crossings, and a spineless cactus which its creator saw as having immense potential as cattle forage in desert areas was produced. Now and then a spine still occurred on the stems, but after a careful search De Vries was only able to find one such. Burbank demonstrated the harmlessness of his cactus by softly rubbing this cheek against the pads. It was a remarkable achievement. But it was no miracle.

What, then, was the secret of his success? First of all, there was the sheer scale of his experiments, which no other plant breeder could match. In this sense he was the Henry Ford of the art: he brought mass production to hybridizing, raising thousands of seedlings to obtain a single improved variety. This naturally increased the chances of finding useful specimens, inasmuch as the likelihood of discovering a valuable "sport" among thousands of plants was obviously better than among hundreds. And since the chances were that out of five or six desired qualities only three or four ordinarily appeared in combination, thousands of seedlings had to be produced to find one that would incorporate them all. In a single year, Wickson observed, fifteen huge bonfires were lit on Burbank's grounds to

---

*Almost all cacti are originally native to the New World. Burbank was in effect reimporting varieties naturalized elsewhere in the hope of finding variants resulting from selection in different environments.

destroy rejected material, one of them alone burning sixty-five thousand two- and three-year-old hybrid seedling berry bushes. As it was just after fruiting time that the rejected specimens were destroyed, it was hardly surprising that his neighbors wondered at "the man who used to have a big nursery, but now raises acres and acres of stuff and every summer has it all dug up and burned."

There were hundreds of stock trees on his place, each of them grafted with dozens of different hybrid plums and covered with an amazing variety of fruit and foliage. No doubt but that he had to be given credit for demonstrating the possibilities of breeding on a large scale. From the perspective of the present day, it is in this that he stands between the small-scale farmer-breeders, who through most of history slowly but steadily built up mankind's stock of useful plants, and the modern scientific hybridizer. De Vries, from his uniquely informed standpoint, was quick to recognize this.

Another factor which De Vries conceded was that Burbank seemed to be guided by a "special gift of judgement, in which he excels all his contemporaries." That was high praise indeed, coming from a man who had studied the work of plant breeders all over Europe, including that of the great cereal hybridizer Hjalmar Nilsson, director of the Swedish Agricultural Experiment Station at Svalöf. This "gift of judgement" was no insignificant part of Burbank's secret. Without it, De Vries felt, his imitators were bound to fail. No one could easily "steal his trade" for "without the special disposition for it nobody will succeed, and for simple imitation, the entire process is too complicated . . ."

Apart from this, and the scale of his experimentation, his techniques were essentially the same as those used by plant breeders in Europe. But since the procedures and results of European horticulturists were, at this time, little known in America, he had had to rediscover many of the common European methods of working on his own—in itself no small achievement.

De Vries freely recognized that in the number of fruits and

flowers which Burbank had improved—they ultimately totaled more than eight hundred over a span of fifty years—he had no equals. Where other breeders had tackled a few genera, usually as a business proposition, in order to create a greater demand for their nursery products, he had taken for his province the whole catalog of cultivated plants and abandoned the seedsman's trade so as to devote himself exclusively to the work of improvement.

On the purely scientific side, the Hollander had some serious reservations, however, which he voiced to a young Dutch gardener named John Zuur whom Burbank had working for him. Zuur understood English well enough but could not speak it, and he was naturally only too happy to be able to talk to his famous compatriot in his own language. He told De Vries that he found Burbank eccentric and suspicious of his help. The men weren't allowed to talk to visitors, and if Burbank caught one of them talking to someone over the fence, he was likely to be fired—not for wasting time but for talking about his business. Burbank *was* afraid that people would steal his secrets. To prevent seeds, bulbs and scions from being stolen, it was his practice to search the men's pockets as they left their work. "He treated us as 'high-graders,'" as one former employee complained, using the term applied to workers in the goldfields who stole bits of high-grade ore. One could never tell when he was likely to do or say some unexpected thing. "See here, Zuur," he had remarked out of the blue one day, "I think I am about two hundred percent overrated!"

For his part De Vries told Zuur that Burbank's failure to keep proper records of his experiments was a disappointment, and also expressed regret at his failure to produce new characters by his method of breeding. The first criticism was destined to be voiced repeatedly in the years to come. It was valid enough: Burbank's records were usually intelligible only to himself, if then, which meant that vital details of the ancestry of his hybrids were frequently lost or uncertain. The second was more than a little unfair. After all, no one else had ever successfully produced significant new characters by breeding either. Selection and hybridization could only combine and enhance existing traits, and mutation was a factor then outside human control.

But, as we have seen, even the scientists tended to expect miracles of him, and were disgruntled when he failed to come up with them. Academic training and distinction do not necessarily make for superhuman objectivity. De Vries had behind him the experience of finding in Mendel an amateur observer who, almost unknown to the world, had arrived at a solution to the problem of inheritance which had gone unnoticed by formal biology. By virtue of his own rediscovery of Mendelian law, and his theory of mutation, he was finding himself hailed as a second Darwin. But there were many who rejected the theoretical edifice he had constructed—among them the venerable Alfred Russel Wallace (1823–1913). Wallace, whose authority was that of joint originator of the theory of evolution by natural selection, and whose independent findings had initially prompted Darwin to publish his work, stubbornly held out against Mendelism, as did many other scientists. The theory of dramatic mutative leaps proposed by De Vries was even more contentious. Its author was, in other words, a man with an ax to grind.

Perhaps he had secretly hoped to discover in Burbank a new Mendel, who would produce confirming evidence of massive mutations as the source of new species. At very least he must have expected to find materials in Burbank's collection that might illuminate his theory. Burbank, he said, was "a gardener touched with genius"—and was that not, in some sense, just what Mendel had been? Like Mendel (who at least once failed to pass an examination in natural history) Burbank had scant academic training. To the hopeful De Vries the parallels with the saintly Augustinian abbot must have seemed remarkable. It was tempting, to say the least, to suppose that answers to the complex problem of how species arose and differentiated could be had for the asking from the sage of Santa Rosa.

But he was doomed to disappointment on that score. On the

evidence, in fact, Burbank probably gave his theory of saltative mutation something of a jolt. If, conversely, as has been suggested, his own visit caused the latter to do some serious thinking in the general field of the biological sciences, there is no evidence that it had the slightest effect on his working habits or results.

At this period very little was known about the physical mechanisms of inheritance. Nuclear division in cells had been observed as long before as 1844, and the word "chromosome" had been introduced in 1888 by W. Waldeyer to describe the threadlike bodies in the cell nucleus, visible in stained material, which, in dividing, initiated the formation of new cells. But it was not until the science of cytology (the branch of biology dealing with cellular structure, evolution and function) had developed that it became possible to grasp the operation of Mendel's statistical laws. August Weismann (1834–1914) had identified the hereditary substance with the chromosomes in 1893, and he and other German researchers were gradually accumulating the understanding of cell mechanics which would provide a physiological foundation for genetic thinking. The term "genetics" itself was first used by the English biologist William Bateson in 1906, and only in 1909 were the words "gene," "phenotype" and "genotype" introduced by the Danish botanist W. Johanssen.

De Vries knew as much about chromosomes and genes and their significance as carriers of heredity as anyone alive. Burbank, who does not seem to have read the scientific literature of his day and probably never owned a microscope, was almost certainly ignorant of them. In any case he remained a stubbornly old-fashioned Darwinian. "Read Darwin first, and gain a full comprehension of the meaning of Natural Selection," he was afterward quoted as saying by one of his ghost writers. "Then read the modern Mendelists in detail. But then—go back again to Darwin."[5]

And Burbank, who had (by admission in a letter dated January 1909) not read the *Origin of Species,* was a Darwinian of a special kind. He had learned his Darwinism from another work, *The Variation of Animals and Plants under Domestication,* which he first read in 1868—the year of its original publication—at the age of nineteen. (Later he also acquired a copy of *The Effects of Cross and Self-Fertilization in the Vegetable Kingdom,* published in 1876, but by then he was already living in California and had, in effect, begun his life's work.) If by 1909 he still had not got around to reading the *Origin,* it is perhaps safe to say that he never did read it. His Darwin was, effectively, the Darwin of the *Variation,* which is of considerable significance to the understanding of his own views.

This book was based on the great mass of material Darwin had accumulated prior to writing the *Origin.* It examined the changes in domesticated animals and plants that had been effected by artificial selection. While Darwin restated his principle of natural selection and argued against the possibility of design in variation, he also attempted to come to terms with the most serious criticism that had been leveled at his system, that advanced by the engineer, Fleeming Jenkin. In the *North British Review* for June 1867, Jenkin had demonstrated that mathematically speaking the "blending" view of heredity, and for that matter the theoretical assumptions of animal breeders up to that time, must be invalid. Single variations could not, on such a view, be perpetuated, but would be swamped by the mass of population. Though Darwin does seem to have envisaged the properties of progeny as something more than a mere blend or mixture of parental attributes, this was the received opinion of the time, and he was in possession of no clear alternative.

Inheritance is not (as was generally supposed prior to the rediscovery of Mendelian law) simply a combination of parental characteristics. Traits are inherited independently, and preserve their independent identities in succeeding generations. But unfortunately Mendel's crucial monograph establishing this, though actually published in 1865, several years *before* the *Variation,* was unknown to Darwin. This was sheer bad luck:

the "Proceedings" of the Brünn Society for the Study of Natural Science, in which it appeared, was a journal exchanged with those of more than 120 other societies, and copies undoubtedly went to England. Darwin did not see it, however, and Mendel's brilliant insight on this score escaped the grasp of most contemporary scientific investigators. The statistical approach to the study of hybridization which Mendel adopted was too much of a novelty to find acceptance with the run of nineteenth-century biologists, and it was never reviewed or discussed by his contemporaries.

Darwin, though well aware of the inadequacy of existing views of heredity, was stumped. In 1869 we find him writing pessimistically to Wallace: "Jenkin argued in the 'North British Review' against single variations ever being perpetuated, and has convinced me . . ." In an effort to come to terms with this difficulty, he reverted to an idea which, if not Lamarckian, has nonetheless smacked of Lamarck to some critical observers. ("He panicked and ran straight into the opposite camp," writes C. D. Darlington. "Lamarck became a posthumous Darwinian."[6]) Now the identification of the doctrine of "the inheritance of acquired characters" with the French evolutionist Jean Baptiste Lamarck (1744–1829) is no more than an intellectual convenience, and not a very constructive one at that. In fact the concept was accepted by almost everyone, up to the time of its rejection by Weismann in his germ-plasm theory of the 1880s. It is handily damned, however, by association with Lamarck's teleological views: the use of the term "Lamarckian" is almost invariably polemical, and should be treated with caution.

The *Variation* suggested a theory of "pangenesis," very different from that later put forward by De Vries, postulating hypothetical particles called "gemmules," which are thrown off by the cells of the body, and find their way into the reproductory system, forming the hereditary constituents of sperm and ovum. Environmental conditions affecting the parent are thus to some extent able to modify inheritance: acquired characteristics may be preserved in future generations.

Regardless of the ongoing arguments concerning the "provisional" nature of what Darwin ruefully referred to as "my well-abused hypothesis of Pangenesis," and its significance to Darwinism as a system, *this was the Darwin that Burbank knew:* a Darwin, that is to say, receptive to the possibility of the inheritance of characters acquired in the parental generation. (We might note here the contention of one of Darwin's most recent champions, Michael T. Ghiselin, of the University of California, that in some contexts the substitution of "gene" for "gemmule" gives a remarkable similarity to the modern interpretation. "Our newer understanding of position effects, allometry, and pleiotropy makes Darwin's thinking seem almost prophetic," Ghiselin says. "The parallels between gemmules and the heredity material are actually quite extensive."[7]) Burbank, the pragmatist, probably found this compromise between the "particulate" and "blending" theories quite reasonable, or at least an adequate working hypothesis—especially coming to him as it did under the authenticating signature of the master evolutionist.

In any case, he was not much impressed by De Vries' theory of large mutations and of *periods* of mutation in the life of a species: ". . . the varied tribes of evening primrose which Professor de Vries developed in his gardens at Amsterdam were overwhelmingly suggestive of various and sundry forms of hybrid plants that I myself have developed year after year in my experimental gardens at Santa Rosa," he is later on quoted as saying. "Over and over again, hundreds of times in the aggregate, I have selected mutants among my plants, and have developed from them new fixed races. But in the vast majority of cases I knew precisely how and why these mutants originated. They were hybrids; and they were mutants *because* they were hybrids. And so from the outset I have believed that Professor de Vries' celebrated evening primroses had the same origin."[8]

And he was right! De Vries' unusual primroses *were* hybrids, which subsequent study has identified as being of several different kinds. Some were a consequence of incomplete chromosome pairing, some were polyploids involving changes in the number of chromosome sets, two were mutants in the modern sense of the term. "The mutants of Oenothera are therefore nothing more than symptoms of its peculiar hybridity and as such are of little significance in evolution," note C. D. Darlington and K. Mather.[9]

Burbank's genius was practical rather than theoretical. Most of his work was done when genetics was still very much in its infancy, and he was in no position to lay down laws of heredity: he was in fact only drawn into expressing his opinions publicly when his commercial promoters were eagerly endeavoring to secure him scientific stature appropriate to their claims. Nonetheless, the example shows his intuitions on the subject to have been remarkably accurate.*

It seems, moreover, that the old notion of the inheritance of acquired characters may be coming back into fashion. Heritable differences have reportedly been induced in cultivated flax by the use of different fertilizer treatments, and it has been suggested that nuclear changes are involved. D. Briggs and S. M. Walters, two modern writers on the subject of evolution and variation in plants, remark in this connection that "Concerning 'orthogenetic' views, which question the randomness of mutation and attribute direction in evolutionary change to some internal bias rather than to selection, we might observe that in certain respects modern chemical views of gene action and differentiation open the door to more complications. For example, the rather rapidly-developing studies of non-chromosomal inheritance may make neo-Lamarckian ideas on the possibility of the inheritance of acquired characters respectable again."[10]

If anything has been established, it is probably that dogmatic views on the subject of inheritance, no matter how well-founded they may seem, are unwise.

When de Vries and company visited him, Burbank was already

*We might add that contemporary views of the Oenothera complex do not predate H. J. Muller's 1917 publication of his study of "balanced lethals" in his paper "An Oenothera-like Case in Drosophila." They are therefore substantially more recent.

world famous. The obloquy that was later to cloud his name, particularly in scientific and horticultural circles, was still in the future. He pursued his goals with an innocent fervor, as yet unembittered by the experience of commercial exploitation and learned disdain. But the tide of popular adulation that was ultimately to swamp him was rising.

He worked exceedingly hard. Now, in July, the busiest time of the year for the experimental horticulturist, when fruit was ripening, when maturing seeds had to be collected, dried and stored, when the selection of plums took place, he would rise at dawn, and by 5:00 A.M. would customarily be starting his rounds in the Sebastopol experiment grounds, seven miles from his home, sampling fruit, judging it for size, shape, color and taste and recording his observations.

July, Walter L. Howard observed, was also the month of conventions, and, "A state or national convention in San Francisco was never complete unless the delegates could spend a day in Santa Rosa seeing the Burbank gardens. Travel bureaus and chambers of commerce encouraged this."[11]

Now Burbank seldom delegated authority where the work of selection was concerned, and his public, for its part, wanted to see *him*, not just some spokesman. Howard paints a revealing picture of Burbank returning home from his labors in the hot sun at Sebastopol, his stomach soured by sampling too many acid fruits, to face the penalties of celebrity.

Passing from the garage to the house he runs the gauntlet of outstretched hands and cheery greetings. He bows right and left and impatiently tells the callers he regrets that he cannot stop to talk with them. At the door a man waylays him and grabs his hand only to be thrust aside. Another more daring than the rest follows him into his study and insists upon introducing himself and explaining why he should have an interview. He is asked to leave.

After Burbank finally sits down to lunch the telephone announces that a party of seventy-five or a hundred persons have arrived in town and wish to be conducted over his gardens. The local Chamber of Commerce secretary protests that the party was sent over by a travel bureau, a plan Burbank had approved months earlier, and what should he do with them. Burbank capitulates and the party comes, but he is not a gracious host. Some were grateful for having seen him under any circumstances; others considered him to be peevish; while the few that had forced their attentions upon him and were repulsed said he was rude.[12]

Fame, which Burbank certainly enjoyed for its own sake, and had in his way courted, was proving a harsh mistress. We can see him now as an early example of that unfortunate species, the media hero, suffering all the penalties attached to the role. But what was it, after all, that had made him so famous? What about him that appealed so profoundly to public fancy? He had become one of the undoubted idols of his time, an age that led directly to our own, and answering these questions should tell us a good deal about the essential temper by which, willy-nilly, the imagination of the twentieth century was delineated.

There was in him that Emersonian faculty of prophecy; and what he prophesied was a land of Canaan, where blackberries were as big as plums and plums the size of peaches, where everything grew straight and easy and the pastoral republic that had vanished in living memory was restored to a people sickening of the spreading fumes and ashes of the Industrial Revolution. The railroads were all built and all the free land was taken. The star of empire could go no farther west. Henceforth the American frontier would exist only in dreams, and Burbank was a spokesman of the dream. Perhaps he speaks to us still, in the eternal longing of urban man to reconstitute the Garden of Eden (more commonly thought of as a little place in the country) one day.

TWO

Our Most Essential Art

THE STORY OF Luther Burbank belongs to the history of horticulture—the science and art of growing plants and their selection and improvement for use. Of all the relations of man to his world, there is none more basic than this. Soldiers and kings, politicians and philosophers have claimed the lion's share of attention, but in the end peasant farmers have underwritten the history of mankind, in the unending task of cultivating food and culling seed for the next season's planting. Though people recognizably like ourselves may have been on earth for as long as a quarter of a million years, the pattern of life remained relatively static until the primary agricultural revolution, which took place roughly ten thousand years ago by current assessment. In effect, history begins then.

Before agriculture human beings spent most of their time looking for their next meal. It was only with the planting of crops and the domestication of herd animals that energy be-

35

came available for the arts, technology and social niceties which we think of as civilized activity. In the process of domesticating plants and animals, man also domesticated himself. Cities became possible, springing quite literally from the development of the granary. Metallurgy, weaving, pottery making, the basic mechanical principles, the plow and the wheel at once commence to make their appearance.

In the transformation and improvement of plants, we may trace the rise and fall of civilizations. It is not too much to say that we have depended on them absolutely ever since the appearance of the first substantial villages in Asia Minor and Middle America heralded the beginnings of urban life. Wheat, rice, barley, oats, rye, corn, sorghum and millet: one or more of these has lain behind every significant increase in human population. No civilization ever arose without the cultivation of cereals; even now society as we know it would be unlikely to survive without them.

Where other records fail, cultivated plants are, in the words of the great American geographer, Carl O. Sauer, "living artifacts of times past," from which careful detective work can deduce the unwritten history of mankind. The difficulty lies in reconstructing their heritage and translating their message, which faithfully preserves the labor and achievements of the experimenters and cultivators who laid the foundations of our society and culture. In this record, it is not unreasonable to surmise, may lie lessons of vital importance in the coming struggle against ecological catastrophe.

But though civilization, science and empire have from the very beginning followed the plant breeder—the man who could make two blades of grass grow where one grew before—no one was ever more anonymous. "Our civilization still rests, and will continue to rest, on the discoveries made by peoples for the most part unknown to history," Sauer observes. "Historic man has added no plant or animal of major importance to the domesticated forms on which he depends."[1] Thus even the safflower, hailed as a "new" crop and now raised on many hundreds of thousands of acres in the United States for its oil, has been found in Egyptian tombs dating back to 1500 B.C., and was cultivated then for the dye obtainable from its flowers.*

In historic times, too, the work of horticulture has been accomplished with relatively little fanfare. Luther Burbank was the first and is thus far the only plant breeder to have his name become a household word, bestowed indiscriminately on high schools and reformatories, and written into *Webster's* in the shape of a transitive verb:

burbank, *v.t.* To modify and improve (plants or animals), esp. by selective breeding. Also, to cross or graft (a plant). Hence, figuratively, to improve (anything, as a process or institution) by selecting good features and rejecting bad, or by adding good features.

The most likely contemporary candidate for this kind of fame would perhaps be Dr. Norman Borlaug, father of the "green revolution" that has revolutionized agriculture around the world. But Dr. Borlaug, notwithstanding his Nobel Prize and outstanding achievements, shows no signs of becoming the object of a cult, venerated by millions and accorded an almost superstitious reverence as was Burbank during his lifetime.

Yet, even for Burbank, fame has proved relatively fleeting. The verb has failed to endure; and were it not, ironically, for those schools and houses of correction, the name itself might be forgotten by most of us. Even in California, his adopted home and workplace for some fifty years, there is a distinct tendency nowadays either to assume mistakenly that he was the eponymous founder of the city of Burbank† or, oddly enough, to confuse him with the black agricultural experimenter, George Washington Carver (1864-1943).

---

*It is true that an exception here may be triticale, a hybrid of wheat and rye which has recently received a good deal of publicity as an alternate crop.

†It was named for a Dr. David Burbank, originally of New Hampshire, who operated a sheep ranch at the site from 1867 and joined in founding the town twenty years later.

It might be argued, of course, that Burbank was more celebrated in the first place than he ever deserved to be. Orthodox
scientists certainly tended to think so. (To them Burbank might
have replied in the words he used in a lecture at the University
of California's Hearst Hall in 1908: "Orthodoxy is ankylosis—
nobody at home; ring up the undertaker for further information.") They found his failure to keep proper records irritating,
and many of them eventually came to think him a fraud. In the
end they would damn him by silence, a technique all too frequently employed by science to deal with thinkers who cannot
easily be boxed into the conventions of the day. He was an out-
sider with little formal education and, if his achievements were
remarkable, he was guilty nonetheless of failing to maintain a
properly scientific facelessness. They did not thank him for
turning horticulture into a kind of spectator sport—notwithstanding that it had never been his purpose to do so.

The public streamed to his door in their thousands. Henry
Ford, Thomas Alva Edison, Helen Keller, Elbert Hubbard,
William Jennings Bryan, Jack London, John Burroughs, Wil-
liam Howard Taft, John Muir, Sir Harry Lauder, Paderewski,
the Polish pianist and statesman, and the king and queen of the
Belgians* were numbered among his famous visitors.

Something about him drew a responsive chord. There was a
natural constituency of Burbank enthusiasts, and it was not
only in America. He had the mysterious quality that goes by the
name of charisma. His very name (as his friend Paramahansa
Yogananda suggests in the *Autobiography of a Yogi*, which he dedicated "to the Memory of Luther Burbank 'An American
Saint'") became a synonym for improvement. And improvement, or "Progress," was precisely the tutelary genius of the
day.

Significantly enough, perhaps, the modern concept of progress, though it was already very much in the air by the second

---

*The Belgian monarchs seem to have had a royal passion for sages, which also led
them to cultivate the friendship of Einstein.

half of the eighteenth century, derives to a large extent from the evolutionary thinking associated with the name of Charles Darwin. The publication of that great heresy, the *Origin of Species,* in 1859 brought out religious leaders of every description in defense of traditional beliefs, but they were fighting a losing battle. By 1900 Darwinism in its biological aspect had been accepted by most educated people in both Europe and America.

"With its triumphs," says the historian Eric F. Goldman, "came an enormous prestige for anything that could be called Darwinism." The so-called "Social Darwinism" propounded by Herbert Spencer, which applied the concept of the survival of the fittest to the social organism, was particularly successful. Spencer was, in fact, more Lamarckian than Darwinian in outlook, but Darwin had adopted his term "survival of the fittest" at the urging of Alfred Russel Wallace as being more readily understandable than "natural selection." This was a mistake, since, as Sir Gavin de Beer has remarked, "the 'fittest' can survive without any evolution taking place at all . . . the use of the superlative implies more than is intended."[2]

Precisely *because* of that implication, Spencer's philosophy complied perfectly with the needs of the conservative business barons who were running the country and enjoyed an enormous vogue in the last quarter of the century. It was in these terms that John D. Rockefeller could justify the Standard Oil trust to his Sunday-school class as "merely a survival of the fittest . . . The American beauty rose can be produced in the splendor and fragrance which bring cheer to its beholder only by sacrificing the early buds which grow up around it. This is not an evil tendency in business. It is merely the working-out of a law of nature and a law of God."[3] It was perhaps no accident that Rockefeller's analogy was a horticultural one, with Burbank the country's best-known Darwinian.

Of the years following the Civil War, Henry Adams observed that "Unbroken Evolution under uniform conditions pleased every one—except curates and bishops; it was the very best substitute for religion; a safe, conservative, practical, thoroughly

Common-Law deity. Such a working system for the universe suited a young man who had just helped to waste five or ten thousand million dollars and a million lives, more or less, to enforce unity and uniformity on people who objected to it; the idea was only too seductive in its perfection; it had the charm of art."[4]

Burbank, too, was such a young man, ten years Adams' junior but cast in the same generation. Like Adams he found in Darwinism an idea "seductive in its perfection," a system that explained everything, or seemed to. In this he was a modern American of his time. For a nation that sought to put behind it the horrors of civil war, the farce of Reconstruction, the failure, as ever, to heal the open wound called the "Negro problem" and somehow to mask the ongoing genocide which was a necessary corollary (or so it appeared) of its inevitable expansion westward, there could have been no more consoling ideology. And if it was all based on a misconception as to what Darwinism actually was, that was nothing out of the ordinary in the history of creeds. It was a misconception, arguably, in which Darwin himself partook. *He* had accepted that "unlucky substitution," survival of the fittest, and it appeared in the later editions of the *Origin* itself. But nothing is so straightforward at the time as it seems in the simplifying light of perspective.

Burbank was no theoretician. What he did was to seize on a few simple ideas, which he got from Darwin but might have found in other writers, and attempt to put them into practice in horticulture. The prevailing climate of Darwinism, in which he appeared as an exemplar of the faith, provided him with a context for fame, and his own unique talents did the rest.

In order to understand what he did, however, it is necessary to know at least a little of the history of the crucial symbiosis of man and plant: the long process of bringing favored species into domestication, ten thousand years of painstaking selection, largely by unknown individuals and peoples, in the New World as in the Old. For the Massachusetts fields and gardens in which he began his lifework came ready stocked with corn, beans and squash which were the work of Central American horticulturists, potatoes and tomatoes originating in the empire of the Incas, spinach, carrots and peas from Persia and Afghanistan, apples and onions from somewhere in Western Asia, cabbages, turnips and plums brought into service in Neolithic Europe, cucumbers from India and peaches from China, to name only a small part of their contents.

Roots and tubers were probably eaten raw by primitive man for a very long time. But the human stomach does not digest uncooked starches and vegetable protein well, and man quite early gained control of what was to be the most useful of all his tools: fire.

We know, for example, that fires burned in the famous cave at Choukoutien inhabited by Sinanthropus, or Peking man, a quarter of a million years ago. The discovery of cooking was not the only consequence. Millennia before the beginnings of agriculture, men and manlike creatures before them used fire, and set fires, deliberately or accidentally, that drastically altered the plant covering of the planet and had the effect of encouraging the variation and development of some species at the expense of others. People also involuntarily influenced plant life in other ways. Human habitation sites were a novel environmental niche, providing the opportunity for new varieties of plant to grow and adapt. We commenced to exert a selective influence on the vegetable world long before we knew what we were doing. A symbiotic relationship sprang up between the useful weeds that throve in a human context and the hominids who gathered their fruit and flowers, roots and stalks, for food, fuel and other purposes. The instincts of the earliest humans, and even, perhaps, of the primates who preceded them, derived from hundreds of thousands of years of experience, were handed down in unbroken continuity as an increasingly intimate understanding of the inherited food plants.

These processes have gone on for so long that it is scarcely meaningful to speak of a natural balance without man. The dim beginnings of agriculture itself are, however, a matter of debate. It seems probable that it commenced somewhere between nine and eleven thousand years ago, both in the Old World and in the New, at the late glacial/early postglacial time boundary. In an era of intensified food collecting, called the Mesolithic in the Old World and the Archaic in America, perhaps partly as a consequence of increasing populations, actual cultivation began. (Systematic irrigation of wild plants may have preceded it in some areas.) Humankind's botanical lore had accumulated to the point where the leap from simple parasitism to control was possible.

Plant domestication took two basic forms: vegetative reproduction, or cloning, by planting a segment of the parent, as in the case of the potato and the banana, and seed planting, as in the case of wheat and beans. Carl Sauer has argued that the second arose out of the first. According to this hypothesis, the earliest plantings would very likely have been for purposes other than food—perhaps for the extraction of poisons or narcotics used in stunning or killing fish. "It may well be," he writes, "that among the earliest domesticates were multi-purpose plants set out around fishing villages to provide starch food, substances for toughening nets and lines and making them water resistant, drugs, and poisons."[5]

With the selection of varieties for purposes of planting came an increase in extractive technology. Some foods had to be processed before cooking; new food combinations were experimented with. Botany and chemistry—and hence science itself—can in some sense be seen as arising out of these early experiments in farming and eating.

The growing of crops by seed planting may have arisen almost accidentally, Sauer has suggested, in the utilization of "volunteer" weeds that sprang up among the cloned species. Thus rice is thought by some authorties to have originally been a weed in fields of taro, a plant of the arum family grown for its roots, in Indonesia or India. As any gardener will have observed, the planting of crops provides room for self-sown plants. Wild varieties of tomato which are protected but not planted deliberately are, for example, still gathered in the fields in parts of Mexico and Central America.

As time went by, certain of these "weeds" would themselves come to be planted deliberately, and as the "Old Planting" people envisaged by Sauer gradually expanded into areas less favorable to their original cloned plants, and more so to the seeded species, the latter would be increasingly utilized and at the same time selected and improved.

An alternative hypothesis is that seed planting developed from the collection of wild grain. In 1966 the agronomist J. R. Harlan made the experiment of harvesting wild wheat in eastern Turkey using a nine-thousand-year-old flint sickle set in a new wooden handle. He found he was able to gather a kilogram of grain an hour. On this basis a family, working for three weeks when the wild grain was ripe, could have gathered more than they could consume in a year. Harlan's grain was, moreover, found to contain at least 50 percent more protein than modern American bread wheat. In this context Kent V. Flannery, of the University of Michigan, has proposed a period of "preadaptation" when diminished food supplies, specifically in the Near East, but perhaps elsewhere too, laid the basis for the deliberate cultivation of food plants and the domestication of animals.

In the Old World, seed planting agriculture may conveivably have begun before the end of the last Ice Age, in areas now desert and hard to envisage as fertile. During the Ice Age the pressure of cold air over Europe caused the Atlantic rains to follow a more southerly route to the east, and a belt of park and grassland covered the whole area from the west coast of Africa to the mountains of Persia. Old World centers of seed domestication are believed to have been Asia Minor and western India, North China and Ethiopia. (Another area of early cultivation may have been the great bend of the Niger River in West Africa.) In the absence of reliable archaeological evidence, however, the pinpointing of the original hearths of domestication remains a matter of some dispute.

The earliest *known* seed planting took place in the hills flanking Mesopotamia's "fertile crescent." Here the archaeological documentation exists, brought to light by excavations in what is now Kurdistan, forming part of Turkey, south of Lake Van, Iran and Iraq, and in Palestine, where the wild ancestors of wheat and barley still survive. Here, as long ago as 7000 B.C., village farming communities existed, cultivating wheat, barley, field peas, lentils and other leguminous plants, and collecting nuts, fruit and berries growing wild in the area. The process of plant improvement proceeded relatively rapidly. Already by the seventh millennium B.C., wheat and barley in particular had come a long way from their wild ancestors.

The seed planting culture originating in the hill country moved down the river valleys to the alluvial plain of the Tigris and the Euphrates. Now for the first time in history we find people in sufficient numbers and with sufficient control of their food supply to build cities. Somewhere around 4000 B.C., with the rise of the Sumerian city-state, civilization as we know it begins.

Agriculture would appear to have reached Europe via Anatolia some two thousand years earlier, and by the time the first Sumerian cities were being built, had already arrived in the lands bordering the shores of the North Sea. Emmer wheat and six-rowed barley, originally brought into cultivation in Asia Minor, were carried into the Balkans by Neolithic farming peoples who tilled temporary clearings in the forest and moved to a new site when the fertility of the soil was exhausted. As always, the process of hybridization and selection automatically accompanied the movement of populations. The cultivated cereals, in the process of being introduced into environments differing from those in which they had originally been domesticated, slowly changed their nature. No conscious human intervention was necessary.

As these peoples moved north and west, whether as a result of population pressures, the vicissitudes of their slash-and-burn planting or out of sheer adventure, the nature of their crops inexorably altered to exploit the potential of climate and soil.

Natural selection continued to operate, though man was now one of nature's agents. Rye and oats, originating as grain-field weeds in Asia Minor and perhaps accidentally imported into Europe in the seed of wheat and barley, came into their own in the harsh climate of the north. Animal husbandry became an increasingly vital part of the rural economy, necessitating the cultivation of special fodder. "Such were the systems of culture across northwestern Europe for two to three thousand years, systems not seriously modified until the eighteenth century," Sauer says. "Then, with the introduction of the potato, the development of stock beets and field turnips, and the cultivation of clovers, the new agricultural revolution arose and, in part, prepared the way for the industrial revolution."[6]

But in the several dozen centuries which intervened, horticulture had not stood still. Greek and Phoenician colonizers and traders, ranging from the Black Sea to Gibraltar and beyond, greatly promoted the spread of plant varieties and agricultural technology from the eastern Mediterranean. The Roman writer Varro lists over fifty Greek authors who wrote on agriculture and related topics, and one of these, Theophrastus, is considered to be the founder of systematic botany. The Carthaginians, drawing on Greek sources for technical information, developed a system of intensive plantation farming of crops such as the olive and the vine. Mago of Carthage, called the "father of husbandry," wrote a lengthy work on agriculture in Punic, which was translated into Latin at the orders of the Roman Senate shortly after the fall of Carthage in 146 B.C. Rome and the empire were themselves supplied by an elaborate agricultural substructure which has been studied in detail,[7] and much of what was known was preserved into the Middle Ages.

With the collapse of the Western Empire, agricultural technology declined, but there was a wave of land expansion throughout Europe in the period A.D. 600–1300. New inventions like the horseshoe, the heavy Saxon wheeled plow, modern collar-harness, improved wagons with pivoted front axles, brakes and whipple trees, and the introduction of the three-field system of crop rotation under Charlemagne to a great extent underlay the civilization of the Renaissance and the rise of modern Europe.[8]

The agricultural revolution of the eighteenth century, when it came, was based not only on improved methods of cultivation, but also on new food plants. In England, Jethro Tull (1674–1741) invented a drill for planting seeds in rows and in his book *Horse-Hoeing Husbandry* advocated repeated tilling to eliminate weeds, manuring and the rotation of crops. Agricultural experimentation became fashionable among the great landowners. For hundreds of years past, a slow but steady improvement in cereal yields can be observed in Europe. In England the average yield for the period 1200–1249 was 3.7 grains harvested from one sown, for 1500–1700 it was 7 from 1, and for 1750–1820 had reached 10.6 from 1.[9] These impressive gains may to some extent have been the result of slowly improving varieties, though systematic improvement of cereals by selection seems to have begun only with the English breeder, Le Couteur, in the early nineteenth century. But it had been known at least since Roman times (Virgil alludes to the fact) that care had to be taken in selecting the grains destined for sowing or the races would deteriorate. The peasants slowly and silently carried on the work. Science would be some time catching up with them.

Basic to hybridization—the mating together of related varieties and species to produce new types—is an understanding of sexuality in plants. There is evidence that this knowledge existed in the ancient world. Herodotus, writing in the fifth century B.C., remarks that the Babylonians cultivated the date palm as they did figs, bringing the flower clusters of the male trees from the desert and binding them to the fruit-bearing trees, to which alone they gave a place in their gardens. The full significance of doing so does not seem to have been properly understood, and it was believed that the insects from the male flowers directly fertilized the fruit-bearing trees, rather than the pollen which they carried.

The modern study of sexuality in plants begins in 1676, however, when Nehemiah Grew, in an address before the Royal Society in London, recorded his own belief and that of Sir Thomas Millington that the stamens are the male organs of the plant and that the pollen acts as vegetable sperm. Experimental proof that pollen was necessary for seed development in a number of plants, among them *Zea mays* (corn) was provided by the German botanist and physician Camerarius in his classic work *De Sexu Plantarum,* published in Tübingen in 1694, and in 1716 Cotton Mather, the first American to be made a fellow of the Royal Society, reported observations on *Zea mays,* including wind pollination, variety cross and the resemblances of some of the progeny to the male parent. The first hybrid of which there is an authentic record was made the following year. This was Fairchild's Sweet William, a cross between the carnation *(Dianthus caryophyllus)* and the Sweet William *(D. barbatus)* made in 1717 by the English gardener, Thomas Fairchild, who noted that the progeny of the cross resembled both parents.

There is perhaps some reason for believing that hybridization may have been practiced by gardeners much earlier. In Shakespeare's *The Winter's Tale,* written about 1610, Perdita refuses to plant "streak'd" gilliflowers, "which some call Nature's bastards," in her garden, because she has,

> heard it said,
> There is an Art, which in their piedness shares
> With great creating-Nature.

This art, some Shakespearean critics have contended, was the art of hybridizing. (If so, however, it is surprising that in a work on horticulture like Parkinson's *Paradisi in Sole Paradisus Terrestris* published in 1629, there is no mention of hybridizing techniques.)

Modern botany is usually held to commence with Linnaeus, the Swede Carl von Linné (1707–1778), who initiated the system of taxonomy and binominal nomenclature in use today. In 1757 he made what has been termed the first scientifically produced interspecific hybridization, between the yellow and violet flowered Goatsbeards, producing purple flowers, yellow at the base. The great systematic hybridologist of the eighteenth century was, however, Josef Gottlieb Kölreuter (1733–1806). Kölreuter's first hybrid, involving the tobaccos, *Nicotiana rustica* x *paniculata,* was grown in 1760, and during the remaining forty-six years of his life he produced hundreds of others and wrote a number of important scientific papers on sexuality in plants and on hybrids and hybridization.

Some early examples of systematic plant breeding which might be cited are the tulip craze, or "tulipomania," that raged in Holland in the 1630s, when wild speculation resulted in the payment of fabulous prices for tulips of new varieties like the "Semper Augustus," a single bulb of which was sold for 13,000 florins, and the gooseberry fancy that engaged the weavers of Lancashire, England, in the years following 1650, which apparently resulted in the origination of some hundreds of new types.

In his *History of Horticulture in America to 1860,* U. P. Hedrick dates the beginning of gardening by settlers in New England to "Wednesday, 7 March 1621, following the first terrible winter in which the Pilgrims landed in the New World, they planted 'garden seeds.'"[10]

In Mexico and Peru the Spaniards had long previously marveled at the horticultural wonders of the New World: avocados, guavas, cacti, maize, tobacco, tomatoes, potatoes, pumpkins, squash, marigolds and new varieties of cotton, beans and peppers were some of the novelties they encountered. These plants were to revolutionize the diet of mankind. Columbus little knew the significance of the discovery he had made when, on November 5, 1492, two of his men returned from the interior of Cuba with word of "a sort of grain they call maiz which was well tasted, bak'd, dry'd and made into flour." Maize, or corn, is today one of the most important plants in America and vitally significant in the agriculture of many other countries besides.

The northern settlements also found the scope of their farming greatly expanded by New World novelties. "North America is a natural orchard," Hedrick observes. "More than two hundred species of tree, bush, vine, and small fruits were in common use by the Indians when the Whites came. Besides these, there were at least fifty varieties of nuts, and an even greater number of herbaceous plants."

Among other fruits, the Indians had raspberries, blackberries, strawberries, blueberries, cranberries, mulberries and persimmons, plums, crab apples, cherries and grapes. Some of these were deliberately planted and cultivated, others simply harvested from the wilds. The Cherokees and Iroquois are generally credited with having been the best husbandmen. Their horticulture was not entirely utilitarian either. There is some evidence that the Indians grew flowers in the vicinity of their vegetable gardens and orchards.*

The main food crops of these people were corn, beans and squash. Grown together as a complex, these constituted the agricultural triumvirate around which settled life revolved. Melons, sunflowers and tobacco were, however, also grown in some quantity. It remains a curious fact that the North American Indians failed to cultivate root crops—though these were to hand, and they dug wild tubers and roots (particularly the Jerusalem artichoke) for food. It remained in the end for European settlers to introduce the potato as a cultivated species in North America.

The colonists in the New World brought with them the skills and defects of their European motherlands. As agriculturists and gardeners, the Dutch, Huguenot French, Germans and Swedes were preeminent. The main trouble with American agriculture in its early days was summed up by George Washington in 1791, in a letter to Arthur Young:

. . . the aim of the farmers in this country, if they can be called

---

*Carl Sauer has suggested (in conversation) that the fact that flowers were not used ceremonially among the North American tribes, as they were in Mexico, indicates that floriculture was probably of no great significance to them.

farmers, is, not to make the most they can from the land, which is, or has been cheap, but the most of the labour, which is dear; the consequence of which has been, much ground has been scratched over and none cultivated and improved as it ought to have been: whereas a farmer in England, where land is dear, and labour cheap, finds it his interest to improve and cultivate highly, that he may reap large crops from a small quantity of ground.[11]

For this reason, also, systematic improvement of food plants by selection was not much attempted in America until the end of the eighteenth century. Hybridization and the production of new varieties were even more restricted. "A study of records," says Hedrick (who certainly knew them), "would show that only an occasional cabbage, onion, lettuce, turnip, cauliflower, parsnip, or carrot was originated in this country before 1860." More, he admits, was done in the way of breeding flowers.

Nevertheless it is possible to compile a lengthy list of Americans who applied themselves, with varying degrees of success, to producing new and better varieties in the late eighteenth century and the first half of the nineteenth century. Most of these men were denied the popular recognition which their work merited. The public, unaware of what *could* be done in the way of improving plant varieties, also largely failed to notice what was being done.

In the eighteenth century Joseph Cooper of New Jersey, whom Hedrick identifies as the first man in America to undertake plant breeding as his life's work, selected potato, pea, and lettuce seed, and also introduced the Cooper plum. In the 1790s William Prince of Long Island made the first efforts at improving a fruit on a large scale, developing four varieties of green gage plum which held their own for many years. In 1819 John Adlum (1759–1836) introduced the Catawba grape at his experimental vineyard near Georgetown, District of Columbia. C. M. Hovey of Cambridge, Massachusetts, introduced the famous Hovey strawberry in 1838, while Dr. W. D. Brinklé of Philadelphia (1799–1863) produced a number of new strawber-

ries, red raspberries, pears, and other fruit. In 1842 James J. H.
Gregory (1827–1910) of Marblehead, Massachusetts, whom we
shall meet with again, inasmuch as he later became the purchaser of the Burbank potato, introduced the Hubbard squash. The
first recorded hybridization involving native American and European grapes was Dr. William W. Valk's "Ada," the result of a
cross made in 1845, and around the same time John Fisk Allen
of Salem, Massachusetts, produced his Allen's Hybrid grape. In
the 1850s Ephraim W. Bull (1805–95) of Concord, Massachusetts, introduced the Concord grape, still the most important
blue-black variety of the Eastern United States, and in the same
years the New England breeder E. S. Rogers (1826–99) developed some forty-five seedling grapes, more than a dozen of
which became well-known. At Cincinnati, Ohio, Nicholas Long-
worth (1783–1863) introduced new varieties of strawberries,
raspberries and grapes. Jacob Moore (1835–1908) spent a
small fortune and a lifetime's work on the production of new
fruits, among them successful grapes, currants and pears, and
died in poverty. Robert Buist (1805–80) of Philadelphia, a prolific writer on horticultural subjects, was known for his ca-
mellias and hybrid verbenas.

Among vegetable breeders we might consider the work of
the Ohio seedsman A. W. Livingston, whose efforts to obtain a
better tomato led to the Paragon, introduced in 1870. Prior to
that time there had been little interest in tomato culture, and
the tomatoes which were grown lacked the desirable qualities of
smoothness and uniformity. Tomatoes had been canned and
sold since the 1840s, but up to the introduction of Livingston's
Paragon, they had not been an important crop. His description
of his procedure gives some idea of the state of the art in those
days:

. . . I tried the best kinds then known to the public, and selected from these such specimen tomatoes as approached in qualities what was needed, or was in demand. The seed from these
were carefully saved, and when planted were given the best cul-

tivation possible, hoping in this way to attain what I desired. After 15 years of the most scrupulous care and labor of this kind, I
was no nearer the goal than when I started in the race. According to the laws of life now (1893) well known, but which I did not
then (about 1866) understand, such stock-seed would reproduce
every trace of their ancestry, viz., thin-fleshed, rough and unde-
sirable fruits. I ran this method through all its changes . . .

Some improvements were achieved, but these could be attributed to improved conditions, Livingston thought. Nonetheless he found it worthwhile to put the better kinds on the
market under various names, while he went on with the work,
growing a varied selection of plants and keeping a watchful eye
on his fields for any "leadings." Success followed on what he
called his "New Method," selection of particular plants rather
than of individual tomatoes. "Whether this method . . . was
new to others at that time (in the 60's) I did not know," he says,
"but it was altogether new to me; in fact it was a pure discovery
on my part." He noticed a plant bearing heavy foliage and uniform, smooth tomatoes growing prolifically but too small to
have much market value.

The seeds from this plant were saved with painstaking care, and
made the basis of future experiments. The next spring, from
these seeds, I set two rows across my garden—about 40 rods long
each—and to my glad surprise they all bore perfect tomatoes like
the parent vine . . . They were a little larger, for which I also
rejoiced . . . The seeds from this crop were again carefully
harvested, but from the first ripe and best specimens I selected
stock to my own planting. By good cultivation and wise selection
from season to season, not to exceed five years, it took on flesh,
size and improved qualities. I then put it on the market. This was
in 1870 . . . I called it the Paragon tomato . . ."

Livingston believed he could repeat the process and was
confident that he had produced an original distinct variety
which would not deteriorate or "run out," for "they are as capa-

ble of being cultivated into 'strains' as are those of cattle, hogs, chickens, or other plants and fruits of distinct kinds. The same laws of life and breeding govern tomatoes as in any other form of life, for all the processes of nature are so simple that few will believe them, even when they are pointed out to them." He later went on to produce a purple tomato—for which there was a demand in the Western states—by selection. This was introduced in 1875 under the name "Acme."[12]

He believed this to be a sufficiently momentous accomplishment to write an account of it, significantly noting the absence of any kind of patent protection for the introducer of new plant varieties. Presumably he did not get as much profit from his discovery as he had hoped. An experienced grower, working only a few years before Burbank embarked on his career, he devoted over twenty years to the improvement of this one species. Any hybridization that was involved appears to have been accidental.

In these same years, however, the foundations were being laid for the development of scientific agriculture in America. The Morrill Land Grant Act of 1862 appropriated funds from the sale of public land to support agricultural colleges in every state, and the Hatch Act of 1887 established the agricultural experiment stations. In 1889 the head of the Department of Agriculture was given cabinet rank—a surprisingly late date for a farming nation, but official recognition, anyhow, of the importance of agricultural development. Between 1860 and 1900 over four hundred million acres of virgin land came under the plow, and the new agricultural machinery—the McCormick reaper, the Pitts mechanical thresher and the Marsh harvester were all in use by 1858—was on the way to turning the farms into factories. With the mechanization of the land came a new rationalization of methods. Farming was less and less to be left to the traditional rule of thumb.

Even in Europe systematic plant breeding began with the nineteenth century. In England the London Horticultural Society was founded in 1805, and among its aims was the hybridization of economic plants to obtain improved varieties. One of the founders of the society was Thomas Knight, who has been called the "father of plant breeding." Walter Howard has suggested that it is to Knight that Burbank can best be compared.

Knight thought that just as the pear had been adapted to the English climate, and the crab apple had been successfully introduced into Siberia, so the peach and the grape could be produced in varieties that would grow well in England. He also believed that form and quality of fruit could be enhanced or altered for special purposes by breeding. At the first meeting of the London Horticultural Society, he read a paper setting forth his ideas concerning the objects which it ought to promote. No permanent improvement, he observed, was ever produced by grafting. "Seedling plants, on the contrary, of every cultivated species sport in endless variety. By selection from these, therefore, we can only hope for success in our pursuit of new and improved varieties of each species of plant or fruit . . ."[13]

But progress required the impetus of some clear insight into the *process* by which improvements might be accomplished. It came toward the end of the year 1859, when there appeared in the London bookshops a work which threw open public debate on one of the most revolutionary hypotheses of all time.

Charles Darwin had been developing the theory contained in his essay titled *On the Origin of Species by Means of Natural Selection, or the Preservation of Favored Races in the Struggle for Life* for over twenty years. It had germinated, he says, in 1838, when "I happened to read for amusement Malthus on *Population,* and being well prepared to appreciate the struggle for existence which everywhere goes on from long-continued observation of the habits of animals and plants, it at once struck me that under these circumstances favourable variations would tend to be preserved, and unfavourable ones to be destroyed. The result of this would be the formation of new species." [14]

Even he could scarcely have envisaged the effect that this simple idea would have, but he was aware that it would be contentious. In order to avoid prejudicing his case by hasty publication, he put off even writing it down for many years. It was not until 1856 that, at the urging of his longtime mentor, the geologist Sir Charles Lyell, he commenced to write out his ideas in full. He initially envisaged a work three or four times the length of the *Origin of Species* as necessary to deal properly with the great volume of evidence he had assembled, but he was obliged to speed up publication when he received from Alfred Russel Wallace, who was then traveling in Malaya, an essay *On the Tendency of Varieties to depart indefinitely from the Original Type,* containing the identical theory, early in the summer of 1858. Wallace's essay and an extract from Darwin's manuscript were published together in the *Journal of the Proceedings of the Linnean Society* that same year, establishing their joint authorship: one of the most singular coincidences in the history of science. Darwin almost immediately set to work to prepare his ideas for more detailed publication. After "thirteen months and ten days' hard labour" he completed the *Origin of Species,* which would eventually establish him as the best-known natural historian of all time and lay the basis for much of the thinking of the ensuing century.

This last statement may be challenged. Darwin has had his critics. "After almost a century of confusion it is hard to say exactly what single idea it was that 'triumphed' with the *Origin of Species*," says Jacques Barzun. "It was rather a cluster of ideas, a subject matter and not a theory." [15] In Darwin's own day it was argued that "the subject was in the air"—with the prompt and astonishing success of the book cited as proof. (Darwin himself answered this charge by pointing out that prior to the publication of his theory he had never come across a single naturalist who doubted that species were permanent.)

Undoubtedly the idea of evolution had been suggested earlier by writers like Geoffroy Saint-Hilaire, Lamarck, Goethe and his own grandfather, Erasmus Darwin. As long before as 1773 the eccentric Lord Monboddo had contended that the orangutan was related to man. What distinguished Darwin was the argument that natural selection, rather than any form of design or purpose in nature, was the instrument by which evolution took place, and the tendering of a great mass of carefully assembled evidence to show that it could account for all the improbabilities inherent in life. (As R. A. Fisher put it, natural selection is precisely a mechanism for generating a high degree of improbability.) It was this that made the *Origin* so decisive and so outraged the teleologists. If one accepted Darwin's argument—and it was difficult not to—there was no longer any need for design or divine intervention to account for natural phenomena.

Darwin's historical contribution to science may be subject to debate. What is hard to contest is his enormous influence on our way of looking at the world. Darwinism became a pillar of the great edifice of scientific determinism, matching those constituted by the "hard" sciences, physics and chemistry. The extent of his significance to the evolving philosophy of scientific materialism can be gauged from the fact that Karl Marx sought to dedicate the English edition of *Das Kapital* to him. (The honor was politely declined, not for political reasons, but because Darwin did not wish to be connected with an attack on Christianity: he had, after all, once intended to be a clergyman.) Evolution by natural selection became the standard under which generations of ardent materialists made war on organized religion and metaphysics in general.

In those days there was no international copyright agreement, and the *Origin of Species* was soon pirated by American publishers. As we have seen, however, it was not this book of Darwin's which fell into the hands of the young Luther Burbank, but a subsequent one, *The Variation of Animals and Plants under Domestication,* not published until early in 1868.

Burbank was not quite twenty when it reached him in Lancaster, Massachusetts. "It opened a new world to me," he says. "While I had been struggling along with my experiments, blundering on half-truths and truths, the great master had been reasoning out causes and effects for me and setting them down in orderly fashion, easy to understand, and having an immediate bearing on my work! I doubt if it is possible to make any one realize what this book meant to me." [16]

The public controversy, running strongly against Darwinism in the rural New England of the time, merely added fuel to the flame of Burbank's enthusiasm. In later life he would never cease to aver that Darwin was the master in whose steps he walked.

THREE

New England Rock

THE PAST, IT has been observed, is another country. The aphorist probably understated the case. The latter half of the nineteenth century, in so many ways the mold in which our own way of life was originally cast, is already infinitely more remote from us than the surface of the moon. And, unlike the moon, it recedes with every succeeding generation.

"Between 1850 and 1900 nearly every one's existence was exceptional," wrote Henry Adams. For Americans in particular the relative velocity of change was as great or perhaps even greater than it is today. In 1846 (the "year of decision" Bernard DeVoto was to call it) war with Mexico had brought California and the Southwest into the Union and established the geography we now take for granted. The frontiers of the spirit, elusive, eternally debatable and yet just as crucial to the developing nation, were less easily to be determined. Fifteen years later came the terrible half-decade of the Civil War. Luther Burbank

59

was eleven years old at the outbreak of fighting. He was just six-teen in April 1865 when Lee surrendered to Grant at Appomattox Courthouse. By then he was already earning his own living. He had grown up while the world seemed to be falling down, and there was room for every hand in the labor-starved workshops of a nation divided against itself.

Looking backward from a distance of fifty years, Adams wondered, "whether, on the whole, the boy of 1854 stood nearer to the thought of 1904, or to that of the year 1."[1] In the essentials he concluded in favor of the earlier date, so great were the revolutions he had seen, in science and in art, in daily life and in public life. And if this were true of Henry Adams, grandson of one president, great-grandson of another, scion of the greatest American family,[2] graduate of Harvard College and seasoned visitor of the capitals of Europe, how much more so of a boy born of plain people at Lancaster, Massachusetts, not that many miles from the Adams' ancestral home at Quincy, true, but a fair eternity from its Queen Anne mahogany paneling and Louis Seize furniture?

Luther Burbank was born at 11:57 P.M.[3] on March 7, 1849, three days after the Inauguration of "Old Rough-and-Ready" Zachary Taylor, who had earned his hero's laurel and Presidential candidacy across the Rio Grande in the Mexican War. The Gilded Age, as Mark Twain would call it, had not quite begun. America, like its President, who now pastured his war-horse Old Whitey on the White House lawn, was a rough-and-ready nation, so busy growing that even its capital, begun over fifty years before, was only half built.*

Taylor, the Whig candidate, had carried the Massachusetts vote. But he was also a slaveholding Virginian, and already the party had split into "Conscience Whigs" and "Cotton Whigs," foreshadowing the struggle that was to come. From the little we know of Luther's father, it seems safe to suppose that he was

---

*The twelve-year-old Adams, who was taken by his father to meet President Taylor, recalled a Washington of unpaved roads meandering between state buildings "like white Greek temples in the abandoned gravel-pits of a deserted Syrian city."

for conscience, and like most other antislavery Whigs, shortly became a Republican. Luther would be a faithful Republican in his turn until 1916, when he came out for Woodrow Wilson.

The best and only full account of his family and youth is to be found in a somewhat mawkish little book, *The Early Life and Letters of Luther Burbank*,[4] published by his sister, Emma Burbank Beeson in 1926, the year of his death, when she herself was seventy-two. The Burbanks, Mrs. Beeson says, were of English extraction,

> although the name Bermbank (as it is sometimes spelled) glimpses Holland, and no doubt a branch of the family were, in the fifteenth century, Belgian-Dutch.
>
> We are told of five Burbank brothers coming to the New World from the North of England, but the first authentic record is to be found in the Custom House at Boston, Mass. Joseph Borebank came in the ship *Abigail* from London in 1635; and John Burbank, from whom is traced in direct line our family, was made a voter at Rowley, Mass., in 1640.
>
> The following brief record of our line in the Burbank genealogy shows the rather unusual maturity of parents, as five generations cover a period of over two hundred years: John Burbank a voter at Rowley, Massachusetts in 1640; his son, Caleb Burbank, was born 1646; when 35 years of age his son Eleazer Burbank was born 1681; when 26 years of age his son Daniel Burbank was born 1707; when 39 years of age his son Nathaniel Burbank was born 1746; when 49 years of age his son Samuel Walton Burbank was born 1795; when 54 years of age his son Luther Burbank was born 1849.

She lists the various spellings of the name in the roll call of soldiers in the Revolutionary War: Birbank, Burbanck, Burbankes, Burbanks, Burbect and Burbank. The New England Burbanks, she says, were generally farmers, manufacturers, teachers and clergymen, for "throughout their generations it has been easier for them to solve a mathematical problem than to drive a nail, and they could make a political argument more successfully than they could make a flower to flourish," Few New England families, she claims with pride, "were more eminently represented in the learned professions, in civil enactments, and public reforms."

Nathaniel Burbank, Luther Burbank's grandfather, born at Sutton, Massachusetts, in 1746, married "the widow" Ruth Felch Foster and fathered seven children. At the time of his marriage he was a paper-maker at Harvard, but in 1797 he moved to Lancaster, not far off, where he bought the farm on which Luther was to be born. Until his death in 1818 he manufactured bricks and pottery there, making use of the fine clay to hand on his property. He was, reports his granddaughter, "a quiet, peace-loving man." For all that he had a mind of his own. When his wife and sons left the Unitarian Church at Lancaster to join the more recently established Baptist Church at Still River, a small village in the opposite direction from home, he continued to go on foot each Sunday to his own church. Asked why he did not go with his wife and sons, he replied that the first parish in Lancaster had always suited him and he saw no reason to change. The will he left gives a vivid picture of rural life in those days:

In the name of GOD, Amen.

I, Nathaniel Burbank of Lancaster, being weak in body but of sound mind and memory, blessed be God for the same, do this twentieth day of February, in the year one thousand eight hundred and eighteen, make and publish this my last will and testament in manner and form following; that is to say:

I give to my wife Ruth Burbank the use of a good cow, to be kept summer and winter; and also eighty weight of beef yearly, and seventy weight of pork, and nine bushels of corn and six bushels of rye, one bushel and a half of wheat and all kinds of summer and winter sauce sufficient for her use, and also the use of one-third of my dwelling house during her natural life, the said third to be chosen by her; and also a sufficiency of good firewood cut fit for the fire at the door, a horse and carriage for her use, and also a good doctor procured for her when needed, and paid, and all her grain carried to mill and the meal returned to her, and also to be comfortably clothed; and also to have the use of all my furniture during her natural life, and at her decease the said furniture is to be equally divided between my two daughters, Mehitable Barrett and Lucy Ball.

Item: I give to my beloved son, Daniel Burbank, the use of my shoemaker's shop to work in whenever he pleases, and an equal right to work in my brickyard for his own emolument with my two sons hereafter named, and to pass and repass to and from the same, and also one acre of land where the old barn used to stand, beginning at the road leading to Harvard and bounding on land belonging to the sons of Timothy Lewis, deceased.

Item: I give to the heirs of my beloved son Caleb Burbank, deceased, the sum of fifty dollars, to be well and truly paid to them by my executor after my decease.

Item: I give to my beloved son Nathaniel Burbank the sum of fifty dollars, to be well and truly paid to him by my executors after my decease.

Item: I give to my two beloved sons, Samuel Walton Burbank and Aaron Burbank, all my lands and buildings and stock and farming tools not before disposed of in this my will whatsoever, whereof I shall die seized in possession of, by their well and truly paying all my just debts and funeral charges.

Item: I make and ordain them to be executors of this my last will and testament.

In witness whereof I, Nathaniel Burbank, have to this my last will and testament set my hand and seal the twentieth day of February, in the year of our Lord one thousand eight hundred and eighteen.

Signed, sealed, published and delivered by the said Nathaniel Burbank as and for his last will and testament, in the presence of us who at his request and in his presence, and in the presence of each other, have subscribed our names as witnesses thereto.

NATHANIEL BURBANK. (SEAL)

CONSIDER STUDLEY
JABES DAMON
DARBY WILLARD

The language itself is modern and literate; but in every other respect (even to the names of the witnesses), it might be a document of the old Massachusetts Bay Colony. In Lancaster village, the nineteenth century had not yet properly commenced.

Luther's father, Samuel Walton Burbank who, with his brother Aaron, inherited the land, buildings, stock and farming tools at Lancaster, was born at Harvard in 1795, and was only two years old when the family moved to the farm. In 1818, shortly before Nathaniel Burbank's death, Samuel and Aaron had built the Burbank home. A "large, square, brick house, divided by a hall through the center and with an ell kitchen on each side," it was paid for by the manufacture of brick used in the construction of a Unitarian church in Lancaster two years before. "In this home," says Emma, "father spent the remaining fifty years of his life. The home is still occupied* and stands under the swaying branches of a great elm tree, which was set out by father in 1821, about the time he brought his bride, Hannah Ball of Townsend, Mass., to the home."

Hannah died after bearing him eight children, and he presently remarried. His second wife, Mary Ann Rugg, had two children by him, but neither she nor they long survived, and in June 1845, he married Olive Ross of Sterling, Massachusetts who would bear him an additional five. The first two of Olive's children died in infancy. Luther, his father's thirteenth child and the first of Olive's to survive, was born in the fourth year of their marriage. Another son, Alfred, and a daughter, Emma, Samuel Burbank's fifteenth and last child and the author of *The Early Life and Letters of Luther Burbank,* were born later. Among the records in Lunenburg town hall, Walter Howard found a yellowing manuscript with the title, "A History of the Town of

---

*"The land it stood on is now part of the Army's Fort Devens," write Burbank's 1967 biographers, Ken and Pat Kraft, "and the house was razed during the warm-up for World War II in 1941, to make way for a firing range . . ." It was apparently used for target practice by Army gunners.

Lunenburg in Masachusetts from the Original Grant December 7, 1719, to January 1, 1866," by George A. Cunningham, which

1. Susan E., born 2 September, 1822, died 20 July, 1825, aged 3 years.
2. Sarah M., born 21 February, 1826, married November, 1846, A. F. Kidder of Lancaster, where they both died, leaving two children. 1. Marcia L. and 2, Lizzie.
3. Hannah E., born 5 April, 1828, died 23 March, 1843, aged 15 years.
4. George W., born 17 November, 1829, married Apphie R. Blake. Settled in California.
5. Lucy A., Born April, 1831, died 29 May, 1848, aged 17 years, 1 month and 25 days.
6. Hosea Herbert, born 13 October, 1834, married 7 November, 1860, Lizzie H. Anderson, born Grafton, 1833. Lived in Westfield; one son, Henry.
7. Eliza Jenny, born 17 April, 1836, married George Varnum Ball.
8. David B., born 6 August, 1838, married 20 August, 1864, Paulina V. Ball, born 17 August, 1838, daughter of Rev. Hosea and Sarah (Helmes) Ball. They are—1874—living in California.

By second [?] wife Olive:
9. Luther, born 7 March, 1849.
10. Alfred Walton, born 2 February, 1852.
11. Emma Louisa, born 20 July, 1854.

The list omits all mention of Samuel Burbank's second wife, Mary Ann, and her two children, and of Olive's first two babies, who also died in infancy. The terrible mortality rate in the Burbank family—only half of the children surviving their teens—was nothing uncommon in those days. But it may go some way to explaining Luther's lifelong hypochondria. The graveyard where seven of his father's children lay buried was never very far away, and the anniversaries of their deaths came round all too often. Though they had died before he was born, the impressions of mortality must have been powerful in a sensitive child. Fatal illness was only too familiar, and any illness might prove fatal. The century itself, with its thriving horse doctors and host of patent medicines—Universal Wound Balsams, Anodyne Cigars, Chlorodyne (a popular panacea compounded largely of chloroform, morphia and hydrocyanic acid, sometimes with hashish and ether thrown in), Brown's Cholera Mixture, Atlee's Cure for Whooping-Cough, Roche's Remedy for Diphtheria, Dr. Krieder's Ague Pills, and Tinctures, Plasters and Elixirs for consumption, scarlet fever, measles, small-pox *et al.*, formulated out of everything imaginable—was more than a little hypochondriac, with excellent reason.

"My father," Burbank says in his autobiography, written with the assistance of Wilbur Hall, "was a New Englander of pure and unmixed physical strain, but it was not the shallow soil, the rocky structure below, the hardness of labor, the rigor of the winters, and the austerity of the people about him that he saw; he was a man of imagination and a facile mind, and he loved beauty and the sunshine and pleasantness of the land, in its garments of spring and autumn, and was influenced by them."[5] Emma adds that Samuel Burbank "loved his children tenderly, and gave to each the best care and education in his power. His love of reading and classic taste kept the home supplied with good literature. The children had books and papers suited to their taste and ability."

What were the books they had? She does not say, but we may surmise. Inevitably there was the Bible; almost certainly a copy of Noah Webster's "Blue-Backed Speller," over thirty million of which had been sold by 1859; very likely there were the works of Thoreau, Emerson, Whittier, Lowell, Hawthorne and Cooper; if fiction was permitted at all there must have been *Uncle Tom's Cabin;* perhaps *Hiawatha. The Age of Fable* and Bartlett's *Familiar Quotations,* all of them published in 1855; Sir Walter

Scott's *Waverley* novels, the enormously popular Washington Irving and even Susan Warner's sensationally successful tearjerker, *The Wide, Wide World,* with more than half a million copies in print, may have been there. Of magazines there might have been *Harper's,* launched in 1850, the New York *Knickerbocker,* in which the great New England writers frequently appeared, the Boston *Youth's Companion,* and *Godey's Lady's Book,* in which the formidable Sarah Josepha Hale gave the world "Mary Had a Little Lamb."[6] Why not? *Godey's* was the country's best-selling magazine in 1850, and according to Emma her mother had gone to school with the Mary Sawyer who was the original heroine of that poem (though "Mary was her senior by several years, and the incident of the lamb at school which gave rise to the familiar poem occurred before her school life began.") America was in the midst of a media explosion, and by the middle of the century had already surpassed England in book and magazine sales. Massachusetts was the most literate of American states, and the Burbanks lived in close proximity to some of the most famous writers of the day.

Samuel Burbank, Emma says, was never arbitrary, and perhaps too kind and indulgent a father. "Someone once asked brother Alfred if father gave him a whipping for some misconduct. Alfred seemed loath to reply, for he knew he deserved it, but he at last said 'No, but he offered to,' and that is as near as any of us ever came to a whipping." This indulgence he seems to have passed on to his son. All his life, Luther would have a soft spot for children.

Olive, Luther's mother, was the second child of Peter Ross and Polly Kendall Burpee, born on April 7, 1813. Her father was of Scots descent and a cabinetmaker by trade. But, Emma observes, he "was by nature a horticulturist, and was the originator of several new grapes. He was best known at the time by the superior fruits and vegetables produced on his place. He was a rather frail man, suffering all his life from attacks of heart disease, yet he lived to the advanced age of 87 years, retaining his ambition and enthusiasm to the last. He was clearing the brush from a very steep rocky hillside in order to set it with grapevines when he was called by death. He was found one bright summer day sitting on a big rock, apparently resting, as so often he had done, but life had quietly gone out. The active, executive wife and loving mother preceded him but a few years to the other life." Polly Burpee was of French descent (the name is a corruption of *Beau Pré*: beautiful meadow), and Emma remarks on the fact that she belonged to the family which included W. Atlee Burpee, the famous Philadelphia seedsman, who would one day be one of Luther's customers and champions.

In his autobiography, Burbank himself says of his mother that she was "shrewd and practical, of a nervous temperament, quick and impulsive, yet kindly, intelligent, and with a great love of her garden. She had an unusual bent for making things grow, whether from domesticated seeds or from bulbs or cuttings or roots found in the woods all about; one of my earliest recollections is of the beauty and peace and fragrance of that old-fashioned garden of hers." It was evidently from Olive, rather than from his father, that he had his love of gardening and feeling for growing things.

She was a woman of strong character. "Mother [it is Emma speaking] was of a very intense nature, walking with firm step and speaking with the falling accent." When only thirteen she signed a temperance pledge and remained faithful to it throughout her long life. If this seems extraordinary, it should be remembered that in the New England of Olive Burbank's youth, rum, beer and hard cider flowed uncommonly freely, as did a variety of brandies and "bounces" manufactured from cherries, peaches and pears. Strong drink was not infrequently given to small children. "In accord with the general custom," Emma notes, "a large mug of 'hot toddy' was prepared on 'election day' and other holidays. Each member of the family, to the youngest child, was expected at least to sip from the mug. Olive

at an early age became disinclined to follow the custom and refused to taste the liquor." She successfully inculcated at least
one of her children with the temperance spirit: Luther would
scarcely touch so much as a drop of alcohol all his days.

Emma gives a picture of life in the Ross home, which she obviously had from her mother and which seems worth quoting
for its own sake as a portrait of a bygone age and way of life. In
this humble home,

> there was much of family life and companionship. When other
> tasks were remitted the father taught the boys to weave baskets
> from slender willow branches gathered from the banks of mead-
> ow streams; the girls braided hats from [the] finest of the wheat
> straws, which had been carefully selected and saved for this pur-
> pose. These hats were sold at the country store. In the attic
> chamber, where were kept the willow strands for basket-weaving
> and the unfinished work, heaped on the floor, in one corner,
> were glistening brown chestnuts; in another, big, rugged butter-
> nuts, and the plump hickory nuts, in larger quantity, filled a bin
> by themselves.
>
> Work and pleasure were combined in the gathering of the
> nuts, picking the apples and husking the corn, and also in the ex-
> cursions for wild strawberries, low-running blackberries on the
> hillside, and huckleberries in the pasture lands. Olive was espe-
> cially fond of these out-of-door tasks and of rambles in the
> woods gathering wild flowers, lupines, goldenrods and asters.
>
> Books then were few and even those not of a nature pleasing
> to childhood. Only homemade candles by which to read, yet
> around the glowing fireside, with popping corn, roasting chest-
> nuts, and apples, there was enjoyed much more of neighborly
> hospitality than now exists.

It is a romantic picture that leaves out the harshness of life in
the cruel New England winters, the perils of the inevitable
sickbed, the stern morality of a Puritan society where, as Van
Wyck Brooks put it, the congregations "followed the web of the

sermons with a keen and anxious watchfulness, eager to learn the terms of their damnation." But it would be familiar enough to the average American of the 1820s, in whose country the farmer still outnumbered the townsman more than ten to one.

The town of Lancaster, incorporated in 1658, lies in Worcester County, Massachusetts. Here, Emma observes, "less than twenty-five years after the landing of the Pilgrims, a tract of land ten miles long and eight miles wide was purchased of the Indian chief Sholan of the Nashaway or Nashawogs." The Burbank homestead was about three miles north of Lancaster Center, just off the Harvard Road. It was "a typical New England home—the large, square brick house, standing well back from the street, beneath the swaying branches of a stately elm tree. Over the door climbed the white jasmine, while lilacs, roses, lilies, and other old-fashioned flowers filled the yard and looked from the windows of the cheery living-room."

Here lived the families of the two brothers, Samuel Walton and Aaron Burbank. In addition to the house itself, their property consisted of some hundred acres of farmland, divided piecemeal between them in order that each might have the same share of the orchards, fields, pastures, and woodland. The brothers also maintained separate brickyards, which provided them with a supplementary source of income in the summer months. Aaron, a Baptist minister in addition to being a farmer and brick manufacturer, spent a good deal of his time tending to his congregation. Samuel Walton devoted himself to the more mundane pursuits of farm, brickyard and woodlot. Home life was strictly ordered. Each day's work began with family prayers and a text from the Bible. But, this being New England, there was also a lively interest in the secular thinking of the day. Worcester County lay at the heart of the Commonwealth of Massachusetts: this was no intellectual backwater.

"The home was filled with intellectual activity, being near Concord, then the center of American literature, famous as the home of Ralph Waldo Emerson and other men and women whose thought was influencing the world," Emma says. "All the household was greatly interested in the great leaders of the times—Lincoln, Webster, Sumner, Agassiz, the Beechers, as well as Emerson, Thoreau, Longfellow and the Alcotts, some of whom were personal acquaintances and sometimes guests at the home." Burbank himself afterward asserted that "My father was a great admirer and personal acquaintance of Ralph Waldo Emerson, Daniel Webster, Chas. Sumner and Henry Ward Beecher . . ."[7] Beecher was a professional lecturer and pulpit orator, while Webster and Sumner were Massachusetts politicians, and Emerson lectured widely in Boston, Concord and the neighboring towns, of which Lancaster was one, to supplement his income. There was nothing out of the ordinary about their knowing Sam Burbank, who was a prominent local citizen. Luther himself never stressed these friendships in his published writing, and it is unlikely that they were more than casual acquaintances. At the same time, their presence in the house makes it almost certain that the Burbanks were first antislavery Whigs, then abolitionist Republicans. These impassioned public men (Webster had been a Presidential candidate and served as Secretary of State, 1850–1852) must inevitably have had a profound effect in the household, if only in provoking discussion of the great controversies of the day. They were a link with the world of intellect and affairs.

A closer, more constant influence was exerted by Levi Sumner Burbank, Aaron Burbank's eldest son, who was a friend and associate of the naturalist Louis Agassiz (1807–1873). This cousin, who was one of the first members of the American Association for the Advancement of Science, was at various times president of Paducah College in Kentucky and principal of Lowell High School and the Lancaster Academy. He had also served as curator of geology at the Boston Society of Natural History, and was the author of several papers on geology and paleontology. At the time the Civil War broke·out he was president of Paducah College, but resigning this position for obvious reasons became principal of the Lancaster Academy in 1861, when Luther was twelve years old. He possessed a large geological collection, and he often took his young cousin with him on his excursions in search of natural history objects.

Levi lived at home, in the Burbank house, and he was undoubtedly instrumental in turning Luther's mind in the direction of natural history. He had a talent for explaining things in such a way as to make them "alive and exciting and never dull and tedious . . . and had read more books and understood them better than any one else I knew." The boy was already at home with nature, but it was Levi, he afterward said, "who may have crystallized my formless thinking and shaped my vague theories until he had made me want to know, not second-hand, but first-hand, from Nature herself, what the rules of this exciting game of Life were."[8]

See then, in the dark years of the Civil War, Levi and Luther roaming the magical countryside around Lancaster—a wooded landscape almost English in its "low, sloping hills, rich intervals, sparkling streams of pure water and enchanting little lakes like bits of blue sky dropped down to earth," Emma observes. She was the little girl who welcomed them back from their walks and, in listening excitedly to the story of their adventures, developed an admiration for her brother that lasted all her life.

He was a shy, sensitive child. "Not being altogether understood," his sister says, "he sometimes suffered undeserved rebuke. Once soon after he began to make his way among the growing plants in mother's flower garden he was found trying to replace in the ground an uprooted plant. As it was thought he was endeavoring to undo his mischief, he was reproved. Later it was discovered that another had uprooted the plant and it was only the child's sorrow for its destruction that led to his efforts to reset it.

"The story has often been told of the cactus plant which the baby boy made his most constant companion, until one sad day he fell, breaking both jar and plant. This might have been a prophecy of the cactus chapter of his later life."

Half a century later, Luther listed some of the ingredients of an ideal childhood, and he spoke from memory of his own: "Every child should have mudpies, grasshoppers, water-bugs, tadpoles, frogs, mud-turtles, elderberries, wild strawberries, acorns, chestnuts, trees to climb, brooks to wade in, water-lilies, woodchucks, bats, bees, butterflies, various animals to pet, hayfields, pine-cones, rocks to roll, sand, snakes, huckleberries, and hornets; and any child who has been deprived of these has been deprived of the best part of his education."[9] He had been fortunate enough to have had all of these things.

When he was five he started school in the little red-brick school house among the pine trees on what they called the "Dingle Road," a crossroad connecting Shirley Road and Harvard Street. It was about half a mile away from the Burbank house, and his brother, Hosea Herbert Burbank, who at twenty was the teacher, pulled him to school on his little handsled. His next teacher was his sister Jane (Eliza Jenny) who, Emma says, "had recently returned from Pennsylvania where she began teaching when only fourteen years of age." He was a quiet, studious, serious child for the most part, but even his brother and sister, as teachers, found it difficult to get him to recite his lessons in the schoolroom because of his extreme shyness. All his life Luther was to remain diffident about public speaking. Slightly built and not physically strong, he preferred to play with the girls, who often defended him against bigger boys and their bullying. But as he grew up he showed a natural measure of boyish mischief. He loved to skate, and one year when he was about eleven or twelve dammed a trout brook that flowed through his father's farm on the pretext of increasing the cranberry crop on the peat bogs, but actually to make a skating pond. The scheme was successful, and a Christmas skating party was held on his homemade rink the following winter.

When his twenty-five-year-old brother, George, grafted the apple trees in the orchard, the five-year-old Luther had watched with intense interest. He could not understand why so many healthy branches had to be cut off, and George explained the process to him. He took great pleasure in watching the development of the grafts and spent a good deal of time in the apple orchard watching the buds grow, the pink and white blossoms unfurl to attract the bees, and the formation of the tiny apples. He was the one to carry back the news of the first faint coloring of the Early June and Williams. He soon learned to identify these and the other kinds—Baldwins, Greenings and Russets—in the orchard. One of his early treasures was a book with descriptions and pictures in outline of different varieties of fruit.

There was one particular incident that had the effect of profoundly stimulating his inquisitiveness about the processes of nature. He was walking along in the woods, kicking at the snow and wishing that the winter were over. Suddenly in the white landscape he saw a green place in front of him. He could scarcely believe his eyes. The grasses grew tall and the shrubs and vines were fresh and springlike. Even the sunshine seemed to him "almost tropical in its white intensity." He rushed forward to find out if this miraculous oasis could be real and discovered a warm spring that carried enough heat to the surface to keep the ground roundabout free of snow, and give the vegetable life a foothold even in the middle of winter.

"I studied the phenomenon intently. Very dimly there began to grow in my mind vague questions as to how these plants and grasses and vines, their neighbors and cousins and brothers all dead and withered under the snow, or else dormant and waiting for spring, could adjust themselves to this summer-in-winter environment. Why, I asked, didn't they follow the traditions of their families and die with the fall, or droop and shed their leaves and hibernate, no matter what the warm water brought to them in the way of a miracle of equable temperature? Certainly the lycopodiums, the beautiful trailing partridge berry, the sedges and grasses, and here and there an early sprouting buttercup, should have known better, the way they had been raised and with their decent seven-months-of-summer ancestry behind them, than to flaunt themselves so shamelessly in this unfilial winter blooming!"[10]

To this incident he afterward attributed his first notion of the power of environment in plant variation. When he got home it was already late, and his family was not much impressed by the miracle he had found. But to him it was the most wonderful thing that had ever happened in his young life. When Levi Sumner Burbank came back from Kentucky not long afterward with his collection of geological specimens and his fondness for botanical expeditions, he found a disciple eager to learn what he had to teach. Natural history became Luther's passion.* In January 1864 we find him writing eagerly to his brother in California: "We all want to see you very much. When you come will you bring seeds of some of the plants that do not grow here, and some of the minerals, too?"

In the fall of that year, 1864, he entered the Lancaster Academy as a student. For the next four years he spent the winter months studying and worked in the summer at the Ames Plow Works in Worcester, where his uncle, Luther Ross, was a foreman, learning the pattern-maker's trade, for which he showed considerable aptitude. There was a bonus in that his uncle had a garden and even apparently did a little horticultural experimenting as a hobby (*his* father, Peter Ross, it will be remembered, was known as the originator of several new grapes). On half days the young Burbank was allowed out of the shop to work among the seedling grapes and rhubarb.

The Lancaster Academy, which was in the way of being a sort of superior prep school for Harvard and Yale, attracted a number of students from out of state. The course of study was comparatively stiff. Here it is, as listed in the catalog of the school for 1866–1867:

---

*Burbank's eulogist Frederick Clampett says, furthermore, that Agassiz was a close personal friend of Luther's father, and that in 1863 "when Luther had attained his fourteenth year and Agassiz was just fifty-six years old, he formed his acquaintance, so that for ten precious years he sat at the feet of that great master." This, I think, must be taken with a grain of salt. There does not seem to be any supporting evidence.

First Year.   Eaton's *Arithmetic,* Greene's *Grammar,* Losing's *U.S. History.*

Second Year.   Robinson's *Algebra,* Harkness' *Latin,* Grammar' & Reader, Caesar's *Commentaries* begun, Carter's *Physical Geography,* Quackenbos' *Philosophy,* Worcester's *History,* Otto's *French Grammar,* Fulton and Eastman's *Book-keeping.*

Third Year.   Robinson's *Geometry,* Caesar's *Commentaries* finished, Cicero's *Orations,* Crosby's *Greek Grammar and Lessons, Anabasis* of Xenophon begun, Sewell's *History of Greece,* Corson's *Soireés Littéraires,* Comer's *Book-keeping,* Cutter's *Physiology.*

Fourth Year.   Arithmetic, Algebra and Geometry reviewed, *Aeneid* and *Georgics* of Virgil, *Anabasis* of Xenophon finished, Three Books of Homer's *Iliad,* Modern Series of French Plays, Surveying with field-practice, Blockheart's *Chemistry.*

Fifth Year.   (Corresponding to Freshman Year in Harvard College.) Pierce's *Algebra* and *Geometry, Odes* and *Epodes* of Horace, Lincoln's *Livy* (Books XII and XIII), *Memorabilia* of Xenophon, *Odyssey* of Homer (Three Books), Felton's *Greek Historians, Histoire Grecque par Dury.* Regular reading classes continue throughout the 1st, 2nd and 3rd years, and exercises in Composition throughout the course.

Luther did not stay on for a fifth year, and one wonders how much of the rest of the course he was able to fit in, studying only part time. The emphasis appears to have been heavily on classics, and there is no evidence that he knew much Greek or Latin. However, in the catalog for 1867–1868, in which his name also appears in the list of students, Rolfe and Gillett's *Natural Philosophy* and *Chemistry* and Guyot's *Earth and Man* are added to the above list of textbooks, and presumably more emphasis was given to science as the years went by.

His name does not appear in catalogs subsequent to 1867–1868, and the academy, which dated from 1815, closed down in 1873. So far as his schoolwork went, Emma asserts that he did well in mathematics and English composition, but found the afternoons, when the students were required to declaim, a torment. "After one or two ineffectual attempts to stand and deliver a perfectly committed address," she says, "he was excused from this exercise with the provision that he write double the required number of themes, and thenceforth life at the academy was a pleasure to him."

Apart from his studies at the academy, he attended what public lectures he could in Lancaster on the topics which interested him. A series by a German, Professor Gunning, on astronomy, physical geography, geology, mineralogy, paleontology and related subjects apparently made a particularly deep impression. He also took a course of lessons in freehand drawing from Professor George C. Gladwin, who seems to have been connected with the Massachusetts Institute of Technology, and made good use of the Lancaster Public Library, said to have been one of the best town libraries in the state at that time. It was here that he discovered Darwin, here, too, that he read deeply in the works of Henry David Thoreau (1817–1862), a naturalist much after his own heart, and of the German naturalist and explorer, Baron Friedrich Alexander von Humboldt (1769–1859). Humboldt's *Kosmos,* a description of the physical universe in five volumes, has been called one of the great scientific works of the day, and he had had a profound influence on both Darwin and Alfred Russel Wallace. Of him Burbank remarked that, "Perhaps the basic thought I absorbed was the idealistic and intrinsic worth of the work in which I was later to embark." These three writers—Darwin, Humboldt and Thoreau—he identified as the decisive "book influences" that "stand out in my life as having influenced greatly my career." [11]

Reading was for the winter. At his summer job he showed a distinctly mechanical turn of mind. He had a natural bent in that direction, and when he was sixteen constructed a wall clock which was attached to a beam in his father's house and is said to have kept time with a fair degree of accuracy. He also made a set of dumbbells for the academy gymnasium—he was very fond of athletics—and worked at a series of machines and gadgets, waterwheels and steam engines. His wages at the plow works were only fifty cents a day at the outset, not enough to pay his board at his uncle's house. Presently, however, he invented an attachment for the engine lathe which turned out to be so effective as a labor-saving device that, working by the piece instead of by the day as had first been the arrangement, he was soon taking home a fatter pay envelope on Saturday nights. But he hated the noise of the shop and found he was allergic to the sawdust which filled the air, and he began to look around for other work. He was encouraged by his father to think of becoming a physician, and started to direct his studies along these lines.

He was a shy, reticent boy, particularly timid with strangers. Once when his mother was visiting him at his uncle's house, and they sat talking in the living room, his aunt, who was preparing supper in the kitchen, pushed open the door a little—so that she "might hear the sound of Luther's voice," she explained when detected. She had heard him speak so few words since he had come into the household.

Around this time he experienced a "religious awakening," and when he returned to Lancaster was baptized in the Nashua River—named for those long-gone Nashaway Indians—and joined the "hard-shell" Baptist church at Still River. This seems to have been under the influence of his mother. The Burbank women were always veering off in that direction, taking their children with them if they could. Grandmother Ruth had done exactly the same thing in her day. In 1870, however, Luther and his mother transferred to the less severe Baptist church at Groton Junction. In his later thinking he gradually reverted to the milder spirit of the Unitarianism his grandfather Nathaniel had brought with him from Harvard and ultimately to the Emersonian Transcendentalism that sprang from the blending of Unitarian rationalism with the Deism of the eighteenth century.

All the same he showed the distinct stamp of his Puritan background. Now, still in his teens, he came across some lectures on diet and the "water-cure" and took up the harsh regimen advocated. "Taking a pail of water to his room at night, which would be frozen over so hard in the morning that he would be obliged to break the ice with a stick of firewood, he would take a sponge bath in this ice water," says his sister. "The window of his room was always open and sometimes the snow would drift in upon his bed. About this time he resolved to eat no meat and only a very limited amount of food, which he carefully weighed so as not to exceed the quantity he allowed himself. All the regulations he deemed good he carried out to the letter, until he so reduced himself in flesh and strength that our parents called in the family physician, who objected to the strenuous régime. Luther, however, always claimed that his health was permanently benefited by the experience."

In the summer of 1868, he suffered a severe sunstroke while running to get help to put out a fire sparked by a passing locomotive in a timber lot on the Burbank property. "Luther, then a slight youth of nineteen, was five feet and eight inches in height, but became reduced from his usual weight of 130 pounds to 120 pounds," Emma says. "Failing to recover from the effects of the sunstroke, in August 1870, he made a cruise in a mackerel schooner bound for the Gulf of Newfoundland. The vessel was wrecked, but he was so seasick at the time that being taken on board a lumber raft and towed to shore seemed of small matter to him. He returned home minus his baggage, but greatly improved in health."

It seems only too clear that there must have been another element to this protracted convalescence of over two years. Our information is, alas, all too scanty, and the age did not give a great deal of credence to the notion of psychosomatic illness, but an ocean voyage would be an improbable cure for sunstroke, if a likely prescription for a nervous breakdown. After that summer he did not return to the academy and seems also to have given up his job at the Ames Plow Works. He was going through a period of complex psychological disorientation. The intense, ascetic youth was flowering under the influence of new ideas. The hard-shell Baptist was in conflict with the newborn Darwinian. By no amount of contortion could these world views comfortably cohabit. An additional strain was the death of his father, Samuel Walton Burbank, in December 1868. The life of the family was painfully disrupted, and Luther was thrown back on his own resources. He could no longer dally in the choice of a career. Fresh in his mind was Darwin's inquiry into the processes of artificial selection, and even though the emphasis of that inquiry was more on animals than on plants, the idea had begun to form in his mind of devoting his life to scientific horticulture. It was only the vague glimmerings of an idea, more in the form of a realization of the dramatic potential of plant breeding than an intention, but it was there. In a letter dated January 1919, which Emma quotes, Burbank afterward wrote,

When I was about nineteen, in 1868, probably the turning point of my career in fixing my life work in the production of new species and varieties of plant life was fixed by the reading of Darwin's "Variation of Animals and Plants Under Domestication," which I obtained from the library at Lancaster, Mass., my old home. Well do I remember reading that work of Darwin's— that the whole world seemed placed on a new foundation. It was without question the most inspiring book I had ever read, and I had read very widely from one of the best libraries in the state on similar scientific subjects. I think it is impossible for most people to realize the thrills of joy I had in reading this most wonderful work. The reading of this book was without doubt the turning point in my life work.

At once, as soon as I was able, I purchased other books written by Charles Darwin, and today I have still one to read which probably influenced the general public more than all the rest of his writings—"Origin of Species."

I have been so busy producing living forms from the thought inspired by Master Darwin's conclusions that I have never, to the present date, had time to read his "Origin of Species." However, I imagine I could write the "Origin of Species" myself from what I have read of his other works.

Darwin was the greatest man who lived in the past century, and in his thoughtful, truthful, laborious, unobtrusive way, in my opinion, did more to liberate and ennoble the human race than any other man who lived during the century.

The second book which I purchased of Darwin's was "Cross and Self-Fertilization in the Vegetable Kingdom."

The following year, 1869, the family left the old home at Lancaster, selling their half share in the farm and house to Luther's cousin, Calvin Burbank, who had inherited the other half on the death of his father, Aaron. Mrs. Burbank and her children now moved to Groton Junction (subsequently called Ayer Junction), where Olive bought a cottage on the outskirts of the village.

In 1871, at the age of twenty-one, Luther took a step which greatly determined the direction his life was to take. On his father's death he had abandoned the medical studies he had begun under a local doctor. What other profession might he take up? In Lunenburg Township, not far from Lancaster, he found "seventeen acres of unusually fine soil" for sale. With the small inheritance from his father's estate and a mortgage, he bought this piece of land which had on it an old house in good condition. Olive acquired a house in Lunenburg, with property adjoining Luther's piece of land, and moved there with Emma and Alfred.

On these seventeen acres he began truck gardening, producing vegetables for sale at the market in the nearby town of Fitchburg. In this way, he thought, he would have not only a living, but room for experiment. Thus he found the métier which was to make him famous. It was, he later thought, more cold necessity than any particular intention that showed him the way.

FOUR

Burbank's Seedling

DARWIN HAD LIT the fuse, circumstances were the charge. It was the very challenge of those early years that laid out the lines of Burbank's career. He was now obliged to compete with established vegetable producers, which was hard going unless he could somehow gain an edge on them. He learned the secrets of his new trade, the use of cold frames, hotbeds and fertilizer, and he learned them thoroughly, gaining a professionalism that would stand him in good stead all his life. He was in competition with more experienced men long set up in business. By cutting corners in production and marketing, he could produce vegetables more cheaply than other gardeners, perhaps, but what really fascinated him was the possibility of raising better vegetables and getting them to market ahead of the others. "Here," he thought, "was a place to use wits and ingenuity and inventive faculty and another faculty that, at the time, I did not know I had, even latently—the power of choice as between two apparently identical varieties or even between two apparently identical plants!"[1]

The challenge of the task excited him, and his Yankee instincts were in no doubt that this was the road to success. The older men had a lead on him. He would make it up by being that much smarter than they were. He set about reviewing the problems methodically in terms of what he knew.

Thinking about the ways in which Nature produced variations in plants, he remembered the "winter garden" he had found while wandering in the Lancaster woods as a boy, where he had seen summer plants growing amid the snow, nourished by a deep-flowing spring of warm water.

> I knew enough to know that vines and shrubs and flowers grew according to their season and withered according to an hereditary tendency that had impressed itself on them through thousands of generations of growth. The warm spring accounted for the equability of the temperature in that spot, but it did not account for the luxuriant and lush growth of plants that should be dead. What I had supposed was a fixed and immutable law of Nature was not, then, fixed and immutable at all. Or, better, the law was there, but I had misinterpreted it. What was the influence behind this phenomenon?[2]

He began to experiment—in what he admits was "a crude, superficial way, without any order to my trials and without keeping any record of results." He noted what every gardener has noticed: that certain plants grew faster than others in the same row. Later in the season he marked out individuals that bore more or bigger produce than ordinary, or fruit that was of superior quality, or ripened earlier or later than average. Some plants were actually superior in more than one respect.

Those individuals who were "willing to take a step forward" as he put it (in the sort of Lamarckian turn of phrase that runs all through his writings, a style so alien to Darwin that one wonders how deeply he could have grasped the methodology of his professed master, who had banished this kind of anthropomorphism from evolutionary thinking) were tagged, and when time came to harvest they were saved, and their seeds kept for the next year's planting. At first he was far from sure that the improvements would be reproduced in the next generation, "but after a time I began to see that they were, and that there was certain to be at least part of the second year's growth that would show all the finer characteristics of the marked plants, and a tendency to improve on their improvement."[3] Slowly he began to believe that he was on the right track.

Creative horticulture was still very much a sideline, taking second place to his market garden. (He kept a few animals, too—a heifer calf of his winning the second prize of a dollar at the Lunenburg Town Fair in September 1874—and sold honey to bring in a little extra income.) But he persevered at it. In the beginning he used seedsmen's collections, testing, selecting and crossing those which seemed most promising. He also experimented with various Eastern wild flowers, gaining an acquaintance with them that would later prove useful (particularly in the development of the Shasta daisy, in which Japanese, European and wild American species combined to produce a unique hybrid that holds its own even today). He did some work with various kinds of beans, and was able to produce a variety of sweet corn that came in a week earlier than ordinary. "It may be said that in general my garden products were of exceptional quality," he later asserted of this period.

One early failure was an attempt to produce a yellow sweet corn. In those days all sweet corn was white, and yellow corn was thought to be fit only for animals. Burbank cross-pollinated white sweet corn by yellow field corn in an attempt to fix a yellow sugary kernel. But he was unable to get a uniformly yellow ear unmixed with white seeds while he was at Lunenburg. There were some promising hybrids, but when he moved to California the project was abandoned, and he did not resume his experiments with corn until much later. At this stage he does not appear to have realized that it was necessary to continue breeding beyond the first generation. Like other breeders he was working very much in the dark. Ironically, as the geneticist Donald F. Jones (himself one of the outstanding figures in the hybrid corn breeding program which revolutionized American agriculture) pointed out, "Thirty-six miles away, in the library of Harvard University, were the Proceedings of a Natural History Society in Austria. In that publication was a clearly written report, printed a few years before, by a Catholic priest that would have told Burbank exactly how to fix his yellow sweet corn in the shortest possible time. But it was written in German and the pages were uncut."[4] Those pages would remain uncut for another quarter century, and Hugo de Vries, who would be among the first to understand their significance, was still a postgraduate student in Germany. Mendel's time had not yet come.

Burbank's first notable achievement, and the point at which his lifework really began, was the development of the Burbank potato. This called for no understanding of Mendelian law, inasmuch as it was nothing more or less than an amazing stroke of good fortune: the improbable sort of opportunity which proverbially knocks once and disappears forever unless unhesitatingly grasped. Luther was ready to grasp it, and nothing he ever did afterward would be so successful in the long run as this potato.

Potato cultivation in South America may go back to before 3000 B.C. In the Andean highlands it was the most important single food plant in pre-Columbian times, and more than ninety wild species are still to be found growing there, along with several hundred cultivated varieties. Sometime during the latter part of the sixteenth century Spanish explorers brought potatoes back to Europe, probably from Chile or Peru (the exact date and provenance of its introduction into the Old World are unknown), and via Spain they were carried back across the Atlantic to Florida, whence in turn they reached Virginia. In 1586 Sir Thomas Herriot, a companion of Sir Walter Raleigh's, apparently brought the first potatoes to Britain from there. They did not find much favor among the English of that day, though Raleigh tried to interest Queen Elizabeth and managed on one occasion to get a dish of potatoes served at the royal table. Not until the middle of the seventeenth century were potatoes widely grown in England. On the continent of Europe they met with even more resistance. To encourage their use, Louis XVI of France ordered potatoes planted and went so far as to wear a potato flower in his buttonhole. The fields which had been planted to potatoes were guarded by troops with a view to provoking public curiosity, and the king served banquets in which the tubers featured prominently. None of this seems to have overcome the suspicious resistance to the new vegetable. Only in Ireland was the potato favorably received, by an impoverished peasantry who could not afford to be persnickety about their diet, and the first cultivation of potatoes in northern Europe took place in that country in the vicinity of Cork. Perhaps it was because of its relationship to the deadly nightshade (which belongs to the same family, the Solanaceae, as do the tomato, tobacco and eggplant) that the legend that potatoes were unwholesome arose and persisted so long. In his book *A Year's Residence in the United States of America,* published in 1819, the English political writer William Cobbett illustrated this enduring antipathy to them:

> Nor do I say, that it is filthy to eat potatoes. I do not ridicule the using of them as sauce. What I laugh at is, the idea of the use of them being a saving; of their going further than bread; of the cultivation of them in lieu of wheat adding to the human sustenance of a country . . . As food for cattle, sheep or hogs, this is the worst of all the green and root crops; but of this I have said enough before; and therefore, I now dismiss the Potatoe with the hope, that I shall never again have to write the word, or see the thing.

The potato refused to be dismissed, however, and once accepted soon demonstrated its remarkable properties as a food. Seven pounds suffice to supply a man's entire daily requirement in calories (three thousand), protein and iron, as also vitamins B and C, and half the requirement of phosphorus. Ten percent of a man's calcium requirements are also supplied by this amount of potatoes, and all other dietary essentials can be supplied by the addition of a pint of milk.[5] This was precisely the basic diet of the Irish peasantry in the eighteenth and nineteenth centuries, and though doubtless a little tedious (per capita consumption in peasant families reached the staggering total of more than eight pounds a day) proved nourishing. Compared with other staples, potatoes yielded a significantly larger quantity of food per acre. They must have seemed a miraculous answer to the persistent problem of famine which had plagued Europe since the beginning of its history.

In the 1840s, however, potato blight, caused by the fungus *Phytophthora infestans,* first appearing in Germany, destroyed the Irish crop year after year, and in the next two decades an estimated million people died of starvation in Ireland, where widespread dependence on this single plant combined with official indifference to produce a long-drawn-out famine. The blight also ravaged the fields of America during these years, and in 1859 the situation was further aggravated by the appearance of great numbers of potato beetles in Colorado. Native to the area east of the Rockies, where they live on wild plants of the potato family, the beetles spread rapidly through Nebraska, Iowa, Illinois and Ohio, and soon reached the Northeastern states. At the same time a mysterious tendency on the part of the tubers to degenerate manifested itself. It seemed an end to potato growing.

The cause of the potato blight was unknown, and it was regarded as part of the degeneration complex (now attributed to an accumulation of tuber-borne viruses within the vegetative clones[6]). It was thought that the potato had degenerated as a result of being propagated exclusively from cuttings, and though other factors were recognized—lack of care in selecting seed potatoes true to type and storage under conditions which reduced vitality—horticulturists believed that the plant needed sexual reproduction—that is, propagation by seed—to restore its vigor. In 1851 the Reverend Chauncy Enoch Goodrich of Utica, New York, procured potato varieties from Panama (the U.S. consul bought them for him in the marketplace there), one of which he misleadingly called the Rough Purple Chile. In 1857 another type, the Garnet Chile, was developed from this, which in turn gave rise, in 1861, to the Early Rose.[7] These, though an improvement, were generally speaking small, red-dish-colored, and kept poorly. The agricultural papers made much of the need for better potatoes. "It required no genius to know," Burbank later observed, "that if a large, white, fine-grained potato could be produced, it would displace the other varieties and give its discoverer a great advantage over his com-petitors."

With this in mind, he had attempted crossings. Inasmuch as the hybridized blossoms produced no seed, however, the re-sults were negative. And since he was dealing with a cloned plant, selection got him nowhere either. Any potato reproduc-ing from cuttings must be exactly the same genetically as its pa-rent; by definition, no improvement is possible.

Then he had a stroke of unbelievable luck. He discovered a pod of seeds ripening on an Early Rose potato plant. Such seed-balls were not unknown, but they were very rare. In later years Burbank was to offer a standing reward for one, but as long as he lived he never saw another. He watched the growth of this solitary seedball day by day. One morning it had disappeared, and he was devastated. Then it struck him that perhaps it had been dislodged by some dog running through the patch, and he made a careful search of the ground. The seedball was soon found a few feet away from the parent plant. He carefully pre-served and planted the seeds. There were twenty-three of them, and he raised twenty-three seedlings. Though a number of these, he says, were better than any potato then grown, he se-lected only two. They were as different from the Early Rose, he asserts, as modern beef cattle from the old Texas Longhorns. In this alone he was lucky. Like other species propagated by cloning, the potato has a great tendency to revert to its wild form when grown from seed. It is often necessary to cultivate hundreds or even thousands of seedlings before any useful new type is produced.

He was twenty-four when the first Burbank potatoes saw the light of day in his Lunenburg truck garden. "It was from the potatoes of those two plants, carefully raised, carefully dug, jealously guarded, and painstakingly planted the next year, that I built the Burbank potato," he says in his autobiography. (Walter Howard avers, however, that "All but two of the clusters were worthless. One of these was later discarded, while the other was kept and multiplied as rapidly as possible."[8]) It seems probable that the talk of "building" the Burbank potato was simply the kind of vainglory to which he was prone, or perhaps the work of his careless ghost-writer, Wilbur Hall. Further hybridization may conceivably have been involved, but in all likelihood the new potato was simply the chosen seedling and its progeny.

He could not in his wildest dreams have imagined how successful it would be. A presumed "sport" of this original seedling, known as the Russet Burbank, which is nearly identical to it but for its russeted skin, is the most widely grown potato in the United States at the time of writing—one hundred years later. Descendants of the Russet Burbank (also known by the names Idaho Russet, Golden Russet and Netted Gem) are also prominent, among them the Early Gem, Shoshoni, Reliance, Norgold Russet, Targhee, Nampa and Nooksack. Of these the Norgold Russet, a fourth-generation descendant of Burbank's original seedling, released in 1964, now stands in eighth rank among U.S. varieties. (Because of its complete male sterility and high female sterility, the Russet Burbank has been little used in breeding new varieties, but new techniques have been developed to overcome some of the female sterility and more use of it in breeding work is now being made.[9])

Burbank's own profit was largely indirect. In 1875 he sold the whole stock of the potato to James J. H. Gregory, a seedsman of Marblehead, Massachusetts, whom he happened to know. ("My Father taught school in Mr. Burbank's home town and was acquainted with him," his son Edgar Gregory afterward noted.) Gregory paid him exactly $150, but allowed him to retain ten of the tubers for his own use. He also did Luther the considerable favor of naming the new potato Burbank's Seedling.

Later on Burbank would attack the potato again, crossing common cultivated varieties with *Solanum maglia,* the Darwin potato, a wild species from Chile; with *S. cammersoni* from Argentina; with *S. jamesii II,* the squaw potato of the Southwest; and with an unidentified Mexican species. In 1895 he crossed the Pacific Coast variety Bodega Red with the Burbank to produce a hybrid, of which eight varieties were advertised but never introduced. Writing in 1912, the Colorado grower E. H. Grubb indicated that he and Burbank were planning to go to the island of Chiloe, off the Chilean coast, believed to be one of the original sources of the potato, "to study conditions." This trip was never made, however, at least not by Burbank, who makes no mention of plans for it in his writings.*

The high degree of luck which went into the finding of Burbank's seedling is evident from the fact that he was never afterward able to do anything remotely as important with potatoes, despite all his efforts. At the same time, the fact that the new variety bore his name did much to lay the basis for his reputation. Fate, in leading him to that original Early Rose seedball, had undoubtedly smiled on him.

"Perhaps one of the first words I ever heard was California," Burbank remarks in his autobiography, in a somewhat rambling dissertation of the whys and wherefores of his move west. Early in 1847 gold had been found in the race at Sutter's Mill on the American River, sparking a frenzy of interest and activity. The newspapers proclaimed the discovery of El Dorado,

---

*Grubb's book, *The Potato,* written with W. S. Guilford, is jointly dedicated to Luther Burbank, "The World's Greatest Plant Breeder," Secretary of Agriculture James Wilson, and W. C. Brown, president of New York Central Lines.

and from then on emigration to California proceeded in a flood from all parts of the country, notwithstanding the great hardships involved in getting there. According to official census figures, the population of the state increased from 224,000 in 1852 to 380,000 in 1860: an increment on the order of almost 20,000 immigrants a year.

Two of these were Burbank's older half-brothers. George had gone to California in 1854, and David followed him in 1859. They had had to make the difficult overland journey by horse and wagon, five or six months traveling, beset by illness, Indian troubles and endless exertion.

But on May 10, 1869, the last golden spike of the transcontinental railroad was driven home, and this same journey could henceforth be made in nine days, still in relative discomfort, but at any rate safely. In the summer of 1874, Luther's twenty-two-year-old brother, Alfred, followed George and David, finding work in the town of Santa Rosa as a carpenter. The temptation was more than Luther could longer resist. "I had no choice in the matter," he says. "I was bound to go!"

That summed it up. For it is hard to imagine any ambitious young man not feeling the lure of the West in that age. "The forty years that lay between the California Gold Rush of '49 and the Oklahoma Land Rush of '89 saw the greatest wave of pioneer expansion—the swiftest and most reckless—in all our pioneer experience," said Vernon Parrington of this period in America's history.[10] And Burbank, who was precisely of an age with it, and had grown up amid the whole great hullabaloo of expansion and exploration, was bound to be a little swift and reckless, too. "Within sixty days of the time when the definite decision to go to California was reached," he remarks, "I had sold my personal property and closed out my business at Lunenburg."[11]

There was, however, one other reason for his going so far and so suddenly. He was suffering from a bad case of unrequited love and had decided that his heart was broken. There had been a disagreement. She was less ardent than he was and made it clear to him that he was not the only eligible young man in

Massachusetts. After his arrival in California, he wrote to her, and their friendship was reestablished by mail, lasting to the end of his life. Concerning this romance, W. I. Beeson, of Healdsburg, California, the man who became Emma Burbank's husband, observed many years later:

> The name of the girl was Miss May (Mary) Cushing and I know for a fact that they were only neighborhood friends. He may have admired her and she may not have encouraged him, but that was all there was to it. He never asked her to marry him so she had no opportunity to reject him. Miss Cushing married a man named W. S. Bartlett in Massachusetts. She talked this matter over with us when she visited California in 1936 or 1937. She is now a widow.[12]

Mary Cushing and his broken heart, the restrictions he felt in Massachusetts, where the clergy still railed unavailingly against his beloved Darwin, the lure of the Golden West and a sense of the potential of California as a horticulturist's paradise—all these reasons probably contributed to his departure from his native New England.

He was twenty-six, in his own words "a small, wiry, active young man, observant, alert, inquisitive, and full of ideas about what I was going to do." As yet he had seen little of the world outside rural Massachusetts, where his amusements had been the village singing school and the choir of the little Methodist Episcopal Church which stood near the Burbank home in Lunenburg. He had no small opinion of himself, however, and after his success with the Burbank potato his future vocation seemed clear. He went with a purpose: to establish himself in the profession of plant breeding in the new lands by the Pacific. With his land, farming tools and stock disposed of, and his mortgage paid off, he was worth just $660, which included the $150 Gregory had paid him. That was more then than it is now (extrapolating from the consumer price index, he had about $3000 in present-day terms), but it was not a great deal with which to start a new life.

What manner of world was it that he set out to conquer? It was tough-minded and ruthless on the one hand, sickly sentimental on the other. Ruthless buccaneers of the stamp of Cornelius Vanderbilt, Jim Fisk and New York's Boss Tweed strode the land, as did their more lowly counterparts, the James boys and the Younger brothers. On the other hand, thought Henry James, it was "a feminine, a nervous, hysterical, chattering, canting age, an age of hollow phrases and false delicacy and exaggerated solicitudes and coddled sensibilities, which, if we don't soon look out, will usher in the reign of mediocrity, of the feeblest and flattest and most pretentious that has ever been."[13] U. S. Grant was President, and his eight years in the White House, Vernon Parrington thought, "marked the lowest depths—in domestic affairs at least—to which any American administration has fallen . . ." The United States was coming up for its one hundredth birthday. In Philadelphia, the Republic's second largest city, preparations were under way for the great Centennial Exhibition. It was a time of expansion, of public corruption and private gentility, of labor strife and mass unemployment. "Everywhere," says Parrington, "was a welling-up of primitive pagan desires after long repressions—to grow rich, to grasp power, to be strong and masterful and lay the world at its feet. It was a violent reaction from the narrow poverty of frontier life and the narrow inhibitions of backwoods religion. It had had enough of skimpy, meagre ways, of scrubbing along hoping for something to turn up. It would go out and turn it up."[14]

Into this world went Luther Burbank. Slight, something of a hypochondriac, a bit of a mother's boy (even Alfred had struck out before him), he, too, would go out and turn his something up.

FIVE

"The Chosen Spot of All This Earth"

ON THE STRENGTH of the sensational Ralston bank failure of August 1875,[1] and various reports disparaging conditions in California, friends tried to persuade Luther not to go. But his mind was made up, and all the preparations had been made. He would not back down now. In the latter part of October, 1875, probably on the twentieth, he set out.

With natural Yankee parsimony, he had decided that he could not afford a sleeping berth, which was in any case a somewhat unusual luxury in those days. He was therefore obliged to sleep curled up on the seat throughout the nine days and nights of the journey. When on rare occasions he found himself with a whole seat to sleep on and could stretch out, the trainmen moving up and down the cars always seemed to be banging into his projecting feet. This remained one of his most vivid memories of the trip.

His mother had provided a basket of food, which proved

very necessary, as the train was sometimes held up a whole day, far out on the plains, out of sight of even the smallest settlement or homestead, because the axle boxes got so hot that long stops had to be made for repairs. Burbank several times shared his lunch with passengers who were less well provided than he.

He wrote to his mother and sister Emma back in Lunenburg virtually every day—even if it were only a postcard. Emma, who was quite ill at the time, saved some of this correspondence, which gives a better idea of the journey and the young adventurer than any reconstruction the biographer might attempt:

BETWEEN LONDON, IN CANADA,
AND DETROIT, MICH.

Have been going westward steadily since I left Worcester at a great speed. No stops longer than twenty minutes. Slept some last night. Have enjoyed every mile. Had a treat in crossing Suspension Bridge by moonlight. Saw Niagara and the rapids. Cars joggle me. Want to hear how Emma gets along as soon as possible. I wish you were all enjoying the ride and scenery with me. We are in Queen Vic's dominions. Mrs. Ward and son have stood it nicely without any trouble. Don't know where I can mail this. The sandwiches and cake are tip-top. The cars are vastly more comfortable than those on the short Eastern roads.

The forests are too beautiful for one to describe—zigzag fences. Saw Lake Ontario at Lockport last night. Will write again before long.

LUTE

(Card from Burlington, Iowa)

Just crossed the Mississippi. Have had extra good luck in making changes, enjoying myself. Seas of corn, thousands of wild ducks.

L.B.

PACIFIC HOUSE, COUNCIL BLUFFS, IOWA.
Dear Mother, Etc.:
I arrived here at 10 o'clock last night. The passengers all

stopped either here or at Omaha last night. We start for Omaha from here at 9:30 this morning. I have enjoyed myself, been perfectly contented and have taken more comfort than a little in the journey. It has been perfectly delightful except changing cars at 11 o'clock at Chicago when I was sleepy. Have met a number of ladies and gentlemen who are on their way to San Francisco. Several of them stopped at this house last night. There are three ladies and two gentlemen from Fitchburg who have come all the way with us. All the people on the cars are pleasant, sociable, and obliging. All *have to* enjoy the scenery. The babies make some noise at times, but I can settle down in a seat and go to sleep amid all the noise and sleep as sweetly as I ever did in my life. We crossed the Mississippi into Iowa yesterday morning at 8 o'clock. It took us all day till 10 o'clock last evening to cross the state, and we went fast, too. Have seen a few Indians, but no Chinamen yet. Have eaten all my sandwiches, one-half of cake. Shall have enough to carry me twice as far as I have to go. I buy coffee twice a day. It is very nice. Should like to hear from home now. Hope Emma is getting better fast.

This letter is a curious one, but you must take it for what it is worth.

Yours in haste,
L.

(Card from Cheyenne, Wyoming Territory)

NEAR THE BLACK HILLS.
Have been travelling since 8 o'clock this morning without seeing a tree or bush over one foot high. A dusty desert. The passengers are enjoying themselves looking at prairie dogs, antelopes, and at the stations hunting for moss agates. The prairies were on fire last night. A finer sight I never saw, but called by the settlers "Prairie Demon." Wish you could only see it.

Just went through the first snow shed.

Near Pike's Peak.

6040 feet above you—more than a mile!

They are the ordinary communications to his family of an apparently ordinary young man, making a trip that was already (it was six years since the opening of the transcontinental line) commonplace. No one would suppose from them that young

Lute, with his "tip-top" sandwiches and cake from Mama's hamper, and coffee twice daily, carried with him any particular spark to ignite the new land.

He reached San Francisco late on a Friday afternoon. By Sunday he was in Santa Rosa, where brother Alfred was settled. That same day, October 31, he dashed off the promised letter home:

> Here I am in Santa Rosa, and before I give you a view of this place I will give you a glance at the journey across . . . We changed cars at Worcester, Utica, Rochester, Suspension Bridge, Detroit, Chicago, Council Bluffs, Omaha, Ogden, Oakland, San Francisco, and Donahue, but after Omaha the changes are so far apart that they are rather pleasant than otherwise, though it would be very hard for a woman if she had any baggage to look after except what she might carry in her hand.
>
> I made but few acquaintances on the cars until I got to Omaha; after that I made some of the *best* friendships (or acquaintances, as Emma would call them) of my life. Shall always remember with happiness some that I made. On board the cars everyone was contented, pleasant, sociable, and kind, though of course anyone has to look and see who he wishes to associate with. There were several from Massachusetts, New Hampshire, Connecticut, and two from Fitchburg who came all the way. Got acquainted with Judge Miller of Chicago (his son expects to settle in this town), also a wealthy Michigan banker's wife and *daughter!!!* The journey to Nebraska Center was pleasant. After that it is all *desert* for more than a *thousand* miles, and with one exception I saw not a tree the whole 1000 miles. Some of the way, in fact a good share of it, is *more sterile than a bare granite rock,* with poison water, mines, coal beds, salt, and alum springs and every other nasty chemical. Someone made the remark that they thought it must be the *roof* of H——. If you saw it you would see the point. Through the desert there is nothing of special interest except inside the cars, and there the dust *gathers* in drifts, especially in a fellow's nose and throat, which it irritates terribly. Coming through the palisades on the Humboldt River and the Devil's Slide are worth going across the continent to see. Have not space to describe them. They are the only places of special interest on the *Central Pacific* road.

On the *Union Pacific,* which commences at Ogden, Utah, there are about 400 miles of desert, then the rest of the way is *delightful beyond description.* Mountains piled on mountains, snow-clad peaks gilded with sunlight, wild forests, rivers, deep cuts, mammoth trees, leagues of snowsheds, thousands of geese, ducks, swans, antelopes, etc. *I cannot give you any idea of them.* Then on the Sierras, when we were winding up the mountainside, could look down thousands of feet onto the *lovely* Donner, Honey, and Tulare lakes. Then we rushed without steam, except to hold the train back, down the Sierras into the golden land where the old gold washings are. It looks as if there had been two or three earthquakes and a flood or two.

The train stopped a few minutes at "Cape Horn," where we got out and looked *down one-half mile* into the valley. After riding a few miles further gardens appeared with olives, oleander, fuchsias, figs; and all kinds of fruit trees and vines are green and thriving. On down into the great Sacramento Valley, where the gardens and front yards are ornamented with palm trees, century plants, fig trees, etc.—*it was a rare feast for me.* Then on across the valley as level as a floor and as *rich* as mud to Oakland, which is a beautiful place. At San Francisco I stayed two nights and one and a half days. I cannot describe the joys I felt in looking at the gardens and feeling the healing balmy breezes, but liquor-selling is the great business of that great city. No one who has not seen it can imagine the amount consumed. I used to go nearly one-half mile to get a glass of good water, and I knew of only one or two places where it could *be got. I made a vow on my way over that I would not touch a drop of any kind of liquor, and I shall keep it.* Of those who do not drink there are a great many, and they are almost *without exception* the *leading* and most *respected* men, and who also own most of the property and do the important business. A young man who will not drink here and is good-natured and makes folks like him, and who *minds his own business,* has *ten thousand* chances of success where the *same* qualities would have *one* chance in the states.

Now you want to know how Alfred appears to me. His chin whiskers are grown out so he looks some different in that respect. Then he looks more rugged, but is not quite so fleshy as he was a while ago, but is in pretty good condition. The thing that struck me most about him is his great haste to get rich, which thing never bothered him when East. He is in for making money. He is out of a job now and is a little blue—is afraid he cannot get one through the rainy season, which, by the way, is expected every day. He and another fellow have put up an 8 by 10 shanty. I expect to go to keeping house with them tomorrow. We bought crockery, bed ticking, etc., last night. Dave and Lina are coming up after me soon. I shall not look for work for a week. The change of climate has given me a cold, as it does nearly all, but I never felt so *contented* and free from mental disquiet and never slept or ate better in my life. (There are two fellows in the room talking, so please excuse blunders.) There are some Chinamen in this place. I like them very well. They know about four times as much as folks generally give them credit for. They are disagreeable in some respects.

I want to know how Emma is getting along very much. Expected a letter before this. I agreed to write all about things when I got here, so I began today, and I have given you as good an idea of things as they appeared to me as I can, except a description of this city, valley, and surroundings, which I will give you on another piece of paper.

Love to all inquiring friends.

LUTHER

His luggage when he arrived contained nothing much aside from his clothes, books and a supply of garden seeds, including the ten Burbank potatoes Gregory had permitted him to keep. Having chosen Santa Rosa (he had two elder half-brothers living in Tomales, but it seemed to him that that was too close to the ocean, and that the climate would be unsuitable to his experiments), he was determinedly enraptured by the place, then a small village surrounded by great fields of wheat. Designated county seat in Sonoma County by a vote taken in 1854, it dated from a settlement founded in 1833 by General Mariano Vallejo. It was, Burbank declared, on the separate sheet of paper, included with the preceding letter, "the *chosen* spot of *all this earth* as far as *Nature* is concerned, and the people are far better than the average Californians in other places." This last sentiment must have been taught him by Alfred and his friends: he himself had, after all, had scant opportunity as yet to become acquainted with the other places in question.

The cost of living, he was sure, was half what it was in Massachusetts. "Meat costs but little, flour is better and cheaper, fruit is nothing, almost, very little fire is needed, and such warm expensive houses are not necessary." He tacked on a postscript, with further raptures:

> P.S.—A fog is hardly ever seen here—the wind never blows hard. I wish you could see California fruit. I bought a pear at San Francisco, when I thought I was *hungry*, for five cents. It was so large that I could only eat two-thirds of it. I threw the rest away. Grapes are so abundant that all are allowed to help themselves to the nicest kinds at the vineyards. There is no skin to them and very small seeds; the pulp is the whole grape. If you try to squeeze one out it will split like a plum. They are very sweet and nice and are so plentiful that they are often used as hog feed.

Quoting this letter half a century later, he was obviously a trifle embarrassed by this excess of enthusiasm: "The italics were those of my youth: also the hand-made abbreviation for San Francisco." (In his own version the city is called "S. Frisco," but Emma appears to have tidied up the letter in her rendering.) The "8 by 10 shanty" put up by Alfred and friend proved a durable edifice, in fact and in legend. It survived into the twenties, serving its later owners as shed and chicken coop. The first book eulogizing Burbank, Harwood's *New Creations In Plant Life*, published in 1905, drew from this the assertion that, "he had no place to sleep nights, and for months made his bed in a chicken coop, unable to get enough money ahead to pay for regular lodgings." Of such Horatio Alger touches, irresistible copy to the newsmen of the day, was the Burbank mythology, which did so much to obscure his real merits, painted up. Harwood went on to describe the young Burbank "reduced to absolute want" and going to the village meat market to "secure the refuse bones saved for dogs, and get from them what meat he could." In fact, Luther afterward admitted (confessing at the same time to a certain reluctance to spoil "so beautiful and inspiring an error"), he had not begun life in California sharing his roof with the chickens, and had been well-fed and happy at the time.

The separate section of the letter describing his new home was marked "Not Public"—and the explanation (which Emma tactfully omits) was as follows:

> The reason that I give this description of Santa Rosa outside my general letter is because if it is generally known what a place this is all the scuffs would come out here, get drunk and curse the whole country, so don't let on to *anybody* outside the house what sort of a place this is *except* that I am delighted with it.[2]

But if he did not live in a chicken-house and eat dog meat, all was nevertheless rather less rosy than he anticipated. The rains had begun, and there was little work available. Alfred was out of a job and was despondent about it despite his normally buoyant spirits. (He had a tendency, Luther thought, to run a little too much on cheek.) The immigrant's life was a hard one, for all the idyllic surroundings. In the summer there was work in the wheat fields with harvesting and threshing crews, or breaking the soil with gangplows pulled by teams of oxen or mules. But Luther's physical strength was not up to this strenuous kind of work. In the winter there was some construction going on in town, but that was not what he wanted either, and there were many applicants for every job. The coming year was to be one of the hardest of his life.

"So [he says] I found myself almost without means, in a strange land, far from home and friends, and there was no obvious way in which to enter on the specific work that was contemplated." The immediate problem was simply a matter of earning enough to support himself, and he could not afford to be choosy about what he did. Life in the shanty establishment was cheap enough: $1.94 a week each, they reckoned, was what their simple housekeeping cost them. They got their supplies in bulk: "a sack of sweet spuds, one sack of onions, one sack apples, ten pounds oatmeal, some fresh canned salmon, etc. etc.," he informed Emma in a letter home.

Now Luther, since he had paid $140 for his ticket to California and had spent only an additional $6 for "coffee, tea, bread, lodging at hotel, and *all*" en route, should logically have had quite a bit left of the $660 he had started with. But this nest egg he was presumably saving against the day when he would be able to enter on the career he planned for himself. In the meantime, along with the other young immigrants, he eagerly went after whatever odd jobs offered. He was never one to live on his capital. Once, hearing that there was work available on a building that was being put up, he learned on applying that he could have a job if he could supply his own shingling hatchet. He went out and bought one, spending his last spare dollar in the process, he says, but was bitterly disappointed when he went back to find that another man had been taken on in the meantime.

He found time to do some exploring and hiked the countryside all around Santa Rosa. In one place he discovered "enough new and curious plants . . . to set a botanist mad. There is an old surveyor who knows nearly all of the plants here. I am going to take a batch to him this evening . . . My botany tells the names of only a few California plants. Some of them *have no names.*"

All the while he continued to sing the praises of California's agricultural wonders in his letters home, his postscripts and post-postscripts—they are replete with descriptions almost too extravagant to be believed:

. . . there is a large field of squashes here in which there are probably five hundred that two men could hardly lift—some of them three and a half feet long by one foot three inches through. Hundreds of them bigger than the biggest ever seen in

Lunenburg. I asked Alfred why he didn't write home about the climate, squashes, and big things. He said he *dare not. I will* run the risk of being called a whopper teller,

"Bro. Lute" informed his family, and suiting the word to the deed immediately went on to extol in a postscript,

Bunches of grapes half a yard long!!! The white Muscat or Alexandria grape—three and one-half by three and a quarter inches in circumference; if you have a Lunenburg grape to compare, you will observe the difference.

There was the typical young man's desire to impress the folks back home. With this letter (November 9, 1875) he included a Chinese laundry receipt. "Can you read it?" he asks. "I should like to see the white man that could." But he had a natural tendency to exaggerate. He was of a kind with the scouts who sent back the first reports of the land of Canaan, and like those Israelites had the two-handed faculty of making his public believe him. It was not that he was lying. He simply *saw* a little larger (elsewhere he reports "a field of cabbages nearly every head of which was as large as a washtub") than life, particularly when it came to growing plants, which loomed up so vividly in his mind in the first place. To do so was in line with the Western trend. Tall stories were the order of the day. But in later years they would get him into any amount of trouble with the hard-headed scientists busy ordering the universe under the banner of exact measurement.

He found some work lathing at the new Palace Hotel, the largest building in Santa Rosa, but this was only good for about a week, as quite a number of other men had been taken on for the job as well. Santa Rosa was growing apace. Where wheat had been harvested the previous summer, he told his mother, houses now stood by the hundreds. The recent arrival of the railroad had opened up the valley to development. The lathing job he had expected being delayed, he decided to pay a visit to his brothers at Tomales. He spent several weeks with them and, he reported, "had an outrageous good time, but it would take me three months to write all about it. I went to the ocean, San Rafael, to the neighbors, to a party, to several pleasant rides, sawed wood, milked, looked around the country, and enjoyed myself hugely, and got fat and *good natured*. Everybody in California has a 'happy don't care' look and . . . everything is offhand and original, and I verily believe that I am pretty well Californianized. Folks are, however, sometimes awful blue here, and when they do have them it goes bad. I have seen several newcomers in various stages of the blues, but that disease, the blues, has kept so far from me as the East is from the West or light from darkness. It seems as if I had crawled out of an old dirty dungeon into morning sunshine, but of course that is not all California, but partly circumstances."

He seems to have spent most of his time with David and his wife, Lina. George, who was twenty years older than he was, was in a hurry to put the finishing touches on his "magnificent house" before going up to the State Legislature—of which he was a member—on December 6. While at Tomales, Luther investigated Petaluma and San Rafael as possible alternatives to Santa Rosa. At Petaluma he and David searched around for some small farm that he might either hire or buy. "Land about the place on which *anything* in *creation* can be raised can be got at $100 an acre," he says. "Around Santa Rosa for $300 an acre." Nonetheless, he did not find anything which suited him and shortly returned home to bachelor life:

When I came home last night Alfred said Mr. Walmsley had not cooked anything or done anything during the two weeks that I was gone. Mr. W. told exactly the same story. I believe all that both said and I'll be darned if the shanty didn't look more like a *hog's nest* than anything I had ever seen before, except the real thing.

Alfred had found a few days work at odd jobs while he was away. Sick of carpentering, he now proposed to go to work "knocking out paving stones." For his part Luther decided that he would not take any job lasting more than a few weeks: he was eager to rent his own place and set up for himself. But the rains had put a stop to all work. Many immigrants were returning east, because there was nothing for them to do. "Mr. Walmsley is going to leave *tomorrow*," Luther wrote his mother on December 5. "Alfred is going to board nearer his work. Mr. Hayes left some time ago and a new set are going to occupy the shanty (so our home is busted)."

Luther's hope now was to find a place where he might earn his board. "After fishing two days like a drowning man for a little piece of work about this place, I found myself nearly 'dead broke' or 'strapped,' as they call it here. Had nearly made up my mind that there is *no place* in the great machine that I was fitted for." The immigrant blues seemed to be catching up with him, but he was not the type to turn tail and head for home at the first taste of hardship. He plugged away manfully:

> Thursday morning I decided to make a strike into the country toward Petaluma. After doing up the housework I started (7:30 a.m.). The first ten miles of the way was through *adobe* land. The mud, or rather *mud-slush*, was knee deep to a giraffe. As I had no boat with me, I walked on the fences where I could. Stopped at several farm houses to get a chance to work for my grub till the rains were over, but found no such chance to make my fortune, so I trudged on by the roundabout Sebastopol road toward Petaluma, where I arrived at 6 p.m., a little more than nineteen miles. I thought I would sleep in a haystack, but could find none near Petaluma, and had to put up at a hotel. (By the way, I had nothing to eat after breakfast except a very small slice of bread.) The next morning I got up and addressed myself to breakfast. There was such a panic among eatables about that time as I never saw one man produce before.

After breakfast he looked around the carriage and cooper shops in Petaluma and then applied to W. H. Pepper, owner of the Petaluma Greenhouses and Nurseries. Pepper protested that he had too much help already, and that he was going to have to let some of his men go, but Luther persuaded him to take him on, and he would give me $50 a month or $30 and live in his family. I thought that was a pretty good offer to *commence on,* at least it was a little better than running into debt for grub. I think the work is just what I was *got up for.* He has large greenhouses, two great nurseries, a fruit farm, and a ranch. Besides, he has two splendid houses in which he lives, sometimes in one, sometimes in the other.

Saw George Burbank in Petaluma a few hours later. He says I am a lucky bugger. Now *if* I can suit Mr. Pepper and *if* the job don't fall through before tomorrow morning, and *if* I can stand the work, and *if* and *if,* etc., etc., and I have "struck ile" at last, but things are uncertain in this state. Fortunes made and lost in a day.

SIX

Plums from Yokohama

HE SPENT THE winter and the spring of 1876 working at the W. H. Pepper nursery near Petaluma. With the hundredth anniversary of the signing of the Declaration of Independence there were unusual festivities through the country that year. A general amnesty was granted all unpardoned Confederates, and on May 10 the great Centennial Exposition was opened at Philadelphia by President Grant. One sensation at the exposition was the telephone invented by Alexander Graham Bell. Bell, a mere two years older than Burbank, had come to the United States from Britain in 1872, and was a professor of vocal physiology in Boston, where he had developed his amazing new device. The world was moving forward, and other young men were accomplishing great things. And where was Burbank? Earning his keep as a common laborer and obliged to live in a room over a steaming greenhouse, where he sickened and came down with a fever that came near to ending his life. He went back to Santa Rosa, where he laid up in "the crude bachelor cabin of a workman." A neighbor woman supplied him with fresh milk from her cow, though he could not pay her. But for this, he said, "it is doubtful whether I should have pulled through. These were indeed dark days."

How was he to get his start? He could have borrowed from his brothers, but he was averse to doing this, "both from an inherited sensitiveness about money, which is almost as universal a New England heritage as the Puritan conscience itself, and because I knew that my relatives, in common with such other people as knew of my project, were skeptical as to the practicality of such experiments in plant development as were contemplated."[1] Even to people who accepted the Darwinian theory of evolution, the idea of altering the form of living things seemed grotesque. The degree to which cultivated plants were human creations was not generally recognized in those days. Even those botanists who were familiar with the history of plant breeding emphasized the fact that plants had been under cultivation for millenia and questioned that significant improvements could be accomplished in a single generation. Those people who knew of Burbank's plans regarded his project as half-mad and predestined to fail.

Luther allowed his ambitions free rein. He had plans to improve ornamental trees and shrubs, to look into the possibility of breeding better lumber trees, to produce finer varieties of flowers and to give the farmers and gardeners of the world a whole range of earlier, sturdier, more productive fruits and vegetables. Everywhere he looked in the fields and gardens around him he saw potential for improvement. What were his assets? He felt he had a pretty good background in scientific reading. He had been interested in plants all his life and had behind him ten years of practical experience working with them. He thought he had the fundamental rules of plant breeding pretty clearly worked out. Even so, he sometimes wondered, "how could one man, in his single lifetime, have much of an influence on the vegetable world, when about all that most experimenters in any line had been able to do was to specialize on one single branch and die leaving the work unfinished?"[2] But he was confident, with a young man's confidence, that he would outdo his predecessors.

Naturally his brothers gave what support and assistance they could. The ten Burbank potatoes Gregory had allowed him to keep, which Luther regarded as his greatest tangible asset, were planted on George's land at Tomales. The first season's crop was carefully saved and replanted, and by the end of the second season the yield was great enough for the potato to be put on sale. He ran an advertisement in one of the local papers:

BURBANK'S SEEDLING

This already famous Potato is now for the first time offered by the originator for trial on this Coast. For description see *American Agriculturist,* for March, 1878. PRICES: 1 lb. by mail, 50 cts.; 3 lbs. by mail, $1.00; 25 lbs. by express, $5.00.

LUTHER BURBANK, Nurseryman.
Santa Rosa, Sonoma County, California.

This supplemented his income a little, but he had to contend with a certain amount of consumer resistance. People in California were used to red potatoes, and it took awhile to convince them that a white one, though larger, smoother and more productive, was an improvement. Later Burbank's Seedling became the chief potato grown on the Pacific Coast—by which time, however, Luther himself had long since ceased to grow it. He had no patent. It was only in those first few years before it became widely cultivated that it was worth his while to raise it for seed.

In the summer of 1877, worried perhaps by news of his illness, his mother and sister had followed him to California. Olive bought a house at the corner of Tupper and E streets in Santa Rosa, with four acres of land adjacent, part of which, Emma says, "Luther immediately rented and began his nursery. This land he later purchased, building a greenhouse thereon." It does not seem as though he struck out in business on his own, aside from taking steps to propagate his potatoes, until Emma and Olive arrived. Was this merely a matter of money? Probably not. All the evidence is that Luther was a shy, somewhat diffident young man who needed his family—and particularly his mother—behind him.

During the day he still worked as a carpenter. In the evenings he took care of his growing plants and trees. He started with fruits and vegetables that seemed likely to be salable locally. At that time Santa Rosa was still largely wheat country. It was only after the exhaustion of the soil that the local farmers began to think in terms of fruit growing. The market for seedlings was, therefore, an uncertain one. And, he remarks, even had it been more certain, "it would doubtless have been difficult for me to get a start, because fruit trees cannot be brought to a condition of bearing, or even to a stage where cions for graftings are available, in a few weeks. And I had neither capital nor credit, being virtually a stranger in a strange land."

But he had a good local reputation as a carpenter by now, and whatever he could earn with his hammer, over and above the barest necessities, went back into stock for his nursery business. "He was also employed by several American and European seed firms as collector of seeds of California's native plants," Emma tells us. "This gave him a very delightful way to become further acquainted with the trees and plants growing in this state. The knowledge thus gained of the locality, time of blooming and seed ripening, and other particulars, afterwards was of great value in his work."

In many ways the time was ripe as far as the nursery was concerned. The first shipment of California fruit (it consisted entirely of Bartlett pears) had left Sacramento for New York within a year of the completion of the Central Pacific line. The consigning of California produce to Eastern markets would soon be facilitated by the introduction of refrigerated cars. Already, Howard observes, "daring spirits were shipping fruit to faraway Chicago and receiving fancy prices . . . The times were favorable for starting a nursery as existing concerns could not keep up with the demands for planting-stock. Especially was this true of prunes because that fruit could be sun-dried and sent to distant places with little danger of injury in transit. This looked like a safe crop and plantings, accordingly, were large."[3]

According to Burbank's old account book, sales for "Nursery stock and ornamental and flowering plants" totaled only a modest $15.20 in 1877, but since he had not begun planting till the summer of that year this was hardly surprising. The following year he recorded sales amounting to $84 ($70, according to Emma, who was teaching in Santa Rosa public schools to supplement the family income), and by 1879 they had reached $353.28. In 1880 the earnings of the nursery had climbed to $702, and the year after that they reached the not unimpressive total for those days of $1112.69. Thereafter business improved by leaps and bounds. Within ten years the quality of his trees and the general reliability of his stock had become so widely known that he was doing more than $16,000 worth of business annually.

Even in those early days he showed the sort of initiative that was to put him ahead of all competitors. His first catalog, a twelve-page brochure issued in 1880, lists a hundred species of seeds "all gathered in South and West Australia and New Zealand during the past season." How he obtained them is not clear. He would later make good use of varieties sent him by foreign collectors and correspondents, some of whom he employed for this specific purpose, but that source of supply had yet to be developed. In any case, it shows notable enterprise, foreshadowing by years the later work of the Division of Foreign Plant Introduction of the United States Department of Agriculture.

In March 1881 Warren Dutton, a prosperous Petaluma merchant and banker, who had had the opportunity of seeing some of Burbank's work, approached him with an order for twenty thousand prune trees, ready to be set out that fall. Dutton had

taken a sudden interest in prune growing as a commercial prospect, and wished to start out on a large scale as soon as possible.

Burbank's first thought was to say that no one on earth could
undertake to supply an order like this at such short notice. But
after a few minutes' reflection he decided that it might just be
done, if almond seedlings were used for stock and prune buds
"June-budded" onto them.

Dutton agreed to provide financial support during the summer to pay for the almond seedlings and the additional help
that would be needed. The project would depend on the fact
that almonds, unlike most other stone fruits, sprout almost at
once. June-budding, if it is to be successful, calls for a long
growing season.

Luther set to work immediately. He had two acres of land
available at the nursery, and he found another five he could
rent. Almonds were bought for the planting and spread on a
well-drained bed of creek sand. They were covered with coarse
burlap cloth, and another inch of sand was spread on top of
this. The almonds could thus be examined when necessary simply by lifting up one end of the cloth.

In less than fourteen days some of the seeds were sprouting.
These were taken out and planted in the nursery rows. The
others were covered up again and planted out as fast as sprouting occurred, four inches apart in rows four feet from each other, by men hired especially for the purpose. The ground was
kept carefully cultivated, and in the meantime Luther arranged
with a neighbor to get a supply of twenty thousand prune buds.
By the end of June the almond seedlings were large enough to
be budded, and in July and early August he labored with a
large force of skilled help to bud the prune buds into them. After about ten days the buds had made good unions with the
stalks, and the tops of the little trees were broken and left hang-
ing—in this way forcing the growth into the bud without en-
dangering the trees themselves, which might have been killed if
the almond twigs and leaves had simply been cut off. When the
prune buds began to grow, they were tied up along the stalk,
and when they were a foot or more high, the old almond top

was removed. By December 1, 19,500 trees were ready. The remainder could be supplied the next season.

Dutton was naturally delighted. He had been assured by other nurserymen that it would be impossible to produce the trees in the allotted time. Burbank, he let it be known, was a "wizard"—probably the first time this fateful title was applied to him.

"Although this was a horticultural stunt that had been employed by others," Howard remarks, "Burbank deserves full credit for having had the enterprise and initiative to do something that was new to his locality if not to the state. In the southern states the process is known as June budding or force budding, and is widely used in the propagation of peaches." This achievement was the beginning of Burbank's reputation as a producer of prune stock. Other purchasers,who bought prunes in smaller lots, were equally satisfied. He took great pains to ensure that no tree left the nursery unless it was exactly what it was represented to be. The prune industry was expanding, and sometimes there was quite a crowd of would-be purchasers at his door, waiting their turn. It became something of a local jest in Santa Rosa when someone was being looked for, to say, "Well, if you can't find him in town, he's probably out at Burbank's Nursery waiting for some trees."

By 1884 Burbank was well-established in the nursery business, with an income from it in excess of ten thousand dollars a year. "Nothing more was required," he observes, "than to continue along the lines of my established work to insure a life of relative ease and financial prosperity." But in fact he had just reached the point at which he could afford to turn his attention to his true lifework. The Burbank story had only just begun. For his ambitions went beyond being a mere nurseryman. The ferment that had begun with Darwin, and the talk of his cousin Levi, the pupil of the great Agassiz, was coming to a head. "So," he says, "from the very hour when my nursery business had come to be fully established I began laying plans for giving it up."

Nursery and market garden had been a necessary apprenticeship. He had learned a great deal about the art of growing plants that was basic to his later work. At the same time he had come to know the native California plants, the seeds and bulbs of which he had collected for Eastern and European seedsmen as a way of adding to his small income. In 1880 and 1881 he had made trips to the Northern California geyser country, where he found promising new material. Everywhere he went he carefully studied the vegetation with an eye to its possible use in his future work. In the years to come this knowledge would suggest novel ingredients for his hybridization experiments.

He would have liked to have carried these botanizing expeditions farther afield. After 1884 it would have been perfectly feasible to have done so. The work of the nursery could have been left to assistants, while Burbank himself traveled the world in search of plants that could profitably be imported. But at heart he was an experimenter rather than a collector, and he was too eager to begin work to allow himself the luxury of travel.

He had already ordered seeds and cuttings of "a great variety of fruits" from Japan, and in anticipation of their arrival had bought the "Dimmick place" on Santa Rosa Avenue, four acres of neglected, run-down land which had been on the market for a number of years. This property, which was to be known as the Experimental Gardens, he immediately set about improving. Tiles were laid for drainage, and his neighbors marveled as eighteen hundred loads of manure were brought in. The first batch of Japanese seeds and seedlings arrived on November 5, 1884. "I felt," he says, "that a new era had begun for me."

While browsing in the Mechanics Library in San Francisco in the early eighties, he had come across a book describing the travels of an American sailor, who in the course of a visit to the province of Satsuma in Japan had eaten plums with deep red flesh. This prompted him to order a shipment of seedling plum trees from Isaac Bunting, an export-import agent in Yokohama. Those which reached him in November 1894 had, alas, failed to survive the journey as a result of not being properly cared for in transit. Burbank wasted no time in reordering, and a second consignment arrived the following year, on December 20, 1885. This time the trees were in good condition.

There is some question as to exactly what Bunting sent. According to Howard, a memorandum found among Burbank's papers after his death listed twelve varieties of plum in all: one hundred specimens of the Blood Plum of Satsuma, and ten each of the others. Burbank's editor and ghost-writer, Henry Smith Williams, makes him refer to only twelve seedlings. This discrepancy Howard attributes to Williams' desire to "glorify Burbank and make a great hero of him." A professional popularizer, he tended to make the story as dramatic as possible, without too much regard for accuracy.

California is the leading plum-producing state in the country, accounting for about 90 percent of the U.S. output of commercially grown plums and prunes. ("Plum" and "prune" were originally synonyms, used to describe hundreds of varieties of fruit falling into at least fifteen different species, but the latter term has come to designate those kinds that lend themselves to drying without removal of the pit, and refers both to the fresh fruit and to the dried form.) Even before the planting of plums in the gardens of the Spanish missions, the California Indians made use of the fruit of the wild native species. The early settlers made some effort to cultivate these wild plums, the Pacific, Western or Sierra plum, and the Gray Branch or Sisson plum, and one observer noted in 1858 that this indigenous fruit was potentially "a worthy competitor for flavor among our best varieties of gages and damsons." As the Spanish settlement proceeded, European plums were imported, and on his visit to California in 1792 George Vancouver came across them at Mission Ventura. The Mission prune, a variety about which little is known, is said to have been grown at Santa Clara as late as 1870.

It was not, however, until the American take-over that

named varieties began to be introduced, the first of these being brought to Sacramento from Oregon in the spring of 1851 by Seth Lewelling. That same year a Mr. Shelton of San Francisco is recorded as having imported six varieties from Valparaiso, Chile, and by 1853 a Sacramento nursery, Warren and Sons, was listing eighteen kinds of plum. Another Sacramento nurseryman, A. P. Smith, who started business on the American River as early as 1848, listed twenty-eight plum varieties in his catalog in 1856. In the early days California growers were largely stocked by Eastern nurserymen, but shipping by boat around Cape Horn was expensive, and the trees did not always arrive in the best condition. California nurseries soon sprang up to supply the demand. B. S. Fox, who was brought to San Jose from Hovey's nurseries in Massachusetts in 1852 by Commodore Robert Stockton, a naval officer who had helped conquer California in the Mexican War, lost no time in setting up in business for himself, and by 1858 had some fifty-eight varieties of plum. A census of 1859 found a total of 105,631 plum trees in California. Plums sold for about 50 cents a pound in Sacramento at that time. Nursery trees were sold for as much as $6 apiece in 1856, but in 1858 and 1859 northern California nurserymen combined to fix a code of fair prices. A price of 50 cents to $1 was established for year-old plum trees, and $1 to $2 for two-year-old trees.

The United States Patent Office is said to have imported the French prune in 1854, but California prune production is dated to December 1856, when Pierre Pellier brought scions of the French and Gros (Pond) prunes to San Jose. Some of these were top-grafted onto orchard trees by George W. Tarleton and J. Q. A. Ballou, and in 1859 Ballou sent the first shipment of California-grown French prunes to market in San Francisco. Some years later, in 1867, he was also the first to ship prunes around the Horn, sending a consignment of five hundred pounds. The following year he was able to ship eleven tons, on which he netted between 18 and 20 cents a pound. The California prune industry, today worth some forty million dollars a year, had begun. By 1870 there were already more than nineteen thousand prune trees in the state.

Prior to 1870 the only plums grown in California, if we exclude the wild species, were European varieties. In that year, however, Hough of Vacaville imported the Kelsey plum from Japan, through the U.S consul there, paying $10 a tree. His stock was bought by John Kelsey, a Berkeley nurseryman, who subsequently contributed his name to this variety, also known as the Botankin. Another Japanese plum, the Chabot, was imported in the late 1870s by M. A. Chabot, of Oakland, along with Japanese tea and bamboo plants. Burbank later acquired this variety from Chabot and put it on the market. There were, therefore, at least two varieties of Japanese plum growing in California when Burbank began to import them. (Japanese plums are, generally speaking, larger than the European varieties and crimson or red rather than blue or purple.) Of these, the Kelsey remains among the important late varieties grown to this day.

In his nursery catalog for 1887, Burbank offered the new Japanese plums for sale, along with numerous other items. Howard, who had investigated Burbank's introductions with some care, comments:

> The contents of the catalog showed that he was going in heavily for new things—novelties he called them—and although he did not claim to be the originator of these unusual things, he left that impression, a trick that was not unusual among nurserymen. Several promising seedlings were listed, among these were apples, pears, plums, peaches, figs, persimmons, olives, and oranges. He refers to himself, about this time, as a dealer in novelties. But while most nurserymen were content to let others find new and promising things as chance seedlings, he was importing from Japan things that for the most part were entirely new.

Among the plums listed were the Botan, the Chabot, the Long Fruit, the Masu, or Large Fruit, the Botankio, the Botankio No. 2, and the Blood Plum of Satsuma. The announcement was relatively modest. "He had not yet learned to make the fullest use of the printed word," Howard observes.

> It is true that he did expand slightly in describing the Blood Plum of Satsuma by stating that he had the only tree growing in America and that it had cost him $40 in Japan, but the statement was made in 8-point type! The price quoted was one dollar per tree or seventy-five cents each for dormant buds. The only explanation I can offer is that he did not realize what he had. This mistake was remedied to some extent in the supplement that followed the catalog, but even here his walnuts and chestnuts from Japan were given more publicity space than the plums. As it turned out, the walnuts are merely a curiosity and the chestnut only of minor importance, while the plums laid the foundation of a huge industry, particularly in California and South Africa, and are of considerable importance in many other states and countries.[4]

Just before his death in 1932, Leonard Coates, a veteran California nurseryman, who had introduced a number of plum varieties and originated a prune called the Coates 1418 (also known as Cox, Date, Saratoga and Saratoga XX) which had considerable success in the twenties, informed Howard that J. E. Amoore, a tea buyer in Japan, had come to San Francisco in the eighties and set up a company which imported thousands of plums under Japanese names—one of which, he thought, was probably the Satsuma. Howard comments that Coates, even if he did have some basis to his claim, should not be taken too seriously, since, "they were professional rivals and business competitors. Coates had the reputation of being a man of high and honorable principles but in this case he seems to have been obsessed by envy or jealousy." Admittedly Burbank did obtain some trees from other importers—among them Chabot—and stated that "The Satsuma and Burbank were the only two among my 12 seedlings that were directly introduced, although sundry of the others subsequently had a share in the production of hybrid races. It should be recalled also that I had somewhat earlier introduced three plums of Oriental origin—the Abundance, Chabot, and Berkmans, that were also a direct product of Oriental stock grown and fruited by me *from seedlings purchased from other importers.*"[5]

So many synonyms have been used at one time or another that it is virtually impossible to trace the provenance of some of these plums. The variety called Abundance, for example, seems previously to have been known as Botan, Botankio, Chase, Yellow-fleshed Botan and Yellow Japan. The Berkmans, or Berckmans, was variously also called Botan, Sweet Botan, and White-fleshed Botan. To make matters even more complicated, another variety, the Willard, also went by the name Botan. In any event, it seems plain that the two important varieties received by Burbank in this batch were the Satsuma and the Burbank, the latter named after its importer at the suggestion of Professor H. E. Van Deman, pomologist of the United States Department of Agriculture. In a letter to Van Deman, dated August 22, 1888, Burbank wrote:

> The yellow fleshed plum with which you were pleased is, in my opinion, *far superior*, taking everything into consideration, to *any other* of the Japan plums. . . . I have and shall call it Burbank (by your suggestion) as nothing like it has been seen here and no Japanese importer knows it. It and the Satsuma were imported by myself with 10 other kinds, arrived here Dec. 20, 1885. As in all Japanese trees this was mixed in a lot of inferior plums. In the 12 varieties (received under number and Japanese names only) I obtained 20 or more kinds. The first Satsuma was obtained by me by *sending a man* from Yokohama to Satsuma for the original tree which cost me $50.00 and $55.00 delivered in Santa Rosa. All the Japan Importers of San Francisco confess they do not know either of them, that they never saw or heard of them. Also that they are delicious.[6]

The Burbank proved to be enormously productive and was particularly successful in home orchards throughout the country. Not a plum of the highest quality, it nonetheless raised the standard in many areas where only native varieties could previously be grown.

It seems clear from Burbank's own statement that Abundance, another variety that became very popular, was not one of the seedlings imported directly from Japan by him, though Howard identifies it as such. According to Liberty Hyde Bailey, the doyen of American horticulture, it was the same as a variety called Wassu, introduced by J. L. Normand, but conversely H. M. Butterfield of the University of California's College of Agriculture identifies Wassu with the Burbank![7] *Et voilà justement comme on écrit l'histoire,* as Voltaire once remarked. It is devoutly to be hoped that we have not here added to the confusion: the present author denies any special competence in the history of plums and refers future investigators back to the "original" sources.

A little more than a week after the arrival of the second and successful shipment from Yokohama, Burbank negotiated the purchase at Sebastopol, in the hills near Santa Rosa, of the Gold Ridge farm. These eighteen acres, acquired on December 28, 1885, were intended solely as an experimental garden. "With the development of the Sebastopol place," Burbank says, "a new phase of lifework began."

The original farm consisted of about ten acres of sandy soil some seven miles from Santa Rosa. Burbank purchased an additional five acres on one side and three on another, making the total of eighteen. "At the time the place was purchased," he says, "about two-thirds of it was covered with white and tan oaks, the native Douglas spruce, manzanita, cascara sagrada, hazel and madrona, while beneath the trees grew brodiaeas, calochortus, cynoglossum, wild peas, fritillarias, orchids, sisyrinchiums—yellow and blue—and numerous other wild plants and shrubs."[8] The land had the advantage of being well-watered, and after it was cleared numerous species of clover made their appearance. Turning these under in the spring provided an excellent source of nitrogen for the soil. Burbank was always very much aware of the importance of good soil culture.

In 1888 he sold part of his nursery business to R. W. Bell, a partner he had taken in. Bell took over the growing and marketing of the standard varieties, along with the old nursery buildings and about an acre of the old sales ground, while Burbank kept control of the novelties he had developed. A miscellaneous announcement of 1888, in the form of a postcard, introduced Bell as "my successor in the standard fruit and shade tree business . . . I shall confine my business in future to olive and nut trees and horticultural novelties exclusively." To prevent confusion Burbank retained the name "Santa Rosa Nurseries," while Bell's establishment was to be called "Bell's Nurseries."

In September of that year, divested of what was perhaps the more troublesome side of his business, Luther allowed himself the luxury of a trip back to Massachusetts. Though he was now very much a financial success, he still did not indulge himself by taking a sleeping car. The Puritan instincts died hard. He slept curled up on the seat "like a jackknife." A $1.50 comforter helped, he remarked in a letter home.

He reached Lunenburg on the stage from Fitchburg on the evening of September 19, and was immediately in the thick of his old friends. "You cannot imagine the handsqueezings and questions that I was put to for about eight hours," he wrote. "One of my old Lancaster Academy schoolmates (Nellie Day) said she waited hours before she could get an opportunity to speak." This was at the Fitchburg Fair, where he was among the speakers of the day.

"The old place looks as it did," he reported. "Mr. Gregory expects to have a monument raised on the spot where the Burbank potato originated, so I pointed it out." Meanwhile, he gathered seeds and plants to take back to California and avoided the usual importunities of an expatriate's visit home. "Fanny Peabody says she has a kitten for Alfred, but I will be darned if I will carry a circus back. She will have to send it by mail."

He stayed scarcely two weeks. By October 3 he had said his good-byes, and was sight-seeing in Boston. From there he went on to Washington, where he arrived on the ninth, on what

seems to have been an organized tour. "Saw the original Declaration of Independence, visited the White House, the President's reception room, Weather Bureau, Senate while in session, House of Representatives, Supreme Court (which is trying
the Bell Telephone case)." There were eighty in his party. They
were put up at the Willard Hotel, which cost the noteworthy
sum of $4.50 a day, and taken by steamer to Mount Vernon.
There was even a Presidential reception given by Grover Cleve-
land. "As his wife is off visiting, we shall not see her," Burbank
observed. He had acquired "a great quantity of very rare wild
and cultivated seeds" and paid a visit to the Department of
Agriculture before he left.

On October 15 the party returned to Boston, and a few days
later he was in Lancaster again. He was, he says, "healthier,
happier, and handsomer than ever you saw me; and if business
would live through it, in any way, I would extend my time, for I
have got more real happiness out of the last month than for
fifteen years." All the same, he confessed, "I should never be
contented to live here and no sensible Californian would either."

By comparison with Santa Rosa he was finding New England
weather distinctly disagreeable and remarks that he will "probably have to buy a suit of oil clothes, rubber boots, and a boat,
and some lightning rods, etc." Attending a town fair at Harvard, an old friend asked him, "If you had a farm here what
would you raise?" Luther replied, "I think I would try to raise
enough money to get to California."

By early November he was home in Santa Rosa again.

SEVEN

"New Creations"

HIS HOLIDAY HAD one distinctly fateful result. On the train (it was probably on the way back to California) he had met a lady, Helen A. Coleman by name.[1] She is described as being a "youngish widow" from Denver, Colorado.

Long after his death, a reputation as an "adventuress" and a vamp would be spoken of. Burbank—they said—had had little experience of women and was an easy mark. What transpired between the couple in transit there is now unfortunately no way of telling, but it is true that she presently followed him to Santa Rosa—and stayed put there until they became formally engaged.

The headlong passion that Walter Howard suggests is probably to be doubted, for Burbank cannot be charged with undue haste. (The notion that he was grievously smitten seems to rest largely on his "extravagance" in buying a horse and phaeton for his fiancee's entertainment. But surely this was hardly out of the way for a man with an annual income now in excess of $10,000 and the prospect of doing better every year. In 1889 his contemporary, William Allen White, found a salary of eighteen dollars a week "beyond the dreams of avarice."[2]) More likely he simply felt that it was time he had a wife and children of his own. Himself one of fifteen, he was no stranger to family life. His love for children was widely publicized. He was an advocate of the eugenic view of things and exceedingly proud of his own Scots-English ancestry, which he lost few opportunities of extolling in print. Above all, he must certainly have wanted a son, or sons, who would one day be able to carry on his work.

Smitten or not, horse and carriage notwithstanding, the couple waited nearly two years before going to Denver, her home town, to be married. Only then did he feel sufficiently sure of his feelings to take the plunge. Evidently he had doubts, and in the outcome they were fully justified.

In Denver he "entertained her royally for about two weeks," Howard says, implying evidence of infatuation. But one thing no one has ever accused Burbank of is miserliness, and this was in any case hardly recklessness worthy of reproof. The wedding itself took place on September 23, 1890. He was forty-one ("a highly susceptible age for a man," Howard remarks in further innuendo) and well on his way to being a national figure. Of Helen we know very little.

"She was peculiar in her dress and speech and even at home her manner was silly, simpering, and affected," informants who had known her in Santa Rosa afterward suggested. But that was almost half a century after the event, and such sources are notoriously unreliable. Judge Rolfe L. Thompson, of the District Court of Appeals, Sacramento, allowed that she had had some good traits of character. She was something of an artist, and he remarked that his family still possessed a picture she had painted. She was interested in literature, he remembered—a great reader.

In the squabbling that ensued it would be only reasonable to suppose that, as is usually the case, there was a degree of justice on both sides. Helen had perhaps expected something very different. Denver, her home town, was a burgeoning, rip-roaring Western metropolis. Santa Rosa was a small country place, with little excitement to speak of, once the initial romance had worn off. And Luther himself was hardly as gregarious as a wife might reasonably have hoped. If, as we may surmise, her ambitions had been kindled by meeting and marrying a dynamic and exuberant Burbank, newly returned from a triumphal tour of the native places that had once doubted that he would ever amount to "a hill of beans," she was probably in no proper frame of mind to settle down and keep house for Burbank, the reclusive horticulturist.

In the end there was really little in common between them. He cared only for his work, and she took no interest in that. She was "high-strung," as they used to say, and had a nervous temperament. From the beginning trouble was inevitable with Luther's mother. Old Mrs. Burbank was almost eighty, but she was also of a very positive disposition, set in her ways and used to getting them. She had occupied the position of head of the family for a long time, both before and after coming to California. She was not about to surrender it to the intruder.

Emma may have been another problem. She, too, had lived with Burbank the greater part of his life. She had an almost absurd faith in his abilities. "She worshipped her brother as a divine dispensation," wrote George Shull, as reliable an observer as any. "She was very religious, and was quite convinced that God had specifically sent her brother to do His appointed miraculous work. With this viewpoint you can understand her solicitude that her brother should not be unduly imposed upon. He must be guarded and protected in every way possible so that he could achieve the specific results he was divinely appointed to get for the welfare and redemption of mankind."[3] She sang his praises to whoever cared to listen, kept up his scrapbooks of clippings and stood between him and the hero-worshiping public that might otherwise have taken up more time than he could afford. "A true friend and disciple, devoid of ulterior motives, she never let him down," says Howard. "Incessantly she fed his natural ego and cultivated the Messiahship idea."[4]

No, Helen could have found no ally among the women of the house, given her own strong character and intellectual and artistic bent. And what of the "Messiahship idea"?

In 1938 Howard interviewed Dr. D. B. Anderson, then a practicing dentist in Santa Rosa. Anderson had done secretarial and accounting work at the Burbank home during the evenings in the years 1887–1889. He recalled Burbank telling him "that the world had experienced many Christs—at least thirteen; that they assumed different forms and might continue to arise from time to time, and hinted that he, himself, he felt, was approaching that status." On another occasion he compared himself to Napoleon, saying, "See, I am about the same height as Napoleon and my hat is about the same size as his, although my head is growing and increasing in size all the time."[5] Anderson was of the opinion that these remarks were made in all seriousness, and although they bear the stamp of Burbank's whimsical sense of humor, it is very possible that they were nonetheless at least *half*-serious, as whimsy often is. Although admitting that Mrs. Burbank was cantankerous and led Burbank a dog's life from the first, Anderson did not go along with the general belief that she was crazy: she was, he said, merely trying to get rid of all his relatives.

It is hardly difficult, in this context of a vain but retiring husband, a possessive mother and sister-in-law living on the premises and friends and neighbors little appreciative of her Denver clothes and manners, to envisage the conflicts that must have lain ready-made in wait for the new Mrs. Burbank. And underlying all that, who knows what else? There were, in the upshot, no children.

Helen indulged herself in fits of temper of which Burbank bore the brunt. They were both very unhappy. He loved children and had always encouraged them to play in his yard. Now she humiliated him by loudly ordering them off. When he came in from his work, she began to nag, and continued till after they had gone to bed. She would not, he later testified, let him sleep. Once she had tried to push him out of bed, and when she found she couldn't, got up, took hold of a revolver and threatened to shoot him. Slamming a screen door in his face one day, she blacked both his eyes.

She declared that his version of this last incident was greatly exaggerated, and that she had by accident let the screen door in the kitchen loose, not knowing that he was about to pass through. But he, for his part, felt so humiliated by his black eyes that he moved into a workroom above the stable, where he could lock himself in and have some peace. There he remained for two years.

And these were years in which his work load was particularly heavy. It was around this time that he first began to attract world attention (particularly after the appearance of his *New Creations* catalogs of 1893 and 1894). In a one-page announcement in 1892 he observed of his varieties, "My time is so wholly occupied in their production that I cannot attend to their introduction and will sell the stock and complete control of some of the most promising new fruits and plants, or would be a member of a joint stock company, for their introduction. Correspondence on the subject solicited." There seem to have been no satisfactory offers, and he was obliged to soldier on alone. There were hundreds of experiments under way on his grounds, needing daily attention and observation. It was always his tendency to take on more than he could handle. Perhaps he was glad to keep busy, to escape the unhappy atmosphere of his home. But he had never been robust, and work and wife combined were almost too much for him. "Under the double load," Howard says, "his health failed and he almost became a nervous wreck."

Ever since 1877 he had been working with walnuts, using more than a dozen species and varieties as breeding stock, among them the eastern and Californian black walnuts, the Persian or cultivated walnut (also called the English walnut, this variety is actually native to southeastern Europe and Asia), the butternut and several Asiatic species, including the Japanese walnut, or Heartnut, *Juglans sieboldiana.*

His greatest success was with the northern variety of the California black walnut, *Juglans hindsii.* Crossed with *Juglans regia,* the Persian walnut, and with the black walnut of the eastern United States, *Juglans nigra,* this gave rise to the "Paradox" and "Royal" walnuts respectively. Another noteworthy Burbank walnut was the "Santa Rosa Soft Shell," a cross between two Persian varieties, introduced in 1906.

In the Royal and Paradox* walnut trees, Burbank felt he had a major triumph. Both were notable for their size and rapid growth, and although the Royal also produced great quantities of nuts—as much as a ton from a single tree in one season— their greatest potential seemed to be as lumber. The Paradox, resulting from a wider cross than the Royal, showed the partial sterility found in many interspecific hybrids. The hybrid trees produced very few nuts, and though these readily germinated on planting, the second-generation seedlings showed an extraordinary degree of variation. Burbank said:

> In the same row there will be bush-like walnuts from six to eighteen inches in height side by side with trees that have shot up to eighteen or twenty feet; all of the same age and grown from seeds gathered from a single tree. This rate of growth continues throughout life, and the fraternity of dwarfs and giants has been a puzzle to layman and botanist alike.

This was a major disadvantage, as unlike most fruit trees, walnuts cannot easily be propagated from cuttings. What Burbank encountered here was the familiar difficulty in crossing species only distantly related to each other. Its explanation

---

*Under the name *Vilmorin* the introduction of this hybrid is sometimes attributed to Felix Gillet, a pioneer nurseryman, of Nevada City, California.

Luther Burbank with Jack London in 1908. *Courtesy of the Jack London Room of the Oakland Public Library.*

The Dutch botanist Hugo de Vries (1848–1933) working on the artificial cross-fertilization of flowers in an experimental garden. *Courtesy of the Bettmann Archive.*

Luther Burbank in 1898,
his "Silver Jubilee Year."

*Courtesy of the
Oakland Public Library.*

George Harrison Shull.

*Courtesy of the Carnegie
Institution of Washington.*

Thomas Alva Edison, Burbank and Henry Ford in 1915.
Courtesy Stark Brothers Nurseries and Orchards Company.

Luther Burbank, probably in the early 1900's.
Courtesy of the Oakland Public Library.

Burbank in his study. *Courtesy Stark Brothers Nurseries and Orchards Company.*

Luther Burbank with Elizabeth Waters Burbank, his second wife, at Santa Rosa, "photographed when he announced that he had presented to the world a new corn." *Courtesy of the Oakland Public Library.* (right)

"All Hail to Luther Burbank," from *Luther Burbank, Plant Lover and Citizen; with Musical Numbers* by Ada Kyle Lynch. Harr Wagner Publishing Co., San Francisco, 1924. *Courtesy of the Bancroft Library, University of California, Berkeley.* (top right)

Luther Burbank in his garden, about 1916. *Courtesy of the Oakland Public Library.*

would have to wait on the coming of Mendelism. The marked increased capacity for growth in cross-bred individuals, both in plants and in animals, had long been known. This phenomenon is known as "hybrid vigor," or heterosis (the latter term, introduced by George Shull in 1914, has now become general). It is exemplified in that best-known of F_1 hybrids*, the mule, which, though sterile, can, as they used to say, "get along with less food than a donkey, do more work than a steam engine, and has more horse-sense than a horse." Sterility in reproduction, which may be partial, as in the case of Burbank's Paradox walnut, or complete, as in the mule, is the first indication that the limits of hybridization are being reached. Even where the hybrid is fertile, subsequent generations may show a failure to breed true, and there may be a rapid falling off in vigor. "The mule would quickly forfeit its place in the estimation of teamsters could it bring forth the mongrel progeny which would certainly ensue if it were fertile," remarks the geneticist Donald F. Jones. "Animal husbandry men have learned by sad experience that those cross-bred cattle, sheep and swine which are so profitable to feed for the market are of no value for breeding purposes." Burbank's second-generation seedlings could not, he points out, be expected to equal the first-generation hybrid trees which he described in such glowing terms and upon which the calculation of probable returns was based.[6]

The fact that Burbank willfully overlooked this smacks a little of dishonesty, but it would be many years before these processes were even vaguely understood, and his attention was focused on his amazingly vigorous first-generation hybrids. He had the faculty—perhaps it is one of the attributes of genius—of ignoring the difficulties and sailing ahead regardless. The Paradox walnut, he declared, "so far outstripped all competitors in the matter of growth that it might fairly be said to represent a new type of vegetation." At sixteen years of age the trees

*In this notation "F_1" means first filial generation, "F_2," second filial generation, and so on.

stood sixty feet high, with an equivalent span in branches. Four feet above the ground, their trunks had a diameter of two feet, whereas thirty-two-year-old Persian walnuts growing nearby averaged only eight or nine inches in diameter and had a spread of branches only about a quarter that of the hybrids. Moreover the wood of the Paradox was harder and more close-grained than that of the ordinary black walnut. This was remarkable, in that trees that grow rapidly usually have soft wood. Burbank pronounced that:

> All in all the production of the Paradox hybrid, and the development of a race of hard-wood trees of exceedingly rapid growth, constitutes a genuine triumph in tree culture. A tree that grows to the proportions of a handsome shade tree and furnishes material for the cabinet-maker in six or eight years, has very obvious economic importance.[7]

The Royal walnut, like the Paradox, grew more rapidly than the parent varieties. Not being the product of a cross between such distantly related types, the second generation did not show such a wide range of diversity, and it was also extraordinarily fecund."The first generation hybrids," Burbank said, "probably produce more nuts than any other tree hitherto known." He conceded, however, that seedlings grown from the nuts could not be relied on to reproduce all the good qualities of their parents, because of the tendency to "throw back" to the grandparent strains. Propagation was therefore best accomplished by grafting, and he suggested that Persian walnuts might be grafted on Royal root stock, arguing that "a tree grafted on this hybrid will produce several times as many nuts as a tree of corresponding size growing on its own roots. The trees are also much less subject to blight when they are thus grafted."

This would, however, be an expensive process if the trees were to be grown solely for lumber, and the nuts themselves, like the original black walnuts, were thick-shelled and difficult to crack. "The slimy deep-staining hull is not easily removed," says Donald Jones. "In spite of these objections black walnuts are becoming increasingly popular on account of the rich delightful flavor and absence of bitterness characteristic of the Persian walnut but so far they are not of much commercial importance. Black walnut trees have been found which bear nuts that yield unbroken meats when cracked. Variations of this type combined with a vigorous and productive tree should do much to increase the use of black walnuts."

Both the Royal and Paradox walnuts were offered for sale (though not yet under those names) in the first edition of what was to be Burbank's most important single catalog, *New Creations in Fruits and Flowers,* issued in June 1893 and bearing the bold subscription, *"Keep This Catalogue For Reference.* You will need it when these Fruits and Flowers become standards of excellence."

This fifty-two-page brochure was the means by which Burbank first became internationally famous (he was already well-known in the United States), and announced some of the best and most lasting things that he was ever to produce. It went out from "Burbank's Experiment Grounds"—with "great care being taken to confine it to the trade only," according to a note in a subsequent catalog. Burbank wanted it to be clearly understood that he was an experimenter, an innovator and not just another nurseryman. An announcement in front drove this message home with unusual forcefulness, and what to some might have seemed no small degree of arrogance:

The Fruits and Flowers mentioned in this list, and to be mentioned in succeeding lists, are more than new in the sense in which the word is generally used; they are new creations, lately produced by scientific combinations of nature's forces, guided by long, carefully conducted, and very expensive biological study. Let not those who read suppose that they were born without labor; they are not foundlings, but are exemplifications of the knowledge that the life-forces of plants may be combined and guided to produce results not imagined by horticulturists who have given the matter little thought.

Limitations once thought to be real have proved to be only apparent barriers; and as in any of the dark problems of nature, the mental light of many ardent, persevering, faithful workers will make the old paths clear, and boundless new ones will appear by which the life-forces are guided into endless useful and beautiful forms.

We are now standing just at the gateway of scientific horticulture, only having taken a few steps in the measureless fields which will stretch out as we advance into the golden sunshine of a more complete knowledge of the forces which are to unfold all the graceful forms of garden beauty, and wealth of fruit and flowers, for the comfort and happiness of Earth's teeming millions.

This catalog, Burbank advised his public, gave the results of more than twenty years' work: these were "the *best of millions* of cross-bred, hybrid and seedling plants, which are now and have been produced at the rate of a million or more a year." Besides the new walnuts (prices on application), *New Creations* offered a "New Japan Mammoth Chestnut"—to produce which, Burbank said, he had for many years grown and fruited seedlings by the thousand. There were two new quinces, the "Van Deman" and the "Santa Rosa," each offered for $800. The Van Deman was named, with consent, for Professor H. E. Van Deman, head of the Pomological Division of the Department of Agriculture; along with other Burbank seedlings this quince had received the Wilder Medal from the American Pomological Society in 1891. The Santa Rosa came with a testimonial from W. A. Taylor, Assistant Pomologist with the U.S.D.A., to the effect that it was "very choice . . . can be eaten raw like an Apple." There were, besides, a new Japan quince, the "Alpha," and a new flowering quince called "Dazzle," each offered for $300.

Among the most spectacular offerings were his new hybrid plums and prunes, ten of them in all. Two crosses between the *Petite d'Agen,* or French prune, designated "A.P.-90" and "A.P.-318," were offered for $1500 and $3000 respectively. This was for stock on hand and complete control. A.P.-318 which, Burbank contended, might "change the whole Prune industry of the world," could also be had in half-shares: he would sell half his stock and half control for $2000. The "Golden" plum, a cross between the Robinson Chickasaw and the Sweet Botan, of which Burbank noted, "I have never seen a Plum tree which perfects so much fruit, and has it so evenly distributed as this one," was priced at $3000. Stock and control in another hybrid plum, "Perfection," a cross between the Kelsey and the Burbank, were offered for $2000. "Among the many thousand Japan Plums which I have fruited, this one, so far, stands preeminent in its rare combination of good qualities," Burbank said. He was not wrong. Renamed the Wickson, after Professor E. J. Wickson of the University of California, it was to prove one of his most enduring varieties. Six other hybrid plums, most of them with ancestors in the original Yokohama shipment, were listed at prices ranging from $300 to $500. Rarely in horticultural history can so many important new varieties of plum have been announced in one catalog.

Burbank was particularly proud of his work with berries. Nothing like it, he said, "has anywhere ever been attempted even by Government aid; and no one will question the claim that I have made more and greater improvements in Blackberries and Raspberries during the last fourteen years than have otherwise been made during all the past eighteen centuries."

He goes on to list thirty-seven species of *Rubus* which have gone into the production of his hybrids, remarking that, "the combinations are endless; the results are startling and as surprising to myself as they will be to others when known." Among those on offer was the Japanese Golden Mayberry, or "Improved Rubus palmatus," with a list price of $800. This Burbank claimed to be the earliest raspberry ever known. He gives a short account of its history, which is highly descriptive of his methods:

> Some ten years ago I requested my collector in Japan to hunt up the best wild Raspberries, Blackberries and Strawberries that could be found. Several curious species were received the next season, and among them a red and also a dingy yellow unproductive variety of Rubus palmatus (described by botanists and collectors as being unproductive and having an insignificant berry). One of these plants, though bearing only a few of the most worthless, tasteless, dingy yellow berries I have ever seen, was selected solely on account of its unusual earliness, to cross with Cuthbert and other well-known Raspberries. Among the seedlings raised from this plant was this one, and, though no signs of the Cuthbert appear, yet it can hardly be doubted that Cuthbert pollen has affected some of the wonderful improvements to be seen in this new variety.

Another berry of great interest, offered for $600, was the "Primus." This was a cross between the hardy Siberian raspberry, *Rubus crataegifolius,* and the cultivated variety of the dioecious* California dewberry, *Rubus vitifolius,* known as Aughinbaugh. Five hundred seedlings were raised, but only a few showed any promise. One of these, a trailing plant showing many of the properties of both parents, was selected. The fruit, which was of a dark, mulberry color, was something like a blackberry in form. "The flavor is unique; nothing like it has ever before appeared; all pronounce it superior when cooked, and most people like it raw, while some claim it is the 'best berry they ever tasted,'" the catalog declares. The most remarkable feature about this cross was, however, that *the progeny came true from seed.* Seedlings closely resembled the parental bush. Jones has speculated that what Burbank had here is what afterward came to be known as an amphidiploid or allotetraploid†, a spe-

---

*That is, with staminate and pistillate flowers borne on different individuals.

†See Appendix.

cies hybrid that bred true because of an increase in the number of chromosome sets. If so—though Burbank could not have been aware of *why* his hybrids were fertile and bred true—this may be the first recorded report of this phenomenon. In the early years of genetics, when Mendel's rules of segregation and recombination were being tested and proven, scientists tended to discount such findings. Here, Jones observes,

was a case where a plant hybrid bred true in the second generation where, by the rules, it should have shown the greatest breaking up into variable types, especially where the parental stalks were so diverse. Away with this imposter who claims such unorthodox results! Either the cross was never made in the first place or else the plants were mixed up with something else while being grown. Such results simply could not be.

Many years later, with Mendel's law carefully proven, biologists have gone further into the subject and have found many species hybrids: in tobacco, in cabbages, in tarweeds—strange plants from unholy marriages—that have given offspring that breed true right from the start. From Russia comes the weird report of a cabbage-radish hybrid that produces neither succulent head nor fleshy root and has flowers and seed pods unlike any brassica ever seen before. When it is examined under the microscope this plant is seen to have 36 chromosomes, those rod-shaped carriers of the inheritance, instead of the 18 of the radish and cabbage. Abnormal chromosome distribution and duplication of chromosomes are topics of interest at the present time in biological laboratories devoted to the study of heredity and related subjects. This cabbage-radish plant also bred true from seed and comes the nearest to being a new species that has actually been produced under experimentally controlled conditions, unless the Primus berry that Burbank made before 1889 is a better example.[8]

More than a dozen other varieties of berry are offered for sale in *New Creations* for 1893. Among these we might note two crosses between the Improved California Wild Dewberry and the Cuthbert Raspberry, listed at $800 each. These were larger than the largest berry ever before known, Burbank claimed, asserting that individual berries often measured three inches around one way by four the other. When they were exhibited the question asked was, "Will they be sold by the dozen?" A hybrid raspberry designated "S.S.-147" was said to be "the first practical cross of the cap and sucker Raspberries ever made . . . no berry has ever been introduced which so delightfully combines the best flavors and aromas of both these species." This was listed at $400. The hybrid berry called "Paradox," which seems to have closely resembled the modern Boysenberry, was priced at $800. This was said to have "appeared in the fourth generation from a cross of Crystal White Blackberry and Shaffer's Colossal Raspberry. The plant is in every respect a most perfect balance between the two species."

Aside from its cornucopia of new berries, plums and prunes, *New Creations* goes on to list five new seedling roses; a number of new callas, with prices in the $1000-$2000 range; two new hybrid lilies; a new myrtle; a new poppy named "Silver Lining"; hybrid nicotianas; a "Begonia-leaved" squash described as "mammoth . . . produces abundant crops for stock-feeding"; three new varieties of potato; an ornamental tomato, "Combination"; and a new plant, the "Nicotunia," produced by crossing the large flowering nicotianas with petunias. Of this last Burbank says proudly,

> If one thinks he can take right hold and produce Nicotunias as he would hybrid Petunias or cross-bred Primroses, let him try; there is no patent on their manufacture; but if the five hundredth crossing succeeds, or even the five thousandth, under the best conditions obtainable, he will surely be very successful; I do not fear any immediate competition.

Though the Nicotunias produced no seed, they could easily be propagated from cuttings. The whole stock, however, was killed off by frost not long afterward.

The catalog concludes with a list of other hybrids Burbank is experimenting with. They include crosses of peaches with almonds, plums and apricots, of almonds with plums, of apricots with plums, of quinces with apples and of potatoes with tomatoes. "Not only one of each of these is growing, but many, in some cases several hundreds each, and of some, thousands," he asserts.

Finally, at the end of the catalog, there is a sort of Burbankian position paper, titled "Facts and Possibilities," which is worth quoting at some length, inasmuch as it is the clearest statement of Burbank's theories as of that time. It cannot be doubted, he says,

> that every form of plant life existing on the earth is now being and has always been modified, more or less, by its surroundings, and often rapidly and permanently changed, never to return to the same form. When man takes advantage of these facts, and changes all the conditions, giving abundance of room for expansion and growth, extra cultivation and a superabundance of the various chemical elements in the most assimilable form, with abundance of light and heat, great changes sooner or later occur according to the susceptibility of the subject; and when added to all these combined governing forces we employ the other potent forces of combination and selection of the best combinations, the power to improve our useful and ornamental plants is limitless. But in crossing, as in budding or grafting, the affinities can only be demonstrated by actual test, which often involves long, tedious, and expensive experimenting.
>
> In budding or grafting, the nurseryman finds every conceivable stage of congeniality between stock and bud or graft, from actual poisoning to a refusal to unite; or uniting and not growing; or growing for a short time and dying; or separating where united; or bearing one or two crops of fruit and then suddenly blighting or separating after years of growth up to complete congeniality. So in crossing, all grades of hybridity are to be found. Crossed plants generally have the characteristics of both parents combined, yet, owing to prepotency of the life-forces in certain directions or congeniality of surroundings sometimes show only

their parentage on one side producing uncertain results in the first generation, and these cross-bred seedlings often break away into endless forms and combinations, sometimes even reverting to some strange ancestral form which existed in the dim past; or the break may not occur until after many generations, but when once the old persistent type is broken up the road is open for improvement and advance in any useful direction. Sometimes hybridized or crossed seedlings show considerable or even great variations for weeks and then change at once to one or the other of the original types; or they may show no change in foliage or growth from one or the other parent forms until nearly ready to bloom or bear fruit, when they suddenly change in foliage, growth, character and general appearance.

Tomatoes may be grown from seed pollenated from Potato pollen only, and Juglans regia from nuts pollenated only from Juglans cinerea or J. nigra. The common Calla has often been grown from seeds pollenated only by Calla albo-maculata; also pure Wheat from Rye pollenations, and *vice versa;* pure Blackberries, Raspberries and Dewberries from Apple, Rose, Quince or Mountain Ash pollenations.

Seedling Lilies very rarely show the effect of foreign pollenation, though often producing seed much more abundantly than with pollen of the same species.

These facts have been observed by me so often, and have been worked on so extensively, and can be proven so readily, that the common theory of parthenogenesis must, in these cases, be set aside.

There is no barrier to obtaining fruits of any size, form or flavor desired, and none to producing plants and flowers of any form, color or fragrance; all that is needed is a knowledge to guide our efforts in the right direction, undeviating patience and cultivated eyes to detect variations of value.

The descriptions in this list are necessarily short and incomplete, but in all cases exaggeration has been studiously avoided.

It is fair to suppose that one who has had extensive experience in any special line should be able to give judgment approximating impartiality. All the new plants mentioned in this list and the supplementary lists which are to follow will have to be judged by the great discriminating public, and will infallibly stand or fall by its verdict, without regard to what the originator or introducer may see fit to say.

It should be remembered that this was written at a time when the results of hybridization could not be predicted. It was only with the rediscovery almost twenty years later of Mendel's principles of heredity that what was called "prepotency" was identified as Mendelian dominance and "reversions" or "atavism" as the reappearance of Mendelian recessives. Until that time, as Professor Edwin G. Conklin of Princeton University has remarked, "The fact of evolution was accepted by practically all scientists, but the factors of evolution were largely matters of opinion, and in general persons believed what they preferred to believe. Indeed this whole subject had become so speculative that it seemed to be a field for the exercise of the imagination rather than of scientific research . . ."[9]

The nearest approach to the Mendelian interpretation of heredity was made by Haacke, in a paper published in Germany in 1893, recording his experiments in crossing albino mice with waltzing mice. Burbank did not subscribe to the *Biologisches Centralblatt* in which Haacke published his results, and the latter's findings were in any case overlooked by those of his contemporaries who did.[10]

Meanwhile Lamarckian or neo-Lamarckian views were held by many perfectly respectable scientists. One might, for example, cite the views of Professor Edward D. Cope, who held that variations were the basis of evolution, and that they were caused by (1) the direct action of the environment on developed organisms, which he termed physiogenesis, (2) the inherited effects of use or disuse, or kinetogenesis, (3) the energy of growth forces, or bathmogenesis and (4) sensations or consciousness, to which supposed influence he gave the awful title of archaesthetism.[11] Compared with this, Burbank's theories are tentative and restrained and much in line with contemporary thinking outside Germany. He probably knew as much about the subject of inheritance as anyone in America. The science of genetics did not yet exist. The generation of geneticists who would judge and dismiss him were still schoolboys.

New Creations is Burbank before the Burbankians—before the puffers and front office men who are generally credited with having inflated his reputation out of all proportion to the truth. Yet already it makes amazing claims—some of them a little hard to believe even with the best will in the world. "Exaggeration has been studiously avoided," he insists. Yet we know that he was by nature given to exaggeration. (George Shull held that he had an "exaggeration coefficient" of about ten; that all his figures should be divided by this number to get an approximation of the truth.) As a nurseryman he almost *had* to exaggerate. It was considered fair practice in the trade, his competitors all did it, and if his varieties were to hold their own, they needed the customary boost. His experiments were entirely funded by himself. Their continuation was dependent on sales. If he could not make a healthy profit, he might as well shut up shop.

He refers his introductions to the judgment of the "great discriminating public," and if we judge by the reception they got— at this date there is hardly any other way—they must have had a substantial part of the merits he claimed for them. They sold and went on selling.

His prices were high, but Andrew J. Coe of Meriden, Connecticut, bought the Mammoth Japan Chestnut and the hybrid raspberry "S.S.-8940" for $300 each; John Lewis Childs of Floral Park, New York, took the Santa Rosa quince (he promptly renamed it the "Childs") for $800, the plums Delaware, Shipper and Juicy for $500 each, the Golden Mayberry for $800, the Primus berry for $600, the hybrid berry "V.C.-16407" for $800, a pair of dewberries for $200 each, the Eureka raspberry for $300, the "Sugar Hybrid" raspberry for $400, the "Dwarf Pardalium" *(sic)* lily for $500 and some lesser items besides; A. Blanc & Co., of Philadelphia, purchased the whole stock of his

gladiolus "California strain" for an unknown amount; and the
Sunset Seed and Plant Co. of San Francisco bought the seedling
roses "M.-11,120" and "M.-19,928" for $300 each. The biggest
single purchaser was Stark Brothers' Nurseries of Louisiana,
Missouri, who bought the "Golden" plum for $3000, the
"A.P.-318" prune for the same amount, the "Van Deman"
quince for $800, and a half-interest in a hitherto uncatalogued
plum, the "Doris," for a probable $300.

According to one version, Clarence Stark, the head of the
firm, told Burbank, "I don't think you will ever make a real success in the nursery business because your heart is not in it. But
if you will carry forward the type of hybridizing you are doing,
I think you will go very far in your chosen field. To demon-
strate our sincere belief in your work, our company will give
you $9,000 if you will let me pick 3 of these new fruits you have
shown me." Burbank is said to have remarked in this connection,

> I had been getting very nominal and insufficient prices for my
> new fruits, and when Mr. Stark made this offer to me that is
> when I really became the Luther Burbank that horticulture has
> known. I could see a vision of the great possibilities of plant im-
> provement if only sufficient time, money and effort were put be-
> hind the work by those who understood it.[12]

That Stark Brothers was not motivated solely by altruism is
evident from the fact that at least one of these purchases—the
Van Deman quince—is still listed in their 1974–1975 catalog
more than eighty years later.

Stark Brothers spent more than $7000, and perhaps as much
as $9000, on Burbank's "new creations" in 1893, while John Le-
wis Childs spent over $5900. These were very much more con-
siderable sums of money than they would be today and should
probably be multiplied by at least four or five to get a rough
modern approximation. He was well on his way to becoming a
wealthy man. These customers were all experienced nursery-

men. They were not likely to be taken in easily by inflated claims, and that they were not disappointed in their purchases is evident from the fact that a number of them remained steady customers in the succeeding years. Stark Brothers retain an equity in his work to the present day, half a century after his death.

EIGHT

Burbank the Wizard

IN THE MONTHS that followed the publication of *New Creations,* orders came pouring in. The catalog itself was in great demand. "Probably no horticultural publication ever created more profound surprise or received a more hearty welcome," Burbank wrote in the introduction to a new edition, *New Creations in Fruits and Flowers,* June 1894. "Almost every mail brings requests for them from colleges, experiment stations, libraries, students and scientific societies in Europe and America, and it has been translated into other languages for foreign lands, even where it would seem that scientific Horticulture was hardly recognized; some asking for one, others for two or three, or a dozen or two or more."

Henceforth there would have to be a charge for the catalog. Letters came pouring in by the thousands, many of them from amateurs who had long lists of questions they wanted answered. Unless this avalanche slowed up, Burbank said, "there will soon be no one here to answer them." Nonetheless, the sudden fame he was experiencing seems to have gone a little to his head. He now addresses his audience in the royal style:

> We love to produce new fruits and flowers, and our heart is made glad beyond expression to know that our work is appreciated far and wide; but most of the *questions* which amateurs ask could better be answered by some horticultural paper, which would welcome them, or by the experiment stations, or by someone who has more leisure at his command.

At the same time he endeavors to answer the criticisms that have already begun to be heard. His products, he insists, will not be found any less hardy as a consequence of being raised in the mild California climate. "Are those already before the public any less hardy or any less valuable than most of the Russian fruits which have been so extensively advertised for years? Are not the various Plums, Walnuts, Chestnuts, etc., which have been distributed from our establishment, proving to be *hardier* even than most of the Russian fruits, and more valuable in all other respects?" Those nurserymen who have been enterprising enough to invest in his trees, he observes, are reaping a rich reward. And the best ones are yet to come. "What better gift has American Horticulture lately received than these fruits and nuts, and the greatly improved seedlings and crosses from them?" he asks. And yet,

> we have the fullest sympathy with all nurserymen who desire to introduce only those trees, fruits and flowers which have been widely tested, and which will prove better than any before known; delicious, productive, handsome, hardy and reliable in every respect. *We would very much prefer to have all our new fruits and flowers fully tested everywhere* and by everybody; but those who know the facts are too well aware that it would be a perilous risk or utter ruin to the originator, as a single bud or seed in the wrong hands may place an unscrupulous person on an equal footing with the originator, who may have spent worlds of pa-

tient thought and toil, during the few short years of the best of his life, in producing the beautiful creation. Having no Government aid or even protection, or college endowment to back us and to pay our bills, we must receive early returns, in part at least, for our tremendous expenses. Most of the horticultural world now knows that we would not send out a plant which was thought to be unworthy; else would the keenest and most level-headed business men—men who have built up mammoth horticultural establishments which are a wonder far and near—pay thousands of dollars for a single plant or tree which they had never seen, to one living in a far-off State or nation whom they had never met?

The originator should not be blamed, he points out, for indiscriminate and unwarranted praise on the part of the purchaser. "Indiscriminate commendation has a tendency to discourage all the honest efforts of originators who might, perhaps, otherwise receive some reasonable compensation for their labors." This was certainly to be true in his own case. Some of the most severe criticism that was to be leveled at him had its origins in the overpraising of varieties that bore his name by other nurserymen. On the other hand, he was too often guilty of professional exaggerations himself to expect much sympathy from his colleagues on this score. If anything, they had merely followed his lead.

The 1894 edition of *New Creations* offers a number of new varieties for sale and reiterates some of the announcements in the previous catalog. Prominent among the new offerings is the Wickson plum, named for Burbank's friend, Professor Edward J. Wickson of the University of California, author of a popular book on *Calfornia Fruits and How to Grow Them.* This cross-bred Japan plum was to be one of the most enduring of all Burbank's introductions. "A year ago I was convinced that this was perhaps the best of all the Japan Plums," he says, "and have yet no reason to change that opinion . . . There is wood enough now for twenty thousand grafts or half a million buds; and if not sold before September 1st, shall introduce it myself to the general trade. Price, $2,500." It was the "Perfection" plum of 1893, now permanently renamed, a *P. triflora X P. simonii* hybrid that for several years became the leading shipping plum. "As the namesake of this plum, the writer has inherited both joy and embarrassment," Wickson himself later noted. "To read in some eastern horticultural reports that 'Wickson is a worthless cross-bred Japanese' has caused him some anxiety lest he might be deported to Tokio."[1] The charge was made that the Wickson and other Burbank varieties were simply Japanese plums brought to this country and renamed. There is scant doubt, however, that they were the hybrids they were said to be. Evidence, Jones remarks,

> was sought from Mr. T. Tanikawa, pomologist in charge of the Horticultural Experiment Station at Okitsu in Japan. His reply was to the effect that the Wickson variety resembled most closely the native plums in tree, fruit and leaves but that he had never seen exactly the same variety in Japan. Most of the other Burbank plums of this type, he said, are quite similar to Japanese varieties in fruit but the tree and leaf characters are different.[2]

Stock and control of the "Giant" Prune ("A.P.–90" of 1893) were offered for $2500. Not having found a buyer the previous year, he had evidently had this reproduced for marketing himself, and there were now several thousand yearling trees "which are growing east of the Mississippi, so that any Eastern purchaser will have a good start *this season.*" If it was not sold by September 1, he said, he would introduce it to the general trade himself. Also offered were the "Prolific" plum ("J.–3,972" of 1893), now priced at $500 as against $300 the year before, the "Doris" plum—Stark Brothers had already purchased a half-interest in this, and the other half was offered for $300—and the "Honey" prune, another seedling of the French prune, priced at $300. A quince, No. 80, stated to be a seedling of Rea's Mammoth, was offered for $600.

One of the most interesting items in the catalog was the "Iceberg" white blackberry. Burbank's attention had been initially attracted to the possibility of producing a white blackberry as a novelty by the Crystal White variety. This had been known in Illinois before 1859, but it was not a true white blackberry as the fruit was more of a brownish yellow when ripe. Burbank's approach to the problem was entirely experimental. He crossed the Crystal White with the Lawton, a black variety. In the first (or E_1) generation of offspring, the seedlings produced only black fruit, but when they were interbred, a few plants with light-colored fruit turned up. The seed from these was planted, and in the next (F_3) generation four or five bushes were found out of a total of several hundred raised that had almost completely colorless fruit. The best of these was selected, and this was the berry now designated "Iceberg" and offered for $2500. (It was bought by John Lewis Childs of Floral Park, New York, and distributed throughout the United States, but it never aroused more than amateur interest.) Burbank went on to make further selections from the Iceberg, and a variety called "Snowbank" was evolved. Its fruit is said to have been "pearly white, tinged yellowish," and it was probably the closest thing to a truly white blackberry ever produced. It was neither hardy nor productive, and as one of its critics observed, the public didn't want white blackberries; it wanted black blackberries. However that may be, as Jones remarks,

> it is an excellent example of the variation that can be induced by crossing. Thus, a yellowish white berry was made very nearly white by crossing with a fruit entirely black. Since Mendel's principles have become known, plant breeders talk freely of unit characters and modifying factors. The main difference between black and less colored blackberries, judging from similar differences in other plants, is transmitted in a relatively simple manner. Just as is that inherited something that makes one flower red the other white in the same species. Burbank found that his white blackberries when inter-pollinated came true from seed in color of fruit, showing this character to be recessive. Since this

experiment in crossing and from that, the building up of a trait that was not fully expressed in either parent, was carried out before anything was heard of Mendel, the white blackberry has more importance than merely a garden novelty.[3]

Besides the Iceberg, the catalog listed the Humboldt blackberry-raspberry hybrid ("V.C. 18,234" of 1893), now offered for $850 as opposed to $800 the previous year, and "Rubus Capensis," a novelty introduced, Burbank said, "by way of New Zealand from South Africa," priced at $300.

There was also a spectacular offer of lilies. "All the earth is not adorned with so many new ones as are growing at my establishment," Burbank avers. "Though not having a very large stock of some, yet the number of varieties being so great, I will offer the control of some very handsome, hardy ones at from $250 to $10,000 each; and, having a multitude of other new things to absorb my attention, will offer *all these lilies* to any responsible party or parties for $250,000, including all unbloomed hybrid seedlings and all the hybrid seed produced this season; this offer holds good only to November 1, 1894." He could hardly have been serious. This would be the equivalent of at least a million dollars in our terms. Obviously no buyer was going to come forward to claim his hybrid lilies, however numerous and fine, at that sort of price. Putting a shutoff date on the offer is even more suspicious. It smacks distinctly of the sort of publicity gimmick then strongly associated with the name of the late P. T. Barnum.

Yet Burbank did do interesting work with lilies, and his achievements in this field were described by Carl Purdy, of Ukiah, California, a contemporary authority on Pacific Coast lilies and himself a commercial lily grower, as "monumental." He gave particular attention to the native California species, crossing the leopard lily, *Lilium pardalinum* with *L. parvum*, *L. parryi* and *L. washingtonianum*. A particularly difficult cross was made between *L. humboldtii*, a fragrant white with large spotted flowers, and *L. parryi*, which is tall and slender with clear yellow flowers. The hybrid, described as "a delightfully fragrant, pure yellow lily," propagated vegetatively, was named *Lilium burbankii* by a New York nurseryman and long grown in England and Holland.

New Creations of 1894 also listed three named varieties of clematis, "Snowdrift" at $300, "Ostrich Plume" at $250, and "Waverly" at $200. These hybrids between *C. coccinea* and *C. crispa,* which he described as "a *New Race* of Clematis," were subsequently introduced by J. C. Vaughan of Chicago. Other clematis offered were about "a dozen new *double* seedlings of various forms and colors, and some single ones with *largest flowers* and unusual colors and habits of growth" at between $100 and $300 each.

His new calla, "Snowflake," is listed again, still at $2000, and another variety, called "Fragrance" because of its unusual scent, was mentioned. Finally, the "Peachblow" rose, which had made its appearance the previous year, was once more on offer—fifty large bushes for $300. The Sunset Seed Co. of San Francisco bought it in 1895, along with two other roses called "Coquito" and "Pink Pet."

These, then, were the catalogs that made Burbank famous. That he was already well-known is testified to by the laudatory testimonials with which they are sprinkled. There are endorsements from nurserymen like Stark Brothers, from scientists like Van Deman and Liberty Hyde Bailey ("You are certainly doing a great work in your hybridizing, and the wonder to me is that you accomplish so much in the midst of business cares.") and from agricultural papers, like the *Pacific Rural Press,* which his friend Wickson edited for forty years, the *Rural New Yorker* and *Orchard and Farm* ("Burbank, the wizard of horticulture," the latter journal called him, in a phrase that stuck better than he might have liked.). Local papers, like the Santa Rosa *Democrat* and *Republican,* were naturally ecstatic. "Luther Burbank has established a world-wide reputation for the excellence of his products," the *Republican* announced proudly.

Praise flowed in from horticulturists in other parts of the country. "Allow me to thank you most heartily for a copy of your unique presentation, *New Creations in Fruits and Flowers*. It is a rare, rich feast, and I congratulate you upon your marvelous accomplishments," wrote Professor T. V. Munson of Texas, himself the originator of a number of varieties of peaches and grapes. "I thank you for a copy received of your pamphlet . . . It is exceedingly interesting and I prize it," wrote G. B. Brackett, secretary of the American Pomological Society. "Allow me to thank you for your catalogue of *New Creations*," said Professor C. C. Georgeson of the Kansas State Agriculture College. "It is the most interesting catalogue I have ever received. Every one of your new plants is a monument in your honor."

Endorsement came from abroad, too. "We cannot say enough in praise of the Burbank Plum; it is superior to all other varieties; the most fastidious cannot find fault with it. This is without doubt the best and most profitable Plum in cultivation," wrote D. Hay & Son, of Auckland, New Zealand. "The Gladioli received by me last spring fully supported your claims for them. Thanks for your catalogue. It is a revelation to me," said H. H. Goff of Ontario, Canada, another professional nurseryman. In 1894 the Santa Rosa *Democrat* noted that "Fred C. Smith, Horticultural Commissioner for the South Australian Government, accompanied by Wm. Brooke, also of Australia, and Mr. Cillie of South Africa, spent Tuesday in this city. One of the chief objects of their visit was to meet Luther Burbank, who is one of the best-known horticulturists. Mr. Smith says his works are extensively read in Australia, and are looked upon as eminent authority. He was as much pleased with the man as with the author." (The "works" in question can at that date only have been Burbank's sales literature, numbering then almost forty separate items. This would tend to indicate the seriousness with which the *New Creations* catalogs in particular were received. But on the other hand, perhaps Mr. Smith didn't really know what he was talking about, or the reporter got him wrong.)

Meanwhile, sales proceeded steadily. In April of 1894, H. H. Berger & Co. purchased "Little Gem" calla bulbs, A. Blanc & Co. bought gladiolus stock and took over the "Rubus Capensis" for $500, while Jackson & Perkins and John Lewis Childs were customers respectively for his clematis and amaryllis. In September of that same year, J. H. Hale of South Glastonbury, Connecticut, paid $500 for the plum that had been announced in 1893 as "J.-3972" and listed the following year as the "Prolific." The buyer introduced it under his own name, a common enough practice. The "Hale" was widely planted, but unsuccessful because the fruit was too tender for shipping, and the trees themselves insufficiently rugged, though Burbank declared in the 1894 catalogue that "From its appearance I judge it will be hardy as far north as New York and perhaps in central New England." This was difficult to judge without extensive testing, but doubtless the purchaser knew that he was taking his chances.

The press was always only too ready to laud and exaggerate Burbank's achievements. In 1895 a Santa Rosa newspaperman named H. W. Slater reported sensationally that he had contracted with a customer to produce a hardy tea rose for a fee of $5000. Whether the story was true or not, the feat does not seem to have been accomplished.

Certainly, however, he had been working with roses since the middle eighties, if not earlier, and ultimately introduced numerous varieties. Ever since George Washington crossed the wild Prairie rose with cultivated European roses at Mount Vernon, to produce the variety that came to be known as Mary Washington, this flower has had special attention from American breeders. Over six hundred varieties had been originated in the United States by 1920, and here, at least, there was no shortage of competition.

Typically, Burbank did not know the exact ancestry of his rose hybrids. "The parents . . . being themselves hybrids of complicated ancestry," he confesses, "it is obvious that the pedigree in a few generations became so complicated that if one were to attempt to trace them there would be little time left for any other experiments . . . so I have contented myself with watching for results among the hybrid progeny of my roses of multiple ancestry." In June 1896 W. Atlee Burpee, of Philadelphia, paid $500 for a rose named "Burbank," and an additional $225 for the "Silver Lining" and "Goldleaf" poppies and the new tomato, "Combination." The last item was thrown in for a mere $25. An attractive ornamental, its fruit had little or no value.

The Burbank rose, a cross between Bon Silene and a seedling of Hermosa, was awarded the Gold Medal as the best budding rose at the Louisiana Purchase Exposition at St. Louis, Missouri, in 1904. A perpetual blooming pink rose, it was described by its originator as hardy, vigorous and disease resistant. It survived as a variety for many years and was reintroduced by Stark Brothers of Louisiana, Missouri, around 1936.

Tens of thousands of Crimson Rambler seedlings were pollinated by Burbank from other varieties commonly grown in California, in one of his mass hybridization experiments. From these came Corona, described as "a large single-flowered pink with thick waxy petals, that would keep fresh for two weeks." The other parent in this case seems to have been the Cherokee. So proud was Burbank of this variety that he grew it in the place of honor over the doorway to his house.

One of his more widely touted productions was a remarkable blue rose. "This unusual color character evidently was not stable, however," says Howard, "for no blue variety was announced."[4] Whether he did actually achieve a blue rose must remain a matter for speculation.

His domestic circumstances now took a considerable turn for the better. On October 19, 1896, his divorce was granted, and the uncongenial Helen returned to Denver, passing out of his life forever. He had not cohabited with his wife for four years, he charged, in suing for divorce. She had bedeviled him until he was a nervous wreck. He was a sick man and unable to carry on his business affairs.

He was willing to make her a cash settlement of $1800 and allow her to take all her house furniture, if he could be rid of her. A neighbor, whom the court called as a witness, substantiated much of his story, including the episode of the blackened eyes, and the fact that the plaintiff was domiciled in the barn. Helen did not appear, and her attorney did not deny the charges. She was, no doubt, as anxious to be free as Luther. They were thoroughly incompatible. Helen had made her attitude quite plain. Luther's mother, she is quoted as saying, was "a vile serpent, an old vicious cat." And she went further than that. "Luther and all his relations were a nest of cats and snakes and low-lived dogs."[5]

The settlement offer was accepted, and on that note Helen's role in the Burbank story comes to an end. He and his family were so anxious to be done with her that she is mentioned in none of the books produced by Burbank with the aid of his various ghostwriters and editors, not even in his "autobiography," *The Harvest of the Years.* Emma's little volume stops conveniently short of her arrival on the scene and makes only the briefest admission that "Burbank was twice married, but left no children." (She did not, it seems, get on with either of the Mrs. Burbanks.) Were it not for Walter Howard's patient detective work in the two decades after Burbank's death, there would scarcely be any other record of Helen's existence. The first marriage, to the Burbanks, was an episode to be forgotten. Divorce was not a happy word in a family that was deeply Puritan. They got around it, as Puritans do, by simply pretending that it had never happened. Time passed, and eventually few people knew that there had ever been a "first Mrs. Burbank." Helen, the Denver "adventuress," was exorcised by a family conspiracy of silence.

She is heard of on only one other occasion, and it does no kindness to her memory. It seems that one morning around 1900, Burbank was opening and reading his mail when he suddenly burst into laughter. His secretary gazed at him in surprise, and he explained that the letter he had in his hand was from a Denver man who had married Helen some time before and now wanted Burbank's advice in his capacity as ex-husband on how to get rid of her.

In 1897 Burbank was ready to introduce his Improved Beach Plum, one of the things that Hugo De Vries was to find so impressive in 1904. The Beach Plum, *Prunus maritima,* is a wild fruit that grows in the sand dunes along the coast from Virginia to New Brunswick, doing best in Massachusetts and New Jersey. The bushes grow low to the ground in the dunes, and are frequently covered by the shifting sands after they have set fruit. At harvest time the branches have to be pulled from the sand, but the fruit apparently ripens well under these conditions and is protected in this way from the usual insect blemishes.

On Cape Cod local families had long been used to collecting the fruit for jelly and preserves, which found a ready market with summer visitors. Burbank would have been familiar with it as a boy, and it was exactly the sort of thing that would attract his questing mind, always on the lookout for plants that had not yet been subjected to the process of human improvement.

There is no information as to whether the Improved Beach Plum offered in 1897 was a hybrid or a selected seedling, but it is described, in a catalog of that year, as a "Compact, handsome tree, enlarged in all respects and the fruit is a beautiful purple, dotted white, with a white bloom and delicious to eat fresh from the tree, not having a trace of the original bitter taste . . . Flesh deep yellow, freestone . . . Ripens with the common beach plum . . . Trees bloom . . . later than any other plum."

After his work at selection of the Beach Plum was complete, the result was crossed with one of his Japanese hybrids, a task which presented some difficulty, for,

it had been generally supposed that the Beach plum could not be pollinated from, primarily because it blooms very late, after most cultivated plums have passed that stage. But I was not to be thwarted by this obstacle, and used here a device I often used both before and since. What I did was to search out the latest bloomers among my cultivated Japanese hybrids and determine ahead of time that their blossoms would still be capable of fertilization when the very earliest Beach blooms were opened. By cross-pollinating between the latest of the one and the earliest of the others I effected a union that many horticulturists had given up as hopeless.[6]

The end product of this process of selection and hybridization was the "Giant Maritima," not introduced until 1905, but supposedly capable of bearing fruit as much as eight and a quarter inches in diameter.

In 1897 gross sales exceeded $16,000. The following year he acquired his first important foreign customer, H. E. V. Pickstone of South Africa, a prominent nurseryman based at Simondium in the Cape Province. Pickstone, who would remain a lifelong customer, was particularly interested in Japanese plums. These, notably the Santa Rosa and Beauty, formed the basis of a considerable industry in South Africa. The Santa Rosa remains the most important export variety there, along with Gaviota, while Satsuma is grown for the processing industry, and Beauty continues to be cultivated on a smaller scale.

Further supplements to *New Creations* appeared in 1898 and 1899. The 1898 supplement quotes a slew of testimonials on its cover, indicative both of Burbank's swelling reputation and the need to fend off his critics. The Santa Rosa *Republican* declared him "The man who has done more to give the world some idea of the possibilities of Nature's work in the world of horticulture than any other of the great scientists of the age." The *Gardeners' Chronical* of London, England, noted a hint chauvinistically that "The statements made to the number and variety of Mr. Burbank's productions are so astounding that some might be supposed to consider them as so many flowers of rhetoric, such as we are accustomed to from the other side of the Atlantic, were they not authenticated by competent observers of established repute." The San Francisco *Examiner,* keystone of the young William Randolph Hearst's rising empire, waxed poetic: "Not Ruskin, perhaps, nor Tolstoi, with all their love and study of human nature, has learned a deeper wisdom than has come to this patient, studious man who has given his love to the strange, silent forms of life we call vegetable, and which play their parts so quietly that to many they are insignificant and half forgotten."* To the San Francisco *Call* Burbank was simply "The Edison of horticultural mysteries."

The catalog bears the exhortation destined to be increasingly familiar: HOW TO JUDGE NOVELTIES—LOOK TO THEIR SOURCE. He tenders his name as a warranty of excellence. The Edison of the horticultural mysteries (he seems to be saying) is no mere ordinary seed peddler. He goes further. "What Shakespeare was to poetry and the drama Luther Burbank is to the vegetable world," an unidentified admirer asserts in small print on the back cover. It was this sort of thing that was to prove increasingly galling to his competitors—who in the years to come would lose few opportunities of taking him at his word and referring his failures back to their source, no matter what other hands had intervened, and pointing up his exaggerations with malicious glee.

The catalog itself announced three new plums, Apple, America and Chalco; a new prune, the Pearl; a new rose, the Santa Rosa, of the same parentage as the Burbank; and a new calla, called Fragrance, which had been mentioned in 1894, but not then offered for sale. The Paradox and Royal walnuts are also advertised. Since control had not been purchased, Burbank now introduced them himself. Paradox nuts are offered at 50 cents apiece, Royal at 75 cents. One-year-old Royal seedlings are offered for $1.00. (The higher price, notwithstanding the greater profusion of nuts it produced, surely indicates that he thought the Royal the more marketworthy of the two.)

*Of this paper Arthur McEwen, its city editor, remarked that when he looked at the front page, he said, "Gee, whiz!" when he turned to the second page it was "Holy Moses!" while on the third page he roared, "God Almighty!"[7]

Of the new plums, the Chalco was destined to be extensively planted, though it never became an important market variety, while the Apple did well in South Africa. The Pearl, a seedling of the French prune, pollen parent unknown, turned out to be a plum of the best quality. "Its rich, golden color, large size, fine form, melting flesh and sweet, luscious flavor, place it among the best dessert plums," says Hedrick. "In the mind of the writer and those who have assisted in describing the varieties for the 'Plums of New York,' it is unsurpassed in quality by any other plum." It was unsuccessful as a prune because it proved difficult to dry in the open.

As the century drew to a close, Burbank, at fifty, found himself firmly established in the public eye as "the wizard of horticulture."

NINE

Fruits and Penalties of Fame

By 1900 Burbank's plums were grown all over the world. His flowers were listed in virtually every seed catalog that appeared. The Burbank potato had become one of the leading varieties in the United States, especially on the West Coast. "Newspaper and magazine editors, special feature writers, garden club lecturers discovered this man who, to them, was doing something new," Jones observes. "Unusual interest in the breeding of new plants and animals had been awakened in scientific circles by the rediscovery of Mendel's laws of inheritance. Biologists in Europe and America saw that Burbank was doing some remarkable things of real scientific interest."[1] At the same time, fame had its disadvantages. In his early years he had had time to test his introductions carefully before putting them on the market. Now, with increasing claims on his time that had nothing to do with his work, he gave them out faster and faster.

One of his best-known and most lasting accomplishments was

the creation of a new variety of daisy. "While there may be room for skepticism regarding his claims about certain productions," says Howard, "there should be no honest doubt about the Shasta daisy. Though the details of the ancestry are incapable—at this late day—of scientific proof, the fact that he did produce the Shasta daisy by breeding, essentially as claimed, is attested by Professors E. J. Wickson of the University of California and Hugo De Vries of the University of Amsterdam. Both these writers viewed the evidence on the ground."

It has been suggested that he simply improved a perennial wild ox-eye daisy, *Chrysanthemum leucanthemum,* native to the Old World but found by him in the vicinity of Mount Shasta in Northern California, or a garden form of the wild *Chrysanthemum maximum* of Southeastern Europe. It seems most probable that starting with a breeding stock of wild daisies, probably from New England, he introduced pollen from two European species, carefully selected the resulting plants, and finally crossed his hybrids with the Japanese species, *Chrysanthemum nipponicum,* to achieve the pure white flower he was aiming at. This work was completed by 1901, when it was announced in a four-page circular as "the latest floral wonder." It was a happy choice of name, and the quadruple hybrid was hardy and adaptable. "As a type of daisy," Howard says, "The Shasta promises to survive indefinitely. Improvements on the original and its siblings, although given distinctive variety names, will doubtless always be referred to as Shasta daisies."[2] Burbank later distributed new selections under the names of Alaska, California and Westralia Shastas. Shasta became the name of a new type of daisy rather than of a single variety. A hardy perennial, it does well in a variety of climates, is easy to grow and makes a good cut flower. It has retained its popularity to the present day. As with many of Burbank's introductions, the new daisy was being sold (he never disposed of it outright) before it was formally announced: a memorandum note of March 1900 records a sale of Shasta daisy hybrids for several hundred dollars.

He was working hard—too hard. On August 20, 1901, he informed Professor E. J. Wickson that "Having overstrained myself both mentally and physically for some months I am now prostrated from this overwork, and am obliged to be at the Sanatarium at Altruria, Sonoma County, most of the time perhaps for a week or two, probably not longer. I notify you so that if you desire, you can come to the Sanitarium if you wish to see me, just a little ways out of Santa Rosa, getting off at Fulton, where there is a stage . . . I can talk with you all you want at any time, as I am not allowed to do much else."[3]

If there is a distinctly wistful note to this letter, he must have been considerably cheered when, in the September 1901 edition of *World's Work,* the new monthly magazine established by Walter Hines Page and published by Doubleday, which billed itself as "a history of our time," he received what was probably his earliest solid endorsement by a prominent scientist (if we except Wickson's encomia in the *Pacific Rural Press,* as reproduced in Burbank's own catalogs.) The *World's Work* piece was entitled "A Maker of New Fruits and Flowers," and was by none other than the great American botanist and horticulturist, Liberty Hyde Bailey (1858–1954), who had visited him not long before. From such a source, it was bound to carry a good deal of weight.

Dean of the New York Agriculture College at Cornell University, and an internationally famous botanist,* Bailey was also widely known for the books on practical horticulture and agriculture which he wrote and edited. His assessment, which was both fair and unexaggerated, must have come as balm to Burbank's soul. "Luther Burbank is a breeder of plants by profession," he wrote, "and in this business he stands almost alone in this country . . ." He drew attention to the harm done Burbank's reputation by calling him "the wizard of horticulture," inasmuch as,

This sobriquet has prejudiced many good people against his

---

*According to one account, it was Bailey who, in copying a reference to Mendel's paper in a German bibliography of the literature of plant hybridization, originally led De Vries to the rediscovery. He had not actually seen Mendel's report himself.

work. Luther Burbank is not a wizard. He is an honest, straight-forward, careful, inquisitive, persistent man. He believes that causes produce results. His new plants are the results of down-right, earnest, long-continued effort. He earns them. He has no other magic than that of patient inquiry, abiding enthusiasm, an unprejudiced mind, and a remarkably acute judgment of the merits and capabilities of plants.

There follows a simple, straightforward account of Burbank's working procedures. There are two aspects of plant breeding, Bailey explains, inducing variations and selecting and improving the best of them. Crossing is simply one of the most fruitful means of making plants vary or "break," and for this reason Burbank crosses his plants in a wholesale fashion.

From an entire tree he will pick such proportion of flowers as would be likely to fall from natural causes. The remainder, num-bering hundreds, he will cross. Before the flower opens he cuts off the petals. Thus the bees are not attracted, and they have no foothold. Then he applies the pollen with a free hand. This pol-len is usually collected the day before from flowers that are picked and dried. All the seeds resulting from the cross are sown. Of a thousand seedlings, a dozen may be promising. These are saved, and perhaps they are crossed with some other plant. Again the seeds are sown; and thus the process continues until a desirable form is secured, or until it seems to be futile to carry the experiment farther. The judgment as to what will like-ly be good and what bad is the very core of plant-breeding. In this judgment Burbank excels. Not to many men is given this gift of prophecy. Burbank calls it intuition. He cannot explain it any more than another man can explain why he is a good judge of character in human beings. Long experience and close observa-tion have directed and crystalized this faculty of his, until it is probably as unerring as such faculties can be.

Burbank loves all plants. He has worked with fruits, vegeta-bles, flowers, grains. A strange plant in the fields at once attracts his attention and he tries to cultivate it, even though he may not know its name. His flowers and other quick-maturing things are usually grown in long, scrupulously tilled rows. Fruit trees have so long a period from seed to fruit that cions are taken from them when one or two years old, and these are grafted into the tops of bearing trees. Thereby he secures fruit sooner. In one tree there may be scores of kinds of fruit in bearing. Of most fruits he expects the graft to bear in two or three years from the seed. At the same time he may allow the original seedling to remain, thus securing two sets of the same plant with which to work. The fruit trees are planted very close in rows, and as soon as any plant proves to be worthless it is removed, and another may be planted or grafted in its place. The rows soon come to be collections of the most unrelated curiosities.

Bailey had clearly fallen under the spell of Burbank's personal charm. "You feel his kindly and gentle spirit," he says, "and before you know it you love him." But he was also a hardheaded observer, not to be fooled where matters of fact were concerned. He is remarkably uncritical of Burbank's failure to keep proper records and maintain precautions against self-pollination. He seems almost to exonerate it entirely:

Mr. Burbank no longer makes any serious effort to keep a written record of his crosses. He remembers the parentage. In many cases he applies the pollen of two or more kinds of plants to one flower. He does not know which pollen will "take." Neither does he always remove the stamens from the crossed flowers, as we are always advised to do in order that the plant may not be self-pollinated. In practice he finds that this precaution is usually unnecessary, for the pistil is likely to refuse pollen from the same flower. When the seedlings come up, he can tell what the cross was; or if he cannot, it matters little, for he is not making his experiments primarily for the purpose of accumulating scientific records but in order to obtain definite results in new varieties. Yet, so careful and acute are his judgements that one places great confidence in his conclusions as to parentage; and many times he makes crosses with every scientific precaution. I must confess I was skeptical as to the existence of the "plum-cot," or the cross between the plum and apricot; but now that I have seen many of the trees in bearing I am fully convinced that he has produced plum-apricot hybrids. The marks of plums and apricots are too apparent in the fruits and trees to be doubted.

Mr. Burbank gets unusual hybrids because he crosses great numbers of flowers and uses much pollen. He is skillful in the technique. He also dares. He has no traditional limitations. He knows no cross that he may not attempt. He has not studied the books. He has not been taught. Therefore he is free. The professor of horticulture would consider it beyond all bounds of academic and botanical propriety to try to cross an apple on a blackberry; but Luther Burbank would make the attempt as naturally as he would dig a new lily from the fields.

The visitor also cast an interested eye over Burbank's bookshelf. He found it but sparsely stocked. Aside from Darwin, he notes, Burbank's chief guides in technical botany were Gray's *Lessons* and *Field, Forest and Garden Botany.* He observes that

> some philanthropist could render a good service to mankind if he would endow this experimental garden and allow its proprietor to devote his whole energy to research. The best fruit-growers of California prize Burbank's work and are confident that his varieties will win. In visiting his place, one feels regret that scientific record is not being made of these rich experimental results. Mr. Burbank shares in this feeling, and he would welcome any careful and sympathetic student who should essay to make a permanent record of the work as a contribution to scientific knowledge. His place is an experiment station of the best type. His work makes for progress.

There was no great theoretical gulf between the two men. A botanist of the old school, Bailey saw Burbank's practical goals and seems on the whole to favor them against "academic and botanical propriety." He was a bit of a maverick himself. At that time, moreover, his views on the mechanism of speciation were not far removed from Burbank's, which were by no means so quaintly anachronistic then as it might seem from the standpoint of the present day. "Professor Bailey's philosophy,"

Professor Edwin G. Conklin observed in 1896, "was neither strictly Lamarckian nor Darwinian, although in general it leaned to the former; it was rather *sui generis* and might be called Baileyan. He maintained that variability is the original law of organisms, that like no more produces like than unlike, but that mutability is a fundamental and normal law, while heredity or permanency is an acquired character. The organism is shaped by its environment, and nature eliminates the non-variable and favors the survival of the unlike."[4] The difference between the two men was that whereas Bailey was prepared to amend his views in accordance with the new knowledge which flowed from the rediscovery of Mendel, Burbank remained stubbornly true to his original opinions. The concessions to Mendelism that appear in some of the later writings attributed to him were probably the work of his editors. The fact was that he did not really trouble to find out what the fuss was about before dismissing it.

Professor Edward J. Wickson, head of the Department of Horticulture at the University of California, and for many years Dean of the College of Agriculture and Director of the Agricultural Experiment Station at Berkeley, was also the editor of the *Pacific Rural Press,* probably the most influential of all the horticultural journals on the West Coast. Simultaneously educator and journalist, Wickson, a portly man with a handlebar moustache, was for decades one of California agriculture's most effective publicists. In 1901 he was collecting material for a series of articles which would serve to make Burbank more famous than ever.

Among those he approached was Judge Samuel F. Lieb, a prominent San Jose attorney (he was a member of the original board of trustees of Stanford University and an intimate friend of the Leland Stanfords), who had been a Burbankian for five or six years at the time—after having initially been inspired to visit the wizard by an article in the *Pacific Rural Press.* From this visit, Lieb informed Wickson in a letter dated October 11, 1901, "a friendship sprang up between us which makes us like brothers." He knew Burbank as well, he believed, as any man alive, and

> I have never known a nature more full of absolute sweetness. He is absolutely honorable in every way and is honest to a fault. He lives what is termed in the parlance of the day a strenuous life, far too much so for his physical endurance. He is an intense man, a man who carefully plans for results and then works for their fulfillment with a patience that exceeds that of Job himself. It may be a question of years to arrive at a single result. Necessarily before arriving at success in seeking to accomplish a given result, he must meet with many failures, but nothing seems to daunt him until success finally crowns his efforts.

Lieb goes on to describe some of the things Burbank was attempting at the time. Although the experiments he speaks of never amounted to anything, they give a further insight into the immense range of Burbank's endeavors, extending over the whole spectrum of cultivated plants, far beyond the scope of an ordinary North American nurseryman.

> Last summer I noticed a patch of parsnips at his experiment grounds. I was astonished that he should be devoting his attention to a thing of that kind, and asked him what it meant. He told me that he was trying to evolve a new plant for sugar. The sugar beets have developed so many diseases and so many objections have been found to them that he is trying to get something better. These diseases and objections are all obviated in the parsnip, if it can be gotten full enough of sugar to answer the purpose. He has already improved the variety in that direction so much that it is just on the verge of being successful. I have not the slightest doubt that he soon will have it so that by analysis it will be found to contain as much sugar as the beet, and doubtless then it will be exclusively used instead of the sugar beet.

This attempt at developing a sugar parsnip obviously came to naught. Burbank announced only one variety of parsnip, and that was in 1919. (A selected strain of Hollow Crown, it was called Imperial Hollow Crown.) But it bespoke the far-reaching imagination of the breeder. What is also apparent from Lieb's account is the extent to which the public already looked on Burbank as a miracle worker who could turn out new varieties to order. He speaks of requests for a new cotton, a new sugarcane, a new, improved coffee. Burbank could not undertake these projects, but Lieb is in no doubt that he could do it if he had the time. His enthusiasm for his hero knows no limits.

> What he will succeed in doing before he dies the Lord only knows. I do not. I only hope the good Lord will preserve him to us for the good of mankind as long as is possible, and "May God bless him" is my constant prayer . . . I can but say that a genius like this is only found once in a century, and the general community, who alone is to reap the benefit should see that nothing of that genius is lost. In my judgement the United States should take such a man and put him to work with every appliance and facility which can be afforded him, to make new productions and better old ones, all for the common good of its citizens. It should say to him, "We have employed you for your genius. Here is all the land you need for your experiments, all the water you need for its irrigation, all the laborers you need to carry on the work, all the foremen you need to carry out the details. What we want you to do is to give us the benefit of your genius to the fullest possible extent.[5]

This uncompromising faith is all the more extraordinary when it is observed that Lieb was himself a fruit grower and far from technically ignorant of horticulture. Burbank, Howard remarks, had given him a "sign" by successfully prejudging two sets of seedling fruit trees, and he was henceforth a true believer. "Except ye see signs and wonders, ye will not believe," says St. John. Evidently Burbank was quite capable of providing them for his chosen disciples.

The first of Wickson's four articles on "Luther Burbank, The

Man, His Methods and Achievement" appeared in *Sunset* magazine in December 1901. The remaining three appeared the following year in the February, April and June 1902 issues! They were all subsequently issued in book form by the Southern Pacific Company, which was then publisher of the magazine, with a foreword by *Sunset* editor Charles Sedgwick Aiken, comparing Burbank to the "soldier hero, who at the outbreak of the Spanish war, carried this Nation's message to Garcia." Wickson himself waxed intemperate in the extreme, in language that is the more astonishing coming from a figure of his academic respectability:

> For such a gifted seer neither weird altar fires, nor incense cloud, nor ecstatic state could add to insight. He could hear the "still small voice" without preparatory earthquake or whirlwind. Like David of old he could do his work with smooth pebbles from the brook; and he cast aside the elaborate armament of his scientific brethren lest it should impede his movements.[6]

There is more than one crack at the scientific establishment. "He has worked through a country not yet officially surveyed, above the pathway of the contemporaneous scientists," Wickson asserted, "and it is not wonderful, then, that they should fail to recognize him for a time." Conservatism implied that Burbank was making a travesty of science and playing to the gallery. He had patiently borne "the burdens of distrust and misapprehension which fall usually to the lot of those who extend the frontiers of human knowledge." Future generations, however, would recognize him as "a lone star glowing in the horticultural horizon."

In the long run this sort of thing could do Burbank no good, but in the short term it was amazingly effective. Botanists who had the fortitude to say that many of the things Burbank claimed were impossible, Jones observes

were immediately discredited as being professionally jealous. No one has ever said that American biologists were jealous of Mendel, a Catholic monk whose name is heard more often in scientific circles than Burbank's; they were not considered to be jealous of Darwin who, like Burbank, was not a professional biologist; they were not jealous of Galton who founded the eugenics movement; but whenever any professional botanist or agricultural investigator stated anything in disparagement of Burbank he was immediately put down as envious of his reputation.[7]

True, the botanists were not necessarily right. The existence of amphidiploids, which could conceivably account for some of Burbank's more extraordinary hybrids—as Jones himself was the first to recognize—had not yet been established or even suggested. But in the face of the threat to their professional integrity which Burbankism presented, the scientists were bound to hang together. Almost inevitably the baby got thrown out with the bathwater.

Initially, however, reactions were surprisingly good. "Dear Prof. Wickson," wrote G. B. Brackett, pomologist of the U.S.D.A. Bureau of Plant Industry, on December 27, 1901, "I am just in receipt of a copy of the magazine 'Sunset,' containing an article on 'Luther Burbank, The Man, His Methods and His Achievements,' for which I sincerely thank you. It delighted my soul to see that photo of yourself and Mr. Burbank in characteristic conversation . . . No pen can over rate the great work of Mr. Burbank, and I am glad you have given to the world so just an estimate of the worth of the man we both so greatly admire. He is easily the foremost horticultural experimenter. I prize this edition of Sunset greatly. A Burbank edition for the Christmastide was a happy idea." In May 1902 Arthur A. Taylor, proprietor of the Santa Cruz *Surf*, wrote, "Mr. Burbank is a miracle worker and is as yet as much without honor in his own country as was the Man of Galilee." Here were obviously two more disciples. Taylor's letter suggests, moreover, that Burbank was far from alone in the "Messiahship idea."

A note of almost incoherent dissent was sounded by one Thomas Lyon. "I have just read with interest but with great disgust your second paper on Mr. Burbank's work with plants," he began.

> You spoiled your work by constantly using the "jargon of the schools" in place of words that could be understood by your least educated reader . . . As you well know Burbank has evolved no new method. He is merely working well and honestly in a very old and well trodden road and hence there is no use in trying to cover his work with a halo that does not belong to it. He has done good work and has achieved good results and deserves credit therefore but he is but one in the great list and deserves no more than his work is really worth. I am sure if he comprehends the meaning of your words his modesty will be much mortified . . . Burbank was not working for fame but for dollars . . .

Wickson forwarded this letter to the sage at Santa Rosa, and far from being modestly mortified, the latter responded with a sneer at the "crisis of wind-colic which affects our 'Grape-nut-brained' friend and adviser who calls himself a Lyon."

> Judging from the muddy tracks of this specimen, I should confidently place the thing under the head of Cimex Lectularius, or Bedbug in language less polite, rather than Lyon as alleged. This specimen, however, appears to be a degenerate microcephalus form of the parasite. Did the thing get the idea you were writing for a Sunday School Journal, or a Kindergarten Paper? Well, these things do irritate in spots, but are not alarming. These little fellows don't come out in the daylight much.[8]

He was quite prepared to carry the war into the camp of his critics. Speaking at the Floral Congress in San Francisco in 1901, he observed contemptuously that "The chief work of the botanist of yesterday was the study and classification of dried, shriveled plant mummies, whose souls had fled, rather than the living, plastic forms. They thought their classified species were more fixed and unchangeable than anything in heaven or earth that we can now imagine. We have learned that they are as plastic in our hands as clay in the hands of the potter or colors on the artist's canvas, and can readily be molded into more beautiful forms and colors than any painter or sculptor can ever hope to bring forth."[9] There was sense in what he said, perhaps, but such vainglorious phrasing could scarcely aid the cause.

Burbank's friends, Wickson and Lieb in particular, were constantly urging him to perpetuate his skills and knowledge, either by writing or by teaching. But he had little time or inclination for either. Nonetheless, in 1902 he did send a short paper entitled "The Fundamental Principles of Plant Breeding" to be read at the first International Conference on Plant Breeding and Hybridization held that year in New York, and this was afterward published in pamphlet form. That same year there was an attempt on Wickson's part to recruit him for the University of California. It was politely but firmly declined. "In the first place I am perfectly sure that I can do much better work for the *world* right in the harness where I now am," Burbank wrote him.

> As to remuneration, that would make no difference with me, for I am making absolutely nothing now, just keeping even, anyway. It is all a work of love, or duty to humanity. But if I should look to the financial part, I have received propositions from another University* with ten times the remuneration proposed for the first year, and a promise of much more afterwards, and numerous other very valuable considerations outside of salary; but these facts make no possible difference with my decision either way.
>
> I appreciate your very great kindness in this matter, and years ago when I was younger and not so thoroughly engaged in matters which cannot well be given up I might have thought it best to have accepted such an offer, but at this critical time when re-

---

*Undoubtedly Stanford, where in the persons of President David Starr Jordan and Professor Vernon Kellogg he had two more ardent supporters.

sults of decades of work are ripening, and that too with comparatively little present effort, I am thoroughly satisfied that I
am right in this matter, and yet I am sorry if my decision shall be
antagonistic in any way to the wishes of my kind friend Wickson.

That the proposal was official, and not simply Wickson's own
idea, is confirmed by a note to the latter from President Benjamin Ide Wheeler, dated September 24, 1902. "I share your
regret," Wheeler remarks.

Burbank was more fortunate in his friends than perhaps he
realized. In 1902 the Carnegie Institution of Washington was
set up by millionaire Andrew Carnegie (1835–1919) with a
charter "to encourage in the broadest and most liberal manner
investigation, research, and discovery, and the application of
knowledge to the improvement of mankind." To this end
Carnegie endowed it to the extent of some $22 million. Some-
one, probably Wickson acting through the University of California, soon put up Burbank's name—it appears in the files of
the Institution as early as March 1902—and in November 1903
a formal application for a grant in aid of his work was submitted by David G. Fairchild for the Evolution Committee of the
Botanical Society of Washington. In a letter dated December 9,
1903, President Wheeler notified Wickson of its failure, advis-
ing him of a "communication from the Carnegie Institution
which I know you will read with regret, as I did." Citing the
"many applications received to date for aid in support of or fur-
therance of various scientific projects," Charles D. Wolcott,
secretary of the institution's executive committee, wrote, "It has
been found impossible to comply with these requests in most
cases. I regret to advise you that in the case of L. Burbank it has
not been found possible to make the grant requested." L. Burbank would get his grant eventually, but he would have to wait
until bigger guns could be dragged up on his behalf.

Despite his pious protests about "just keeping even," and the
failure of the first grant application, he was making money.

These were years of steady sales. In 1902 John Lewis Childs paid $1100 for a "Phenomenal Hybrid Berry" and plants and seeds of the "Season's Crimson Winter Rhubarb." In November 1903 the Oregon Nursery Co. bought the "Miracle" plum for $2500. (This was the so-called "stoneless" plum. The buyers advertised widely, and it was extensively planted at the time.) There were, of course, numerous smaller sales, the combined value of which at least equaled the big ones. Toward the end of 1903, or early in 1904, Burbank was sufficiently well off to buy his first car: an Oldsmobile. The tokens of recognition were also piling up. At the opening meeting of the American Breeders' Association at St. Louis in 1903, he was unanimously elected to honorary membership. In the early proceedings of the association a number of articles by him appear, under the titles of "Heredity," "Right Attitude Toward Life," "Another Mode of Species Forming" and "Evolution and Variation with the Fundamental Significance of Sex."

The Carnegie grant, though denied, was obviously still in the offing, for it is mentioned without comment in a memorandum note of January 1904, apparently typed by Burbank himself. Wickson was probably busy pulling strings and may have given him some encouragement around this time. The president and chairman of the executive committee of the board of trustees of the Carnegie Institution was, after all, none other than Daniel Coit Gilman, Benjamin Ide Wheeler's predecessor as president of the University of California. An influential member and later chairman of the institution's finance committee was D. O. Mills, a prominent San Francisco banker and merchant. Another member of the finance committee, Lyman J. Gage, ex-Secretary of the Treasury, could be regarded as distinctly friendly, as could Judge William W. Morrow, of the Board of Trustees, who had lived in Santa Rosa and was married there. It was a common rumor at the time, Howard says, that California would have its share of the Carnegie money and that the "California members" of the trustees were bringing pressure to bear on the others to this end. With the support of Wheeler and other Burbank enthusiasts like David Starr Jordan of Stanford, Wickson must certainly have believed that he would ultimately be able to swing the board in Burbank's favor.

In July 1904, with the appearance of an article entitled "A Maker of New Plants and Fruits" in *Scribner's* magazine, a new champion joined the lists. W. S. Harwood was a professional journalist and popular science writer. Prolific and given to extravagant hyperbole, he would do more than anyone else to spread the Burbank myth and at the same time to ruin Burbank's reputation among serious horticulturists and workers in the new science of genetics.

There were always those who did not fall under the spell of Burbank's charisma. In 1904 he had a visit from his South African customer, H. E. V. Pickstone, who spent the day with him. "I was disappointed with his personality," Pickstone later noted. "I found him too much of an egoist . . . I do not think he can be considered a great man from any angle, but he was not a fakir; I believe him to have been quite honest but perhaps unbalanced." For all that, he remained a customer to the end of Burbank's life, though concluding in somewhat jaundiced fashion as of 1938, that "the only variety of his that has proved of commercial value is the Santa Rosa plum."[10] This was hardly true even in South Africa, so it may perhaps be supposed that Pickstone was venting some undisclosed grievance. These turn-of-the-century nurserymen took offence easily.

In January 1905 Wickson was again on the lookout for biographical material—now apparently with the aim of telling the story of Burbank's life in "simple, bold and stirring English." Burbank having been just about to leave on business when Wickson's letter broaching the subject arrived, he delegated his reply to his faithful secretary, May Benedict Maye, who had worked for him for the past five years or so. Miss Maye was evidently a woman of character and sense and a fervent Burbankian besides.[11] Her reply is instructive both of Burbank's own view of what he had accomplished and of the devotion he inspired in the people around him.

Noting defensively that the "reporters have camped on his trail for some time lately and it seems from what you say that they are not yet by any means satisfied. They have made this their Mecca from before breakfast until as late as midnight on some occasions, and life has been one round of filling their demands for 'Copy,' 'Stuff,' Material and Photographs," she lists the six most important things Burbank has done "from my standpoint and to the best of my ability with some suggestions that I have had from the Boss himself." These are:

1. *Popularizing horticulture* and placing NEW IDEALS of horticulture before the people, giving it a CLASSICAL position before the world. (Perhaps he, more than any other one man has done away with the title "Hayseed" in connection with tilling the soil. People now realize that the scientific farmer or plant creator has a work as great as any other of the artists and can change the destinies of the human race, and create *Masterpieces* that go on *re-creating themselves,* thus *solving perpetual motion* in its truest phase, and making the marble and lifeless statue seem tame in comparison.)

2. The bearings of Mr. Burbank's discoveries in plant life in their relation to the improvement of the human race, and the future biological application that will be made of them in the uplifting of humanity when the laws governing heredity in plant life shall be used in human improvement.

3. Bringing scientific and practical horticulture on one common ground. In fact proving by his discoveries that the best scientific work in the truest sense of the word is also *Practical.*

4. Discovery of *New Tendencies of heredity* and the laws *governing plant improvement,* so that others may avoid mistakes and continue the work with the advantage of his experience.

5. Destroying the preconceived notions of many scientists of the past and *building new ones in their place* so that we may turn from the *old ideas* of the past to the *facts* of today, Perseverance giving place to *pliability,* etc. etc.

6. Last, the new creations in fruits and flowers, grains, nuts, etc., that are a heritage, not only to this, but to all future generations as long as man shall cultivate the soil . . . his true greatness is not measured by the actual fruits and flowers Mr. Bur-

bank has produced. Others have made new roses, new carnations, new watermelons, new fruits—here and there all over the world plant breeders have been at work; our gardens and orchards testify to the facts. But Mr. Burbank has done more than merely by infinite patience produced these new fruits, etc. He has *unearthed* the *laws* that have governed their production and made bare truths that will *live and benefit humanity* even *if they should ever cease to eat plums or care for potatoes.*

"P.S.," she adds, "If this isn't a 'full dose' come up and we can give you some more, Boss will be home after Monday."

This exposition is interesting from several points of view. It lays stress on Burbank's belief in the implications of his work in human eugenics (No. 2), and on the idea that he has unearthed the laws of plant improvement (No. 4). What these were it is hard to tell, since for all the torrents of words attributed to him, he never succeeded in clearly formulating them. It is true that there were implications in his results which, had they been trusted or heeded by contemporary scientists, might just conceivably have led to an earlier understanding of polyploidy. But even this would have depended on comparable progress in cytology.

New laws aside, however, Miss Maye is not far wrong in according first place to his popularization of horticulture and last to his new creations. This in the end must be the verdict of history also. It is to the credit of Burbank's sharp wits (we may be reasonably sure that his secretary was only quoting him) that he perceived this, when his contemporaries—including even the experts like Wickson and De Vries—failed to do so. Long after his death, agricultural scientists and horticulturists would reckon this his chief merit. As Professor Wendell Paddock, an Ohio horticulturist, wrote:

Of course his work has been of great value: it interested people in general in plant life: it stimulated college and experiment workers to unusual activity. They could not afford to have this unlettered man forge so far ahead of them. You and I both re-

member the time when there was practically no plant breeding
going on at the Stations . . . Burbank came later and for a time
was practically alone in the field.

Dr. O. M. Morris, of Washington, who had the impression
that Burbank was "an egotistical maniac," nonetheless conceded that, "he has been a great spur or prod to a lot of technical
workers who are in federal and state institutions . . ." Professor E. H. Hoppert of Nebraska felt "Burbank was highly overrated but . . . the publicity that he received was of some value
in arousing interest in the possibilities of developing new varieties of fruits, perennials, etc." Joseph A. Chucka, a Maine
agronomist, said, "It is my impression that Burbank contributed little if anything to the science of plant breeding. In my
judgement he contributed a great deal to the world in arousing
interest in the possibilities of plant breeding and in actually giving the world a rather large number of useful and ornamental
plants."[12]

The year 1905 saw the introduction of the "Giant Maritima"
plum, a new version of the beach plum of a few years before. In
May of that year J. L. Childs bought the Improved Giant Crimson Rhubarb, a selection from Crimson Winter that was nicknamed the "Mortgage Lifter" by contented growers, for $1500.
In July, Burbank concluded an agreement with George C.
Roeding, president of the Fancher Creek Nurseries in Fresno,
California, "for sale of certain new varieties," and the same
month there was a major deal with John M. Rutland, an Australian nurseryman, who for $1600 bought the "Santa Rosa"
plum for distribution in Australia, and rights in the Southern
Hemisphere, including South America, to the Rutland (previously "Blood") plumcot. The Rutland had been one of a display
of plum-apricot hybrids exhibited at the Pan-American Exposition at Buffalo, New York, in 1901, for which Burbank had received a special gold medal. Burbank believed it to be a cross
between an apricot and the Satsuma plum, but, says Howard, it

is "now definitely regarded as a large hybrid plum, with perfect flowers, but with flesh of poor quality." De Vries, who saw and tasted the results, was convinced, however, that Burbank had successfully made this cross, and other horticulturists subsequently claimed to have duplicated it.

More important than these sales, however, was the financial support of the Carnegie Institution, which was at long last confirmed. In a letter dated December 29, 1904, President R. S. Woodward, who had succeeded Gilman, informed him that a grant of $10,000, "to be available during the ensuing year," had been allotted "for the purpose of furthering your experimental investigations in the evolution of plants." An equal grant, Woodward noted, was contemplated "annually for a series of years, *or for so long a time as may be mutually agreeable*" [italics in original]. A further grant of $2000 was made to Dr. O. F. Cook, of Washington, D.C., "for expenses and salary while engaged in association with Mr. Burbank in investigating results, conduct of experiments, and preparation of a report," the minutes of the institution's board of trustees reveal. But this fell through. Among other reasons, it appeared

> on consultation with a number of leading biologists . . . that Dr. Cook lacked their confidence to a degree which promised to make a report from him deficient in the weight essential to such a document appearing under the auspices of the Institution.

In July 1905, Woodward paid Burbank a visit to study the problem, and concluded that "the best way to carry on the work would be to have it supervised by a committee consisting of the heads of our Departments of Biological Research along with the President." Cook accordingly withdrew, and the committee was set up. Meanwhile, in January 1905, the initial payment of $10,000 had been made. With reference to "Grant No. 221," President Woodward observed in the Institution's Year Book that,

The horticultural experiments and the remarkable achievements of Mr. Luther Burbank are well known in a popular way, though it must be said that the more important aspects of his work remain yet to be interpreted to men of science as well as to the interested public. Owing to the impractability, during the past year, of securing the services of a trained biologist, the preparation of a scientific account of the ways, means, methods, and results of Mr. Burbank's work has been delayed. He has continued his experiments, however, as related in his report, and it is hoped that the necessary arrangements for securing the scientific account of his work contemplated by the Board of Trustees will not be long deferred. Little short of five years will be required for this work if it is done thoroughly well.[13]

That year was also one of widespread publicity for Burbank, some of it from highly accredited sources. In January an article by David Starr Jordan, entitled "Some Experiments of Luther Burbank," appeared in *Popular Science Monthly,* and in August the same magazine published "A Visit to Luther Burbank," by Hugo de Vries. The indefatigable Harwood published two articles, "A Wonder Worker of Science" and "Burbank's Creed," in *Century* magazine, and a third, "Luther Burbank's Achievements," in *Country Calendar.* Of these "Burbank's Creed" is of particular interest, inasmuch as it purports to give an account of his religious beliefs. "My theory of the laws and underlying principles of plant creation is, in many respects, diametrically opposed to the theories of the materialists," Harwood has him say.

I am a sincere believer in a higher power than that of man. All my investigations have led me away from the idea of a dead, material universe, tossed about by various forces, to that of a universe which is all-force, life, soul, thought, or whatever name we may choose to call it. Every atom, molecule, plant, animal, or planet is only an aggregation of organized unit forces held in place by stronger forces, thus holding them for a time latent, though teeming with inconceivable power. All life on our planet is, so to speak, just on the fringe of this infinite ocean of force. The universe is not half dead, but all alive.

Finally, in September 1905, Harwood published the first full-blown book about Burbank. This work, *New Creations in Plant Life; an Authoritative Account of the Life and Work of Luther Burbank,* was full of typical hyperbole, so much so that Howard afterward thought it should have been entitled "New Creations in Plant Life—A Fairy Story," while prior to its acceptance by Macmillan, David Fairchild, who was apparently called in as a consultant, managed to persuade the Century Company that they ought not to publish it. "In it were claims that Burbank should have forbidden publication of or repudiated," said Fairchild, who was well disposed toward Burbank and in his own autobiography described him as "an altogether lovable person, whose intuitive sense with regard to plants was most extraordinary." He did feel, however, that Burbank allowed the people around him grossly to exaggerate the claims of his new creations, which frequently turned out less well when grown away from the climatic conditions they had been produced in. (He had, moreover, been "surprised and nonplussed" to discover that Burbank believed in clairvoyance.) Fairchild makes the particularly telling observation that

> One might describe Burbank as like Tolstoi, in that, when one was with him, one felt the strange force of his simplicity and his profound confidence in his own abilities. But, on leaving him, the impression faded, and one began to wonder wherein lay his power, for his results did not quite seem to justify his claims.[14]

No one else expresses it quite so succinctly, but many another observer seems to have been similarly affected.

TEN

Enter George Shull

The 1880s AND 1890s had been a period of intense interest in the agricultural potential and development of the state of California. These were the years that saw the beginnings of modern large-scale fruit production, preservation and cooperative fruit handling. Canners were beginning to learn what varieties would process best, and the pioneer apricot growers of Riverside had demonstrated the advantages of sulfuring before sun-drying. Some idea was being gained of the preferences of Eastern markets in dried and canned fruit.

In 1892 California passed a law against the introduction of fruit trees from other states, and the effect of the quarantine was inevitably to promote local nursery business. The threats of Eastern nurserymen to boycott California fruit in retaliation came to naught, and the courts maintained the quarantine law, with provisions being made in 1899 for greater powers for inspectors and quarantine officers. All this had the effect of creating an ever-greater demand for California trees, and nurseries multiplied rapidly.[1]

Burbank was far from alone in the field of plant breeding, and neither did he have any monopoly on go-ahead ideas. A. T. Hatch, who had come to California as a miner in 1857, began to cultivate almonds at Suisun in 1872, and around the end of the decade originated three important varieties—IXL, Ne Plus Ultra and Nonpareil—by selection. Francisco Franceschi, an Italian immigrant who settled in Santa Barbara and established a nursery around 1893, introduced avocado seedlings and did pioneer work with a variety of subtropical fruits, including the banana, the guava and the mango. Franceschi even tried to introduce coffee plants, which were listed in his nursery catalog in 1897. Others, like Anthony Chabot of Oakland, attempted to raise tea on a commercial basis. A. B. Chapman and George H. Smith brought the Valencia orange to California in 1876, and Washington Navel oranges, originating as a bud sport near Bahia, Brazil, were introduced through the efforts of William O. Saunders of the Department of Agriculture.[2]

George Christian Roeding, of the Fancher Creek Nursery at Fresno, who in 1906 assumed the marketing of such Burbank productions as the Santa Rosa plum, the Rutland plumcot and the Royal Walnut, made a personal crusade out of promoting Smyrna fig culture. Smyrna figs and the wild caprifig necessary for their pollination were imported from Turkey by Roeding's father, a German forty-niner who had stayed on to make his fortune in land development. Artificial caprification—pollination of female Smyrna fig flowers with pollen from caprifig blossoms—was accomplished with the aid of a goose quill, but the younger Roeding realized that if Smyrnas were to be grown on a commercial basis, it would be necessary to introduce the fig wasp, *Blastophaga grossorum*, which performed the act of fructification in the fig's native habitat. As a result of Roeding's efforts, and with the assistance of the U.S. Department of Agriculture, this was accomplished, and by 1899 the *Blastophaga* had been imported and was established in California.

This was a notable achievement for the new art of economic entomology, opening the way for large-scale Smyrna fig culture. By the 1930s, California would be producing more than twenty thousand tons of Smyrna figs annually.[3]

Other new lines of development found ardent enthusiasts and speculators. In the early nineties the so-called "Great Olive Rush" developed, with the spread of the notion that olives could be grown on land too poor and dry for other kinds of fruit. The Mission olive had been introduced by Junípero Serra and José Gálvez, who planted seeds brought from San Blas, Mexico, at Mission San Diego in 1769. In 1875 another variety, the *Manzanillo,* was brought from Spain, and ten years later the *Sevillano* and *Ascolano,* both mainly pickling varieties, were introduced. The number of olive trees in the state increased from less than fifteen thousand in 1875 to some two and a half million in 1897. Established nurserymen rushed to supply the demand for olive trees, while no less than six new nurseries devoted entirely to their reproduction sprang up, one of the smaller of which offered half a million trees for sale in 1892. Burbank did not neglect the olive. "The nine hundred thousand olive trees which I offer for sale this season are grown by a new process," he announces in a postcard sent out in 1888. This seems to have been purely a business proposition, and he does not seem to have given much thought to improving the tree. Growers found, however, that they could not compete economically with cheap European olive oil and other vegetable oils, and difficulties arose in pickling and shipping. Olives consigned to Eastern distributors in casks spoiled en route, and early canning efforts frequently resulted in botulism poisoning. By 1895 planting had virtually come to a halt, and the hopeful olive nurseries of a few years before were in the process of closing down again. (Production picked up again after 1900 with the introduction of modern canning methods, and today California is the only important olive-producing state in the United States, with an annual crop in excess of fifty thousand tons.)

The "Eucalyptus Craze" of 1906 was a similar phenomenon.

Plantings of eucalyptus, promoters claimed, would yield as much as $2000 per acre every six years, and needed neither good land nor water. Interest was whipped up to a frenzy. Land sharks set to work subdividing desert and dunes, and the demand for eucalyptus trees reached incredible proportions, despite the warnings of university and government experts. Eucalyptus peddlers and backyard nurserymen swarmed to take advantage of the boom. Frost and lack of water killed off many of the young trees, however, and eucalyptus fever went the way of so many other California sensations.

It was against this backdrop that Burbank saw fit to touch off a craze of his own. It had long occurred to him, he said, that every plant growing in the desert was either bitter, or poisonous, or spiny. He had been struck by the hardiness and adaptability of cacti as much as by their potential use as cattle fodder. In the seventeenth century Spanish herdsmen had learned to utilize cactus for feed by burning off the spines over a brush fire. The spines, which are dry and waxy, quickly burn off, while the fleshy, water-holding pads remain undamaged. Alternatively the chopped cactus could be allowed to stand in a mass, which softened up the spines. Later gasoline torches were used to burn the thorns off.

But singeing did not always remove all of the larger spines, and left the rudimentary spines imbedded in the slabs untouched. Cattle that had been fed cactus were often observed with blood dripping from their mouths, and their throats and tongues would tend to become inflamed. This was, therefore, a source of food and water which cattlemen fell back on only in time of need.

But what if a spineless forage cactus could be developed?

The idea appeared to open up a whole vista of possibilities for reclaiming the barren regions of the earth. In the arid regions of the United States, a vast land area, much of it given over to coyotes and jackrabbits, cacti of many species flourish. These are mainly spiny varieties, but Burbank knew perfectly well that there *were* varieties of cactus that were comparatively spineless. In fact, he remarks, in one of his catalogs, "one of the first pets which I had in earliest childhood was a thornless cactus, one of the beautiful Epiphyllums. The Phyllocactus and many of the Cereus family are also thornless, not a trace to be found on any part of the plants or fruit."

He therefore started to build up a collection of cacti, concentrating on the genus *Opuntia,* to which the prickly pear (*O. tuna*) and Indian fig (*O. ficus-indica*) belong. Specimens were obtained from all over Mexico, from Central and South America, from North and South Africa, Australia, Japan and the Hawaiian and South Sea Islands. (All cacti, with one possible exception, are natives of the New World, so that he was, in effect, reimporting species that had reached the latter countries after Columbus, in the hope that they might have sustained significant variation in their new habitats, or undergone mutation.) Eight partially thornless kinds from Sicily, Italy, France and North Africa were obtained for him by the plant explorer David Fairchild, while the U.S. Department of Agriculture supplied him with specimens from a large collection that had been brought together in its Washington greenhouses for a taxonomic study of the family. Frank F. Meyer, later of the Federal Office of Plant Introduction, sent him a spineless opuntia which he found growing in a garden in Mexico. In addition to all these, he had varieties, Burbank said, from Maine, Iowa, Missouri, Colorado, California, Arizona, New Mexico, the Dakotas, Texas and other states. It was a vast collection, one of the largest of his breeding projects ever. Over a period of eight to twelve years the Burbank principle of mass selection was applied—hybridizing, selecting and hybridizing again. The aim of the breeding was twofold: forage and fruit—that is, the prickly pear which formed a common item of diet in Mexico and Central America, as well as in Mediterranean countries. Many varieties combined both objectives, and some had beautiful flowers as well.

By this means some forms which were *almost* spineless and

also possessed the other qualities desired were eventually evolved. Burbank admitted that the cacti sent him by David Fairchild, among others, had been spineless "for all practical purposes." However, he insisted, "I have still to see any form of Opuntia that is of good size and suitable for forage and yet that is altogether free from spines and spicules, except the ones that have been developed on my experimental grounds, and their progeny; and no such variety has yet been reported, although the authorities of the Agricultural Department of Washington scoured the earth to find such a variety." Others, notably Dr. David Griffiths, Senior Horticulturist of the United States Bureau of Plant Industry, disagreed. "Spineless as applied to Opuntias is a relative term," said Griffiths. "I have never seen one entirely spineless and much less spiculeless." W. B. Alexander, of the Australian Institute of Science and Industry, asserted that "The 'spineless cactus' is merely a practically spineless form of the well-known Indian Fig, *Opuntia Ficus-indica* . . . Mr. J. H. Maiden states that specimens obtained from Mr. Burbank are in no way different from plants which have been in the Sydney Botanic Gardens for very many years." It would be fair to assume that Burbank *had* improved his opuntias, but not entirely succeeded in getting rid of their defensive armor. The character of spinelessness in cacti is variable, even when they are propagated vegetatively, and the ones he sent out or which were distributed by others were not necessarily identical with those he had raised himself.

The controversy as to just what he had or had not succeeded in doing with his opuntias was aggravated by the fact that when he commenced to advertise his product, it was in the usual extravagant nurseryman's manner. The Carnegie grant—intended at least in part to support this work—had been insufficient to finance his breeding and development program. He had sunk funds of his own into it. As a businessman he saw no reason why he should not recover his costs by sales. George Shull has a story highly revealing of his attitude in this respect:

Just inside his gate at his Santa Rosa experimental garden, he had planted a bed, some 15 feet square, with the sprawling, thorny cacti from the desert. In the midst of this forbidding-looking culture, he planted a single specimen of Opuntia Ficus-Indica of the spineless variety, in most striking contrast with the thorny cacti around it. Mr. Burbank's visitors, who often came in droves, would look over the fence at this striking demonstration and comment to one another [on] the amazing wizardry which "created" the smooth fat-slabbed cactus from the sprawly thorny ones. I was a bystander on one occasion when a group of representatives of the press stood inside the gate beside the cactus bed, accompanied by Mr. Burbank. The conversation among the members of the press was much the same as that of the *hoi polloi* on the outside. Mr. Burbank listened to their conversation in silence, but when one of the men asked him whether he had actually started with the thorny types to produce the spineless cactus, he quietly gave the monosyllabic answer "No", but vouchsafed no further explanation. This is only one of many examples of his ability to set up an exhibit which was misleading to the uncritical. Mr. Burbank's own explanation of this had some merit, as you will readily agree. He explained that he had given up a successful and fairly lucrative nursery business to devote his time to the creation of new and improved horticultural varieties. In order that his plant-breeding program might be self-sustaining it was necessary for him to secure all the free advertising he could. Consequently, he felt that it would be foolish for him to reply to any sort of fantastic statement about his work if it were couched in terms calculated to enhance his reputation as a successful producer of marvelous new things.

He took pleasure in rubbing a cactus slab against his cheek to show how harmless it was. But visitors were so frequent that he could hardly cut a fresh slab for every demonstration, and the same piece was used again and again, till it was polished smooth by repeated rubbings. The more observant among his visitors sometimes noticed that there were numerous thorns on other parts of the same plant. (He was prepared to suffer for his cactus project, and remarked that he had been pricked,so many times in the hands and face handling the slabs that he sometimes had to shave the spicules off with a razor or rub them down with sandpaper, so that as what was left of them worked into the skin, they would not cause more than a minor irritation.) These ploys should have fooled only the ignorant and the unwary, but the journalists who took up the spineless cactus story so enthusiastically seem to have had no trouble accepting Burbank's presentation at face value.

To the specialists of the Department of Agriculture it smacked of yet another phony promotion, analogous to the olive and eucalyptus booms of recent years. Experiment stations were swamped with inquiries about the value of spineless cactus. Their replies—based on the official conviction that cactus was at best an emergency source of feed to fall back on in bad years—were distinctly negative. They pointed out that cactus had spines for a reason: spineless cacti planted unprotected in the desert would be eaten by rodents before they got a start, and older plants would be killed by grazing animals eating them to the ground. Moreover, if they were to make the rapid growth Burbank advertised, they would have to be irrigated, and in that case alfalfa and other crops, which would give equal or greater tonnage of more nutritious dry fodder, which could easily be handled by machinery, were to be preferred. There was a great deal of acrimony on both sides, and the spineless cactus episode contributed substantially in the end to damaging Burbank's already precarious reputation with horticultural officialdom.

But in 1906 the cactus debacle was largely still in the future, and in January of that year Burbank's confidence in his "new creation" was strengthened when his Australian customer, John M. Rutland, purchased five varieties, designated by name as Santa Rosa, Sonoma, California, Chico and Fresno, for $3000,[4] as part of an order, including also six varieties of plum and his Montecito grape, totaling $5800. On the strength of this, it must have seemed likely that his cacti would prove even more profitable than the plums which had hitherto been his greatest success. So encouraged was he that he built himself a new two-story house, which he was afterward fond of remarking had been paid for "from the proceeds of a sale of spineless cactus to a dealer in Australia."

He was fortunate in that the contract for this substantial, fourteen-roomed dwelling (stipulating that work be begun within a hundred days and setting the cost of construction at $4485) was let only a few days before the great San Francisco earthquake of April 1906, which also did a great deal of damage in Santa Rosa. The earthquake actually served to enhance the myth of his miraculous powers. Much was made of the fact that Burbank's greenhouse had gone unscathed, though the house a few feet away sustained severe cracks and had its chimney knocked down, and that no damage had been done to his plants.

At the Carnegie Institution, the august President Woodward noted hopefully that "In one respect, doubtless, the earthquake was advantageous to him and his work, namely in preventing visitors from encroaching too freely on his time and attention."[5] The Carnegie people, having committed themselves, were eager to see their protege justify their faith.

In May 1906 two members of the institution's committee on Burbank's work, C. B. Davenport (Director of Experimental Evolution) and D. T. MacDougal (Director of Botanical Research), visited Santa Rosa, bringing with them George Harrison Shull, also of the institution's Department of Experimental Evolution. It was mutually agreed that Shull would be appointed to the task of preparing a scientific account of Burbank's work, and he remained behind for the month of June, the first of numerous visits to this end.

Shull was then thirty-two, a well-trained scientist with a doctorate from the University of Chicago, a quarter of a century Burbank's junior but a man who had already begun to make his mark. Since the previous year he had been at work at Cold

Spring Harbor, Long Island, where the Carnegie Institution's Station for Experimental Evolution was based, on the problem of hybrid corn. He had not begun his studies with a view to improving the corn plant, the geneticist Paul C. Mangelsdorf has pointed out. "His objective was to analyse the inheritance of quantitative characters and he chose corn as an appropriate experimental subject for this purpose. He inbred his lines to 'fix' their characteristics and he crossed lines which had been thus inbred to study the inheritance of kernel-row-number." From these experiments he drew important conclusions regarding the effects of inbreeding and crossbreeding, and discovered a new method of corn breeding based on the exploitation of the phenomenon he named "heterosis," otherwise known as hybrid vigor. His brilliantly simple idea was that otherwise worthless lines of inbred corn be developed and maintained so as to utilize the heterosis consequent on their hybridization. This combined with the "double-cross method" invented by Donald F. Jones of the Connecticut Agricultural Experiment Station, who successfully interpreted the phenomenon of hybrid vigor in terms of the chromosome theory of heredity and proposed the use of four inbred strains instead of two, in 1917, revolutionized corn production. Between them Shull and Jones accomplished one of the great feats of applied genetics, which Mangelsdorf terms

the most far-reaching development in applied biology of this quarter century. It has already affected more lives, I venture to guess, than any of the epoch-making discoveries in medical biology of the same period. Insulin and penicillin have saved thousands of lives in the past 25 years, but the new abundance of foodstuffs which hybrid corn has created has saved millions of lives in this period of the world's history.[6]

Shull was also intensely interested in the question of mutation and would study this phenomenon over a thirty-eight-year period, both in the evening primrose, which had drawn De

Vries' attention to it in the first place, and in the shepherd's purse, a plant which was found to mutate just as freely. In the light of his subsequent career, he must be considered one of the foremost American plant geneticists of the day. It is hard to imagine a man better qualified to observe Burbank's work, and in view of his own concerns he must have had a considerable personal interest in making a study of it.

He soon found, though, that there were difficulties here quite unlike those normally encountered by botanists. The study of the man himself, he rapidly came to realize, would be one of the key aspects of his task, for this, he noted, "must be the most important factor in any comprehensive account of his work."

At the outset, Burbank was ill. It was several days before he was even able to talk to him about his mission. Very well, he conceded, he needed a day or two to get settled in himself. Then, however, though he was treated with consideration, and everything necessary to the study of Burbank's collections was thrown open to him, he began to discover, in his own words, that "certain psychological traits of Mr. Burbank made impossible the adequate study of his processes while he is at his work, because chiefly of his great sensitiveness to the presence of another person,—the self-consciousness induced by such presence necessarily lessening the clearness of his ideals and the spontaneity of his methods." (When Shull speaks of Burbank's "ideals," he means, of course, the ideals he worked toward in selecting his plants.) It was a sort of Heisenbergian uncertainty principle—the observer influencing the observed so that accurate observation became impossible.

Nonetheless, Shull persevered. Almost every morning he was out in the gardens by six o'clock. This was necessary if he was to examine the cultures before the workmen, who now did a good deal of the less exact selection, had destroyed any specimens. Remaining to watch this selection on a number of mornings, he found it to be "a complex process which no two workmen carried out on exactly the same lines, the result being that much that was left was essentially equivalent to much that was discarded." For this reason, too, it was impossible to make meaningful comparisons between discarded and saved material. How could there be, when none of the several different workmen doing the selecting appeared to judge according to the same standards?

At about 8:00 A.M., Burbank himself usually came out, and Shull was able to accompany him about his work. He was made aware that his presence hindered Burbank from working as rapidly as he would have done alone. Accordingly, as soon as he had observed all Burbank's methods, he avoided spending time with him while he was working.

All of Burbank's methods, Shull noted, were of the simplest kind. None of them would have been considered satisfactory by an investigator interested in the genetic relationships of the plants he worked with. Burbank himself admitted that had he been conducting a scientific experiment, he would have done things differently. But, he insisted, his work was nonetheless scientific for all that. It was in fact of a *higher* scientific type, he maintained, since he achieved the desired results without superfluous operations or unnecessary expenditure of effort, thus permitting the accomplishment of more work than would otherwise have been possible. Shull discovered, as others had done before him, that Burbank keenly resented suggestions that he was not a scientific man.

Until about 1904, he told Shull, he had done all the breeding and selecting with his own hands. Now, as a result of the great volume of correspondence and the number of visitors he received, he was obliged to delegate much of the less particular work to his men. He instructed them in the common characteristics he did *not* want, and these were gradually eliminated morning by morning, leaving only the task of making the final selections to Burbank. Almost all his experiments were begun at the home tract at Santa Rosa, and those which required continuous attention were carried on there. On the larger experiment ground at Sebastopol were trees and plants that needed only occasional attention. Shull observed that during his stay there Burbank visited the Sebastopol grounds on an average of about once a week.

In general, the methods used by Burbank consisted almost entirely in cross-fertilization and selection. In crossing two plants, he usually removed the anthers before they opened to prevent self-fertilization. The pollen was then applied either by brushing the stigmas with freshly opened anthers or by brushing about in one flower with a camel's hair brush and then using this to pollinate the other, or by collecting unopened anthers in a watch crystal or a tin box lid, drying them and then applying the pollen to the stigma by finger or with a brush. Shull was pained to note that in many cases no attempt whatsoever was made to prevent self-fertilization, and that steps were only infrequently taken to prevent crossing with any other flower that might grow in the vicinity. Visits by insects were occasionally prevented by tying together the corolla after pollinating, but this was more often than not to prevent the delicate stigma from desiccating rather than to guard against the entrance of foreign pollen. Burbank would often examine the stigma with a magnifying glass before applying pollen to it, to make sure that it was free of pollen from other sources. If a few grains were detected, he would simply blow them off with a sharp puff of breath. He would then smear the stigma thickly with pollen and take the chance that even should an insect visit it the likelihood of obtaining a hybrid was strong.

Before pollinating, he usually removed all buds except for one, or a small cluster. Afterward he would mark the branch that bore it with a strip of cloth. When pollen from different sources was used on the same plant or batch of plants, he marked them with different colors of cloth, depending on his memory, for the rest, as to exactly what the cross had been. When a number of different crosses were made among several species, he cut tags into different shapes and assigned one shape to each species from which pollen was being used. One tag of each form was then labeled and kept in the office as an index, while the others, attached to the tree, were left blank, and indicated by form alone the origin of the pollen which had been applied to the flower to which the tag related. When material was scarce and he was especially anxious to obtain hybrids, he would actually use pollen from several species on the same flower. Such methods, observed Shull, in a preliminary report to the Carnegie Institution dated July 1906, "lead to results that can not give any confirmation of Mendelism or any other theory of inheritance that rests upon statistical inquiry." But Burbank was in no way concerned with confirming Mendelism or any other newfangled probabilistic law.

Selection, Shull points out, was the most basic of Burbank's methods, since irrespective of whether or not cross-fertilization was resorted to, it entered into the production of every new variety. As to mutations, Burbank admitted they took place, but held that they differed from the ordinary variation within species only in degree and not in kind. He maintained that any variation could be "fixed" by repeated use as a seed plant in the pedigrees—though some might require more repetitions than others. He used hybridization more often than not simply to increase the range of variation rather than to achieve certain desired combinations of characters. His other methods of increasing variability were the provision of especially favorable soil conditions, and the use of imported material. Shull listed four elements which he felt went to make up Burbank's remarkable talent for selection:

1. Sensitivity to slight variations in any desirable direction, which made for speed and accuracy in selection. "He says that he used to utilize the delicate senses of ladies in making his selections with respect to color, grace of form, scent, etc., but does so no longer because the long training has developed a higher susceptibility in him in these directions than is possessed even by ladies."

2. A quick and vivid imagination, able to visualize ideals by which selection could be guided. Sometimes a general ideal mo-

tivated him in a whole series of selections. In woody plants and fruit trees, for example, he saved only those with short, stocky internodes, prominent buds, and large leaves. In individual cases, his ideal was formed in response to suggestions given by the variation of the material itself. The suggestion for a blue Shirley poppy, for example, was the discovery of a decided bluish tinge in several specimens. The crimson Eschscholtzia was suggested by a delicate line of crimson noted inside one of the petals of an ordinary yellow one. "Sometimes his ideal grows as new possibilities appear in the material; but in the case of the Eschscholtzia it leaped at once to the perfect crimson flower."

3. Persistency. His ideals had to remain unchanged, or in harmonious development, sometimes for many years, "as any inharmonious shifting of the ideal which guides selection would lose all that had been gained by the previous selection."

4. The concentration with which he was able to consider a large number of different qualities without reducing the speed of the operation. In selecting fruit, for example, he had to consider not only size, shape, color, texture, and flavor, but also earliness of ripening, productivity, speed of reproduction, resistance to disease, insects and frost, and cooking, shipping and keeping qualities.

"There can be little doubt," Shull wrote, "that Mr. Burbank's success has been most largely due to the correctness of his economic ideals." In other words, he had an exceptionally keen eye for what the market wanted.

His operation was economical, moreover, in the utilization of space and time. Selections were made at as early a stage of development as possible. Blackberries and cacti, for example, were selected in the seed pan, so that fewer than 1 percent of the seedlings were ever actually transplanted to the garden. Hundreds of grafts were made on the same tree, enabling him to raise the entire progeny of a cross to maturity only two years from the planting of the seed. There were disadvantages to this when the grafts on a tree were from various sources, as it frequently became impossible to determine the origin of any particular graft except by guesswork. These trees, with their dozens of different kinds of fruit and foliage, had the effect of amazing observers who did not realize how easily explicable they were. Effects of this kind inevitably tended to swell the myth of Burbank's miraculous powers, and there can be little doubt that he relished the astonishment of the wondering public. In fact, there was no particular significance to this method of multiple grafting: it simply saved him space.

Shull carefully looked into Burbank's system of record-keeping and confirmed that it was haphazard in the extreme, while conceding that, given the financial and other limitations, "more records could only have been coupled with fewer economic results." Those records that did exist were for the most part simply rough notes on the history and location in the experiment grounds of various plants, intended solely as an aid to Burbank's memory, on which he relied heavily for the more exact details. Only in his fruit records were observations recorded in any sort of scientific manner.

These fruit records consisted of single loose sheets on which the most promising of the selections being made were described. The fruit was cut in half, and a pencil tracing made of the half section on one corner of the paper. Anything noteworthy about the pit or core was then usually sketched in. A working name was assigned to the variety, heading a brief description as to size, shape, color, flavor, prolificness, cooking, shipping and keeping qualities and so on. If Burbank thought particularly highly of a variety, he would mark the sheet with one or more double crosses—###—indicating his assessment of its worth. If, after several years' testing, he decided that the fruit was fit to be put on the market, he would stamp "BURBANK" on the sheet with a rubber stamp as the mark of his imprimatur.

The whole system had more in common with the work habits of an artist than with any scientific procedure. And an artist, it may be confidently asserted, was exactly what he was, following his way among his living materials in almost complete reliance on his own personal instincts and intuitions. "His whole life," Shull observed, "has been one of constant training of senses which were undoubtedly keyed to a high degree of sensitiveness by nature. Preconceptions do evidently affect his observations but principally in making him see the thing he is looking for to the partial exclusion of other things in which he has no interest, and not leading to any notable degree of error in the observations made." Internal moods tended to affect his observations to the extent of his noticing different features in the company of different visitors. For this reason, quite irrespective of any other, he sought solitude when he was at work. In the process of selection the weighing up of the multitudinous factors involved was to a great extent done subconsciously, by intuition, "amounting in its highest development to slight auto-hypnosis, in which condition the two factors, observation and imagination, are so intimately associated that neither he nor any one else could successfully draw the line between them, and this is doubtless the source of greatest error in his observations."

So vivid were the impressions he received from his plants, so graphically did his remarkable memory reproduce them, that it was impossible afterward to determine in what proportions observation and imagination had been mingled in the original critical experience. Shull thought it was probable that the more strongly subjective element of imagination frequently came to dominate in memory, with the result that Burbank's accounts did not always square with the observable reality. Even so, he conceded, "the main features of the original observation are probably reproduced with unusual accuracy." He had only rarely, he admitted, found a man more honest to his experiences than Burbank.

Artistlike, Burbank preferred not to be influenced by others in his perceptions as to the relationships of the forms he was working on. He allowed that he had his own preconceptions and strove to avoid these, Shull says, "with what he believes is success, but which appears to me to lack much of it." One of these preconceptions was the belief, already noted, that only acquired characters could be inherited. This led him to attribute all variations to environmental causes to a degree far beyond what was warranted by observation. To him everything in heredity was explicable as a mingling of forces. He believed that there was purpose in nature, and this teleological faith led him to assign uses to many characters "that present knowledge discredits." Instinctively he took sides—against Mendel, Weismann and De Vries, and with Darwin and the contemporary opponents of Mendelism and mutation theory. In so doing he generally never troubled to read the authorities in question.

Sometimes this partisanship manifested itself as a peculiar, pigheaded arrogance. In later years it would be claimed that Burbank had independently discovered Mendel's laws. (For example, in the supposedly autobiographical *Partner of Nature*, put together by Wilbur Hall, he is made to say, "I slowly came to a realization of the fact . . . that all the best variations and recombinations in a hybrid stock, obtained by crossing, appear in the second and a few subsequent succeeding generations— almost never in the first. This was, of course, Mendel's Law, that I had observed in many experiments long before D. De Vries and others unearthed the Mendel reports and made them belatedly public."[7]) And Shull believed that he *had* sensed early in his career—probably before the "rediscovery" in 1900—that the "break" in hybrid lines comes only in F_2 and afterward, and never, or not usually, in F_1. But neither this, nor the observation of ratios in the offspring of hybrids—which had been noted by Darwin and others long before—is the essence of Mendelism, the revolutionary element in which is the *idea* of segregating alleles.

And Burbank was, for that matter, inclined to dismiss or deny the ratios themselves. Shull notes that on one occasion the Santa Rosan drew his attention to a row of seedlings of a hybrid between a purple-leaved and a green-leaved plum, in which a 3:1 ratio was to be expected in Mendelian terms, but which gave the impression of being about 90 percent purple. This was done with the specific intention of *discounting* the general validity of Mendel's law. When the younger man afterward took the trouble to make an actual count, however, he found an almost perfect 75 to 25 percent relationship between the seedlings of the two colors. The superficial effect of an overwhelming preponderance of the purple-leaved type was an optical illusion.[8] Once, when he pointed out a discrepancy between certain published figures and the true numbers involved, Burbank told him "quite positively" that "I never count anything." And, Shull observes, no one who does not count can discover the Mendelian principle.

Figures presented one of Burbank's real weaknesses, so much so that Shull estimated that those given in published statements should be divided by at least ten to get a true approximation of the size of his cultures. On one occasion he told Shull—and the press—that he had planted 4000 *varieties* of seedling potato out of 14,000 to be planted. Shull counted them and found that there were in fact 4000 *individuals,* belonging to 390 clones. He did not think this was dishonesty on Burbank's part, rather that, "the numbers simply so much exceed his capacity for numerical conceptions that any large number will seem to him to be reasonably moderate." Other trained observers were not always inclined to be so charitable.

Paradoxically almost, honesty struck Shull as one of Burbank's consciously strong characteristics, the product of his powerful sense of self-esteem. He was of the kind, Shull thought, who would rather be right than be President. Though he was inclined to speculate about subjects he knew little about, delivering himself of trenchant generalities unsupported by fact, he was otherwise frankly prepared to admit that he did not know something, even, "in cases where it might appear to his advantage to know, and where his imagination could quite readily supply the information without the possibility of detection if he so desired."

Conflicting with the independence conferred by his self-esteem was his love of approval by others. Though he would do nothing dishonest to earn such approval (for that would have brought self-condemnation), he eagerly accepted it as no more than his due. "There are striking instances," says Shull, "in which the combination of these two dominant traits produces one instant the most profound modesty and the next instant almost blatant self-praise."

In 1906 he told Shull that only Darwin had grown more plants than he had, and that he was therefore [*sic*] the greatest authority on plant life next to Darwin. Two years later "he figured that he had by that time surpassed Darwin in the number of plants he had raised and that *therefore* he was the greatest authority on plant life that had ever lived."⁹ This being the case, he felt that he was better qualified than anyone else to pronounce on the subject of evolution. (Shull stresses the "therefore" to emphasize the extraordinary naïveté implicit in such a view.)

While not claiming the powers of a wizard, he was nonetheless delighted that the public should think him one. He delighted in the role of the great benefactor of mankind. This feeling of superiority naturally had the effect of making him less susceptible to evidence from outside sources which might tend to contradict what he himself had deduced from experience. "He says he read very little of De Vries' 'Species and Varieties' because the author was working along such wrong lines; and he is always impatient of a conversation in which he does not do all or nearly all the talking," Shull observes.

Though his phraseology constantly stressed his own role as "creator" of his products (he "originated" and "trained" his plants, "teaching" them to "behave" in the manner desired), he would nonetheless give a straightforward answer to an informed question from a scientific interlocutor. Shull found that he could depend on sober answers, even though he noticed that other people sometimes received evasive ones. His appreciation of Burbank's love of being intelligently questioned about his work, he felt, materially aided their relations.

It is a psychological portrait of some acuteness that Shull presents: evidently his powers of observation and evaluation in that respect were by no means inferior to his horticultural sense. At once perspicacious and sympathetic, he was able to look Burbank's faults in the face without losing sight of his merits. He made no fetish out of objectivity, but neither was he overcome by the Burbank charisma. It is to the credit of both men that they managed to remain friends of a sort.

A more homely picture of the master is painted by W. C. Williams, an osteopath who attended Burbank from early in 1906 to mid-1908.[10] Williams was living in Healdsburg, about sixteen miles from Santa Rosa, when he received a telegram summoning him to Burbank's house on a sick call. When he arrived, he was told that Burbank had pneumonia, but after examining him diagnosed the problem as acute bronchitis. He visited Burbank daily for nearly a week, and was finally persuaded to transfer his practice to Santa Rosa, Burbank telling him that he wanted a course of treatments himself and assuring him that "with his quietly talking to his close friends he would be able to build me up a nice practice what with Santa Rosa being a large town and all." In the course of the treatments, which took place in the evenings in Burbank's bedroom, he wrote, in a memoir noted down in 1948,

> He told what a struggle he had had to keep up his work on account of being short of capital. He told me that Carneiga [*sic*] Foundation was figuring on assisting him. Then he told me how trying it was on him to have Carneiga men there going all over his business and asking so many private questions. He said, "They seem to think because they aim to grant me money in case

I qualify that they own my place and can come and go as they please." He told me that if he didn't need the money so desperately he would call the whole thing off and forbid them coming on his grounds.

Williams felt that the treatments, including a good deal of massage, did Burbank a lot of good, "because his circulation was poor and he was going through such a strain at the time." For his part, Burbank seemed pleased, telling him that "his experience had been with osteopaths that they would give you a good long treatment the first two or three times and from then on give you a short treatment and he liked a long treatment." He declared his belief in "natural methods" in treating diseases of the human body, saying that he had been one of the first to recognize osteopathy.

One thing that emerges clearly is the extent of Burbank's preoccupation with his health. "He told me he had never been strong in his life, always frail. Then his dry humor asserted itself, 'I never had a constitution—I always went by the bylaws.' " A surgeon had once bungled a hemorrhoidal operation, he said, "and it had been a great handicap to him ever since." They spoke a good deal about diet. Onions, Burbank insisted, "were healthful. Said he never knew a person that eat lots of onions but what was healthful." He was no vegetarian, however, and "told me he never saw a vegetarian but what he could take him by the seat of the pants and throw him over a fence."

Though Williams felt they were good friends, he found he had to keep his distance on anything pertaining to Burbank's private affairs. Questions were only rarely allowed. But Burbank did make a number of remarks that are of considerable psychological interest. "He told me how things would come to him at times," Williams recalled. "How ideas would come in his mind almost as if he had been spoken to." Jack London used to come over from the nearby Valley of the Moon in those days, and Williams remembered how much Burbank seemed to enjoy his visits. One day he asked him, "what he thought of Jack

London plagerizing [*sic*] in writing a book." Burbank replied tartly, "If some one takes an old abandoned house that no one cares to live in and remodels it and makes a fine house of it, is that wrong?" It was his pragmatic approach in a nutshell. One might as well have said, "If Burbank imports a plant from Chile or Manchuria that no one has bothered with, gives it a name and makes it a useful economic crop, is that wrong?"

"I saw the point," Williams admits.

ELEVEN

Burbankitis

BURBANK EARLY ON subscribed to a newspaper clipping service, and these clippings were preserved in scrapbooks. The magazine articles about him by Wickson, Harwood, Jordan, De Vries and others, Harwood's book *New Creations in Plant Life* and the chapter on Burbank in the same author's *The New Earth*, served as a nucleus for numerous newspaper articles. For many years now, too, reporters had been eagerly seizing on any statement Burbank cared to make in their search for "copy," further swelling the flood of newspaper publicity. (He was usually only too willing to provide them with quotable material. "I don't believe I ever called on him that he did not give me a good story for my paper," one of these journalists told Howard.) All these items were clipped, to be filed away by the faithful Emma in large quarto volumes kept especially for the purpose.

The earliest clippings dated from 1874 and were reports from Lunenburg in the Fitchburg *Sentinel* and various other local papers about the Burbank potato. By 1906 the seventh volume of the scrapbook was in the process of being filled, and clippings were accumulating at the rate of some six hundred quarto pages a year. From each original source, the flood of publicity spread out in concentric circles. Volume one, covering the period from 1874 to 1895, had 150 pages. Volume two, running from 1896 to 1901, had 204. Volumes three and four, dating from 1901 to 1905, made up a combined total of 400. This ever-increasing quantity of clippings is a clear measure of his growing fame.

But he, who was so much written about, wrote little himself. Aside from his catalogs, Burbank's only published writings consisted of letters or brief items in agricultural and horticultural journals, and one or two short papers. He had for the most part preferred to get on with the practical side of his work and let others speak for him. When in May 1906 he published a longish article in *Century* magazine (reissued the following year in pamphlet form by the Century Company), it curiously enough had nothing whatsoever to do with his own area of special competence. Entitled "The Training of the Human Plant," it plunged instead into the complex field of human eugenics and child-rearing.

The eugenics movement is now little remembered, having been effectively extinguished by the supererogatory enthusiasm of Adolf Hitler & Co. But, drawing strength from the prevailing Social Darwinist philosophy of the late nineteenth century, it was in the first decade of the twentieth a force to be reckoned with. The movement had begun to take an organized form in the United States around 1900, growing rapidly thereafter until, says Richard Hofstadter, "by 1915 it had reached the dimensions of a fad."[1] There was an influential eugenicist party in the ranks of the American Breeders Association, founded in 1903, of which Burbank, it will be recalled, was an honorary member. When in 1910 the association, of which Liberty Hyde Bailey was then president, set up a Commission on Eugenics with a mandate to study and disseminate what was known about human heredity, David Starr Jordan was appointed chairman, Charles B. Davenport was named secretary and the other members were Vernon Kellogg, Frederick Adams Wood, Roswell H. Johnson and Luther Burbank.[2]

The movement had begun to bear fruit (if so unsuitable a simile may be employed) in 1907 with the passage of a sterilization law in Indiana. California was the second state in the Union to pass sterilization legislation. This was done in 1909. By 1915 similar legislation existed in twelve states. By 1940, twenty-nine had laws of this kind, and over 33,000 people had been sterilized nationwide. Of these 41 percent—13,721 cases—were in California.[3] The prevailing opinion was stated by Burbank's friend and patron, David Starr Jordan, when he wrote that "It is not the strength of the strong but the weakness of the weak which engenders exploitation and tyranny." Inferior human material was held responsible for "poverty, dirt and crime."

The leader of the eugenics movement in America was none other than Charles B. Davenport—Shull's chief and the Carnegie Institution's Director of Experimental Evolution at Cold Spring Harbor, where, with financial help from Mrs. E. H. Harriman, a Eugenics Record Office was set up in 1910 which, Hofstadter says, became "a fountainhead of propaganda." It would be a mistake to think of the activities of the movement as entirely sinister. In many ways they were anything but that. David Starr Jordan, a courageous pacifist, devoted a number of books, for example, to exploring the dysgenic effects of war, arguing that it was a biological evil, carrying off the fit and leaving the unsound, both of body and of mind, to perpetuate the race. Nonetheless it was a time, as Hofstadter observes, when, "Encouraged by the eugenics movement, men talked of racial degeneracy, of race suicide, of the decline of western civilization, of the effeteness of the western peoples, of the Yellow Peril."[4]

Now Burbank was a believer in the eugenic view, but with a difference. He proposed the inheritance of *acquired* characteristics—and, more than that, *only* of acquired characteristics. (This proposition is either utterly naive or extremely subtle. In any case, by carrying it to logical absurdity, it shows up the cant formula "inheritance of acquired characteristics" for the tautology it is.) In his view, therefore, living things were to be molded not so much by selective breeding as by careful nurture. This is the message of "The Training of the Human Plant."

Though superficially, as a statement by a man who had devoted his life to selective breeding, it seems self-contradictory, it is also a work of profound humanism, sane and reasoned by contrast with the eugenic opinions of many of his contemporaries. Though the latter might rest more squarely on the current findings of the geneticists, they were equally founded in pessimism and paranoia. In these terms the biologically fit were handily identified with the upper classes, the unfit with the lower. It was a doctrine from which racists of all kinds could take great encouragement, irrespective of Davenport's concern with the need for "additional precise data as to the unit characteristics of man and their methods of inheritance."[5] In the end it would provide the ideological underpinnings of Hitlerism.

Burbank, on the other hand, makes it clear from the outset that he rejects the notion that immigration is lowering the standard of American intelligence by "mongrelizing" the breed. On the contrary, he feels that precisely because of the "vast mingling of races brought here by immigration" the United States has before it "the grandest opportunity ever presented of developing the finest race the world has ever known." Crossing is, after all, the basis of improvement in plant breeding; so, too, it will be the basis for improvement in mankind.

However, he says, he has never lost sight of the principle of the survival of the fittest. "Selection, wise supervision, intelligent care, and the utmost patience" will be called for if the best results are to be achieved, in human as in plant hybridization. Americans are more crossed than any other nation in the history of the world, and the results are the same as in a much-hybridized race of plants: "all the worst as well as all the best qualities of each are brought out in their fullest intensities." Here is where *selective environment* will count. Care, nurture, the influence of surroundings, selection, the separation of the best from the poorest will be called for. To the extent that we leave the children of the poor to their evil surroundings, to that extent we breed danger for ourselves. The only way to avoid this is "absolutely to cut loose from all precedent and begin systematic State and National aid, not next year, or a decade from now, but today."

He admits that there may be reversions to former ancestral traits but insists that for the most part "by surrounding this child with sunshine from the sky and your heart, by giving the closest communion with nature, by feeding this child well-balanced, nutritious food, by giving it all that is implied in healthful environmental influences, and by doing all in love," the desired traits of "honesty, fairness, purity, loveableness, industry, thrift" and so on can be fixed in it.

But what of the obviously abnormal? Should weaklings be destroyed? No, he answers, again drawing analogy from the experience of the plant breeder, who is constantly on the lookout for "abnormal" individuals and "that which springs apart in new lines." How many plants are there in the world today, he asks, that were not in one sense once abnormalities?

It would, he concedes, be best to prohibit the marriage of the "physically, mentally, and morally unfit." For "suppose we blend together two poisonous plants and make a third even more virulent, a vegetable degenerate, and set their evil descendents adrift to multiply over the earth, are we not distinct foes to the race?"

Ten generations, he feels, should be sufficient to fix the desired traits, given ideal conditions. He bases this on his experience with plants, "varying according to the plant's character—its pliability or stubbornness." Plants, he believes, are in any case more stubborn in their habits than children. "The human will is a weak thing beside the will of a plant . . . When it comes to so sensitive and pliable a thing as the nature of a child, the problem becomes vastly easier."

Total depravity is no more to be found in people than it is in

plants. There has never been any such thing as a totally de-
praved human being. Heredity should be seen not as "some
hideous ancestral specter forever crossing the path of a human
being" but the conditioning of past environments. It is, to use
one of Burbank's favorite phrases, "the sum of all the effects of
all the environments of all past generations." Acquired characteristics, he states quite unequivocally, *are* transmitted. In fact,
all characters which are transmitted have been acquired, "not
necessarily at once in a dynamic or visible form, but as an increasingly latent force ready to appear as a tangible character
when by long-continued natural or artificial repetition any specific tendency has become inherent . . ."[6]

And here is the essence of Burbank's teleology. Simple, yet
not without a certain subtlety, it is utterly wrong-headed from
the standpoint of genetics and stands in sublime and willful ignorance of Weismann's theory of the germ plasm. For all that,
however, it has much more in common with modern liberal belief than any practical application of genetics (as then understood) to human material could conceivably have had. It is the
creed, above all, of a thoroughly humane man, struggling to
merge what he knows with what he feels. In the context of the
time, moreover, it is a revolutionary statement. "A socialistic
dream, but with human appeal," Howard calls it.

It was surprisingly well received, particularly by the clergy
and the popular press. Though more sophisticated eugenicists
might sneer, general opinion was more in line with that of Ella
Wheeler Wilcox, writing in the New York *Evening Journal:*

I wish every mother and every young woman who hopes to become a wife and mother would read Luther Burbank's article on
the "Training of the Human Plant." That article should be printed in pamphlet form and sent by the Government to every woman. It should be read from pulpits and discussed at women's
clubs and talked to young women in seminaries and colleges. Mr.
Burbank gives scientific proofs of many statements (made many
times) in these columns of the power of Mothers and Teachers

to develop in the children under their charge whatever qualities they desire them to possess.

The public had taken Burbank to its heart, and fame and honors were showered on him. In December, 1903, he had been elected to honorary membership in San Francisco's elite Bohemian Club, a distinction only rarely conferred (other honorary members of the day included Samuel Clemens, Daniel C. Gilman, Sir Henry Irving, David Starr Jordan, Pietro Mascagni, Joaquin Miller, Theodore Roosevelt and Benjamin Ide Wheeler). In 1905 he was awarded an honorary degree, along with fifty-six other prominent Americans of the time, by Tufts College (now Tufts University), as part of the celebration of the fiftieth anniversary of the opening of the college in the academic year 1854–1855. He received the degree of Doctor of Science, with the citation:

> *Lutherus Burbank, vir hortorum culturae peritus, qui ab noviciam earum rerum quas terra giguit plurima beneficia in homines contulit.* (Luther Burbank, expert horticulturist, whose discoveries have brought many benefits to mankind from the fruits of the earth.)

The same year he was made honorary life member of the California Academy of Sciences, and a testimonial banquet was held in his honor by the California State Board of Trade. In 1906 the California Federation of Women's Clubs passed a resolution recommending that his birthday, March 7, be celebrated as State Arbor Day, and the following year Santa Rosa named its newest grade school after him.

But his own colleagues in the profession of horticulture were many of them becoming more and more resentful of his reputation. Other horticulturists, the trade felt, had done as much or more than he had, while receiving nowhere near the rewards, financial and otherwise, that accrued to Burbank.

"I am heartily tired of this gush about Mr. Burbank," wrote Ernest Braunton, secretary of the Southern California Horticultural Society. He held nothing against the man himself, he said. "I am not of that envious class of tradesman who ask, 'What has he done,' but really consider him the most over-estimated man, by the general public, that we have in the world today." Braunton observed that he himself did a good deal of breeding, particularly of gladiolus, of which he had some that were superior in size and color to anything he had seen. He failed to see that Burbank had accomplished anything that he and many others could not have done—or did in fact do—in the same time, and he vowed "to do what I can to get the public to look at him through normal eyes." As for the trade, they were so "touchy" that "the best of them rise up in arms at the mere mention of his name." Members of the Southern California Horticultural Society had opposed inviting Burbank to talk, even though, Braunton observes, "I know it would be the best drawing card with the public that the Society could have."[7]

Even the faithful were feeling the effects of "Burbankitis." Horticulture, the loyal Wickson observed, replying to Braunton, was suffering through the exaggerated reports published by ignorant people about Burbank's work. The latter was himself, perhaps, the chief sufferer. "I have done what I could to stem this tide of exaggeration and false conclusion," Wickson says, "but have become somewhat weary of the task, and have rather adopted the policy of waiting until the misrepresentation and exaggeration shall expire by its own unfitness to live. I doubt if there is any use in continually writing against this misrepresentation, and for this reason I have largely retired from the field."[8]

Now Wickson, that "Nestor of Our Horticulture," was one of the chief culprits himself. It could perfectly well be argued that *he* was the one who had convinced the public of Burbank's unique talents and contributions to horticulture in the first place. No other writer of any scientific standing had worked at promoting Burbank with anywhere near his enthusiasm and efficiency. He had in the past been guilty of the most astonishing hyperbole on Burbank's behalf.

His cooling off can perhaps be explained in terms of his

mounting academic prospects. In 1905 he had been elected Dean of the College of Agriculture of the University of California, and appointed acting director of the Experiment Station, stepping into the shoes of the great Dr. E. W. Hilgard. The following year he became a member of the National Horticultural Council, served as expert for the commission which selected and purchased the University Farm at Davis and was a member of the commission organized by the legislature to select a site for and establish the Southern California Pathological Laboratory at Whittier and the Citrus Experiment Station at Riverside. Full professorship at the College of Agriculture and appointment as permanent director and horticulturist of the University Agricultural Station were in the offing (and would come his way in September 1907). In the meantime it doubtless behooved him to be more cautious about his endorsements than he had been in the past.

A warning note was sounded by Patrick O'Mara, horticulturist for Peter Henderson and Company, a New York seed and nursery firm, in a trade publication, the *Florist's Exchange*. O'Mara had visited Burbank in the summer of 1906. Though this was the busiest time of the year for the plant breeder, his firm had bought some of Burbank's productions and listed them in their catalogs, and O'Mara, who was in charge of the plant department of one of the leading seed houses, expected a cordial reception to say the least. For some reason he was totally snubbed. Not only did Burbank refuse to see him, he would not even admit him to his experiment grounds. This would have incensed anybody. It was a particularly unwise thing to do to an Irishman. His pride deeply wounded, O'Mara retaliated by attacking Burbank's reputation at a meeting of the New York Florist's Club, and followed up his initial salvoes with a sarcastic article, "Luther Burbank, A Short Review of His Work in Plant Hybridization and Brief Comparison with Other Hybridizers," which drew most of its ammunition from the writings of Wickson and Harwood.

He began by taking Burbank to task for his claim to "New

Creations." He had, O'Mara said, "no more right to claim the title of 'creator' of new plants than he has to apply it to the bee that flits from flower to flower and carries the pollen . . ." He was particularly scornful of Wickson's set of articles in *Sunset* magazine, collected in *Luther Burbank: An Appreciation.* "Many friends and admirers of Mr. Burbank contend that he is not responsible for the extravagant claims made for him in that publication; but it is well to bear in mind that he helped to circulate it and therefore gave a semblance of sanction to its contents." Certainly the critic did not have to search very hard to find passages that were eulogistic to the point of parody:

> Plant development is one of the phases of civilization, and it makes new conquests as they are needed in the onward rush of mankind. We are now at the beginning of an epoch of accelerated motion in this direction. Burbank is the prophet of this epoch. Obeying the command of the Infinite, he is carrying the gates of Gaza. Let not the Delilah of modern organization shear him of his God-given strength and make him like other men,[9]

And so on. Adulation in such terms was almost as bad as slander. The hero would have had to be a Samson indeed to bear up to it. "Then," O'Mara appended rancorously, "he reaches out and gets the $100,000." This with reference presumably to the Carnegie grant of $10,000 a year for a projected ten years, the second installment of which had been paid on January 1906. Yes, there was more than a tinge of plain envy in the attack. In addition to being heaped with honors and awards, Burbank was making more money than the average horticulturist could ever hope for, *and* getting subsidized by Carnegie into the bargain.

Why had not other deserving men had his rewards? O'Mara ventured that the loganberry, a hybrid between the wild California black dewberry and the red raspberry, originated by Judge J. H. Logan in the early eighties, was better than any of Burbank's productions. He exclaimed over the fact that, "The

Phillips cling peach is of more value to California in my opinion than any fruit which he has produced, and sad to relate, the man who produced it is in the Yuba Co. almshouse, so announced in the Pacific Rural Press of Jan. 6th last." He cited hybrid grapes developed by Rogers, Jacob Moore and T. V. Munson, the work of John Cook, E. G. Hill and Dr. W. Van Fleet with roses, that of Fred Dorner, C. W. Ward and Peter Fisher with carnations, Antoine Wintzer's work with cannas, and Groff's with gladioli, *inter alia,* as evidence that Burbank was far from being the solitary pioneer he was cracked up to be.

Burbank's science he dismissed as "somewhat of the Mary Baker Eddy or Helen Wilmans order." As to all the talk about "educating" plants, "I wish to say, and make it as emphatic as possible, that in my opinion no exercise of the human mind by way of suggestive thought directed upon a plant can change one cell or filament of it." This last is interesting. For though Burbank never wrote that he influenced plants by "suggestive thought"—or indeed permitted himself to be quoted to that effect until much later—it is evidence that rumors of the kind were current. Given the backdrop of the Messiahship idea and his mystical propensities in general, it might not be too much to assume that such rumors originated with Burbank himself. Whether or not he believed it (and he probably did), it was exactly the sort of power he was likely to hint at to a gullible audience—and such he had aplenty. The reference here to Christian Scientist Mrs. Eddy (1821–1910) is also revealing: there was certainly something approaching evangelical fervor to the condition now dubbed "Burbankitis."

O'Mara was not of a disposition to allow his subject much credit for anything. The Burbank potato, he alleged, was a "volunteer" seedling of the Early Rose, not hybridized by him. In the East, he contended, it had outlived its usefulness and been superseded. He was rude about the Shasta daisy, branded the Burbank plum "an importation pure and simple," observed that Carter of London had produced a superior crimson Eschscholtzia, and that Italian breeders had developed better cannas. As to the "Iceberg" blackberry, he said, accurately enough, "Nonsense, people don't want a white blackberry; they want a black blackberry."

Needless to say he took off after the current miracle—the "spineless" cactus. First of all the original plant "was given him right straight out of the Department of Agriculture." Secondly, what was it good for anyhow? "I never crossed the desert myself except on a railroad train," O'Mara observes with elephantine humor, "but I can imagine that if a man is crossing the desert and wants to sit down, how handy it would be to have one of these thornless cacti handy." Here again the hyperbole of Burbank's admirers could neatly be used against him. "They say when a poet gets after a man, he is done for," O'Mara gibed, turning up a deadly verse in evidence:

> He touched the spiculed desert—cacti cursed—
> And turned its thorns to figs; its thistles fruit.
> He nodded to the daisy half immersed
> In dwarfing dust, and lo! a lily mute
> Rose from the weeds—a perfume with a flute.

To this awful celebration, he then appended a bit of comic doggerel, supposedly spoken by one of the "knockers":

> O, Mr. Burbank, won't you try and do some
>   things for me?
> A wizard clever as you are can do them
>   easily.
> A man who turns a cactus plant into a
>   feather bed
> Should have no trouble putting brains into
>   a cabbage head.

The haw-haws in the Florist's Club must have been resounding. But if some of this critical sniping was justified by a few grains of truth, it was not for that reason any the less unfair. Certainly Burbank had imported, certainly he had received

cacti from the Department of Agriculture. But his importations
had been subjected to elaborate crossing, and his opuntias had
been grown and selected on a vast scale before being put on the
market. It was true that other men had done good things in
various fields. But no one had attempted a fraction of what he
had. A more valid criticism would have been that he had tried
to do too much.

Burbank found his defenders, notably W. Atlee Burpee, the
famous Philadelphia seedsman, who had long been appreciative of his work. (Burpee, O'Mara observed, tried "to show me
the light, but I could not see the light.") But the run of the trade
was henceforth increasingly suspicious if not openly hostile.

Every great reputation provokes detractors, and Burbank's
called forth enemies in greater numbers than most precisely because it was so much bolstered by addle-brained sentimentality
and exploited with increasingly incautious puffery. The claque
of hack writers, lady mystics, schoolmarms and man-milliners
who sang his praises so loudly inevitably raised the hackles of a
good part of the nursery trade, which had reason to be jealous
anyway, and of the scientific community as represented by the
workers in the agricultural experiment stations and the staffs of
the land-grant colleges, who were, it was touted abroad, being
put to shame by this unlettered man. Once their enmity was
aroused, it was uphill work to convince them that Burbank
was—despite all that—doing remarkable things. They would
not see the light. O'Mara, with his stubborn Irish pugnacity,
stood for them in that. The dog had been given a bad name.
Hang him.[10]

O'Mara's attack met a warm enough reception to warrant its
republication in pamphlet form, which the author did in Jersey
City in September of the following year. Conversely, however,
1907 also saw publication of Hugo de Vries' book, *Plant Breeding: Comments on the Experiments of Nilsson and Burbank*. A large
section was devoted to Burbank's work, which the Dutch botanist clearly viewed as important. This was a significant compli-
ment and was bound to be influential, particularly in Europe.

Again on the debit side, Harwood's rhapsodic *New Creations* now went into a second edition, and the same author published yet another eulogy, entitled "How Luther Burbank Creates New Flowers," in the *Ladies' Home Journal*.

But whatever the current state of his fame, business was booming. There were candidates aplenty for the Burbank bandwagon. A list compiled by Emma Beeson records the sale, on September 20, 1907, of seven varieties of thornless cactus— Santa Rosa, Sonoma, California, Fresno, Monterey, Chico and Guayaquil—to the Thornless Cactus Farming Company of Los Angeles for a grand total of $26,000. This was undoubtedly a speculative operation, prompted by his twenty-eight-page illustrated catalog of "The New Agricultural-Horticultural Opuntias. Plant Creations for Arid Regions." Appearing in June, this inevitably whetted the appetites of the get-rich-quick brigade, always thick on the ground in California. It may perhaps be doubted that Burbank was paid in full (other figures suggest that only $20,000 was involved), as he may well have been prepared to grant a certain amount of credit in the light of the size of the order. If he was, however, this single sale made him the richer by an amount equivalent to perhaps $150,000 in today's money. It was the biggest single sale he would ever make. Very likely it was the biggest single sale in horticultural history.

His reputation had reached its perihelion along with his earnings. Henceforth it could only decay. The first marks of the decline, so evident to hindsight, were by no means obvious then, however. O'Mara's ranting and the mutterings of the trade could be written off as envy. He had been written up at length by one of the most famous botanists in the world, and the deluge of favorable publicity continued.

He felt so sure of himself that early in 1906 he had begun negotiations with Dugal Cree, president of the Cree Publishing Company of Minneapolis, for the preparation of a ten-volume account of his work intended for popular reading. This was disturbing news to the Carnegie Committee, which was anticipating the publication of its own definitive account. However, Shull advised it in February 1907: "Mr. Burbank informed me that the Cree books can not be in the least conflict with our work. He says that the 10 volumes will not contain as much 'meat' as ten pages of the Carnegie work. It is to be made up mostly of illustrations, on thick paper with very brief statements in large type:—to be sold by subscription."

Mindful of the criticism of Harwood's book, the Cree Company had hired Dr. Leroy Abrams, Assistant Professor of Systematic Botany at Stanford University, to read its manuscript and stand sponsor for its scientific aspects. Abrams, Shull noted, "will be on the ground here until the work is completed, which is expected to be at least a year."

For Shull that year was marked by tragedy. In July 1906 he had married Ella Amanda Hollar, and returning to Santa Rosa in 1907 he brought his young wife with him. She was well on into pregnancy and perhaps ought not to have made the trip. The baby, a little girl, did not survive its birth on May 5, and Ella herself died two days later. She was buried there—her husband would be buried there himself almost half a century later—and Shull returned to Cold Spring Harbor alone.

When he next visited Santa Rosa, early in October 1907, he found relations somewhat strained. Burbank was evidently getting impatient with the delay in publication of the institution's findings and wanted them to bring out at least an initial volume. Shull found it difficult to get to see him at all. "In the nine days I have been here," he reported,

I have had only two hours of Mr. Burbank's time. He comes in each day at the appointed hour to say that he "Simply can not give me the time" and promises to do better later. In view of the urgency on the part of the Committee to hasten the work, you can imagine the strain this puts on me. I am *feeling* it, too. I am not idle of course, for I am pushing the matter of collecting statements regarding Burbank's work from authoritative sources and have also brought with me Station work to which I can devote what time I am not otherwise occupied. I can not avoid the feeling sometimes, however, that I would be accomplishing much more for science if I were back with you and would not then be taking Mr. Burbank from work he is so pre-eminently fitted to do.

In January 1908 the Carnegie Institution made its fourth payment of $10,000 to Burbank. Shull was beginning to wonder whether it was worth going on. Burbank's work was being estimated at more nearly its correct value in the trade than it had been two years before, he felt. Doubtless the general public would in time also come to assess him more accurately, even without any published report by the Carnegie Institution, "as the work of other plant breeders becomes more widely known and appreciated." This tone implies an intent to debunk which could not have been part of his original mandate from the institution. Shull was getting irritated. He felt that Abrams was receïving more of Burbank's time than he was, and that one of the two projected books was bound to be superfluous. Shortly after he resumed his task at Santa Rosa early in March 1908, he wrote Davenport, however, that "I shall not find fault so long as he continues to take an interest in my side of the work, and shows the good spirit he now manifests." Bürbank seemed in better health than usual, and Shull was optimistic of making good progress.

In August of that year, the institution sent him on a European tour of other plant breeding establishments. He visited some thirty of these, from Copenhagen in the north to Naples in the south, from Dublin in the west to Brünn in the east. He gained an invaluable background in contemporary horticultural experimentation and also picked up current European opinions of Burbank.

English breeders seem to have been particularly critical. The Laxton Brothers of Bedford exemplified this attitude. Edward

Laxton complained that "the exploitation of Mr. Burbank was wholly unfair to other plant breeders who had been doing excellent work for many years, and he thought that Mr. Burbank had accomplished practically nothing, as none of the plants that he had sent out have yet found their way into general culture in England or proved of any value there." This insular point of view disregarded the fact that Burbank had been working with varieties intended to do well in California's Mediterranean climate rather than in England's home counties. But the simple lack of charity to a fellow breeder was probably attributable to the hostility already being exuded by the American horticultural establishment itself.

Meanwhile, that same August, the institution's President Woodward paid Burbank a visit to see what was going on. He found him "pretty badly tangled up with the universe, so badly, in fact, that it was necessary to issue a sort of ultimatum to him," he wrote Davenport. "I hope we may be able to extricate him, in part at least, since I feel that he is making good to the Institution on the horticultural side. He has certainly achieved great success with his edible cactus." Unfortunately there is no clue as to what the precise nature of the entanglement referred to was. The ultimatum was a strong hint that the Carnegie grant might be discontinued if he did not straighten out.

Woodward remained personally sympathetic, and evidently Burbank also retained the support of none other than Andrew Carnegie himself. At a meeting of the Board of Trustees on December 8, 1908, Carnegie observed that, "If we can sustain Mr. Burbank in his work so that in the end we will have economic gain, I would even be in favor of increasing the amount given to him." (It is clear that by "economic gain," practical benefit to mankind as opposed to purely scientific outcome is to be understood here, not profit on the part of the institution.) Woodward agreed that the scientific results were "purely secondary," and that the "economic aspects of the case" were almost "the sole justification for the undertaking." He noted, however, that he was often asked "why we, as an institution, are subsidizing a faker." In the upshot the Board of Directors went on record to the effect that it was

> desirous of seeing the work brought to an end. G. H. Shull is to return to Luther Burbank as soon as convenient and shall finish the work with Burbank by the end of 1909. Voted that the year 1910 should be devoted by Dr. Shull to writing up his investigations and gathering illustrations for his final report.

Writing to Burbank on December 21, 1908, Woodward informed him that a further appropriation of $10,000 for the year 1909 had been made, but warned that "by reason chiefly of the numerous misrepresentations of your work in the popular press," he was having difficulty in convincing the Board of Trustees to continue its support, and expressed the hope that "in future we may be able to divest this work of its sensational features to such an extent that its real merits will plainly appear." The handwriting was on the wall.

TWELVE

The Luther Burbank Press

IN JANUARY 1909, at the annual meeting of the American
Breeders' Association, held that year in Columbia, Missouri, a
paper was presented by Burbank under the title "Another
Mode of Species Forming."* In it he reported a phenomenon
which science would be another twenty years in recognizing:
the true-breeding species hybrid. Unfortunately, nobody believed him, and to this day his priority in reporting such hybrids has scarcely been conceded. "Possibly this paper was
ghost-written by G. H. Shull. It bears his fingerprints," the
geneticist W. E. Castle, who seems to have been relying entirely
on memory and got both its title and its contents wrong, later
remarked unkindly.[1] Quite apart from the fact that Shull had
been in Europe for the past four months, he would, had he accepted Burbank's findings on this score, almost certainly have

*See Appendix.

made his own report. He did not, and the existence of what are now known as amphidiploids, or allotetraploids, species hybrids whose somatic cells contain the diploid chromosomes of both parents, would have to wait until the cytological studies of the twenties identified them.

Meanwhile, as far as the rumblings from the Carnegie Institution were concerned, Burbank seems to have made few, if any, concessions. It was not in his character to do so, and as sales remained good, he was not overly concerned about money. In October 1908 the Thornless Cactus Farming Company had bought ten more varieties of opuntia from him for $5460.50. Given this further endorsement of his personal faith in the eventual economic importance of his cacti, it would hardly have seemed necessary for him to go begging. The fifth—and last—Carnegie payment was made in January 1909. When Shull turned up in the spring to resume his work, there was no apparent acrimony. But another visitor that April, the popular philosopher Elbert Hubbard, observed that his "blue eyes . . . would be weary and sad were it not for the smiling mouth."

In February 1909 he had had a new proposition, this one from the brothers Herbert and Hartland Law, owners of the Fairmont Hotel in San Francisco. The Law brothers, who had made their fortunes as promoters of patent medicines, seem to have been brought together with Burbank by the flamboyant Oscar Binner, a partner in the Cree Publishing Company, who though himself a professional promoter, was a true Burbankian besides, and remained associated with his enterprises for a number of years. Burbank was persuaded to sign a contract in terms of which a corporation headed by the Laws, to be known as Luther Burbank Products, Inc., would market everything he produced. Walter B. Clarke was taken on as sales manager at Santa Rosa, but while the project was still largely in the planning stage, Burbank seems to have had second thoughts. He repudiated the preliminary contract and fortunately the other parties were sensibly prepared to bow out gracefully if that was what he wanted.

Binner made a statement to the effect that "For myself and my associates, the Law Brothers, let me say that Mr. Burbank's absolute happiness and contentment are our first consideration . . ." Clarke was placed in a somewhat difficult position, as he had given up another job to take up his post in Santa Rosa, and Burbank was induced to let him stay on. They do not seem to have hit it off too well. Clarke thought Burbank "erratic in his actions and slipshod in his methods . . . a strange combination of childlike simplicity and Yankee shrewdness," while Burbank for his part decided that he did not need a sales manager. Clarke's contract, too, was therefore terminated, with some suitable compensatory payment. This was the end of the first scheme to market Burbank in a big way as a purely commercial proposition.

In 1909 Governor James N. Gillett signed the bill making Burbank's birthday, March 7, State Bird & Arbor Day, as proposed by the California Federation of Women's Clubs three years before. But even as this signal honor was being paid him, a fresh storm was brewing.

In March 1908 he had sold John Lewis Childs, of Floral Park, New York, a hybrid berry, which he called the "Sunberry," but which Childs renamed "Wonderberry" with the inevitable eye to the market. According to Howard it was an F_2 hybrid between *Solanum guineense,* the staminate parent, and *Solanum villosum,* the pistillate parent. Both progenitors produced fruit that was inedible, though not actually poisonous, but the fruit of the hybrid proved good, either cooked or eaten raw when thoroughly ripened. Having bought this berry for a mere $300 (or $375—there is some discrepancy in these figures), Childs proceeded to advertise it widely as a new Burbank marvel, going so far as to issue a recipe book entitled "100 Ways of Using the Fruit of the Sunberry or Improved Wonderberry."

The controversy which followed has been described in detail

by Charles B. Heiser, Jr., in the chapter on "The Wonderberry" in his book *Nightshades: The Paradoxical Plants.*[2] Early in 1909 the battle was opened in the pages of the *Rural New Yorker,* described as "The Business Farmers' Paper, a National Weekly for Country and Suburban Homes," under its crusading editor, Herbert W. Collingwood, whose pet cause was honesty in advertising. Collingwood was evidently suspicious of Burbank from the start, and it seems to have been in an article in the *Rural New Yorker* that the charge was first made that the Wonderberry was nothing more than *Solanum nigrum*—the black, or garden, nightshade, a common enough weed throughout the United States (not to be confused, however, with the deadly nightshade, *Atropa belladonna*). It was reiterated on May 29, 1909, in an article entitled "The Wonderberry and the Wizard Burbank," the author of which observed wittily:

> I'm a very humble reader, with a home among the hills, and the thought of eating nightshade all my soul with anguish fills. I'm the ultimate consumer, and I only want to know, if the berry is a wonder, whether Burbank made it so!"
>
> The "Wonderberry" appeared this season as one of the "novelties" which are sprung upon the public without official test or preparation. We had no chance to test it, but botanists of high reputation were sure it was in no wise different from the well-known Solanum nigrum . . .

The writer went on to cite a letter from Burbank offering to pay $10,000 in cash to "any living person on earth" who could prove that the Wonderberry was the black nightshade, and asserted that since by his own admission it was a cross between *S. villosum* and *S. guineense,* which had been declared to be "nothing other than forms of S. nigrum, a weed in every country," he should "at once hand himself that $10,000 for he has earned it. If, however, he does not consider it good taste to have money or honors thrust upon himself THE R.N.Y. will put in a modest plea for the amount."

In July 1909 the credibility of the Wonderberry suffered a

further blow when the judges at the Boston Flower Show declared it to be worthless. The *Boston Post* of July 18, 1909, noted that "Luther Burbank received the first severe snubbing yesterday when his latest creation the Wonderberry, or Sunberry, was declared a failure . . ." To compound the confusion the *Post* identified the berry as a hybrid produced by crossing *Solanum nigrum* with *Solanum africanum.*

Meanwhile the *Rural New Yorker* kept up the attack. The Wonderberry, Heiser observes, was "mentioned or discussed at length in no fewer than 34 issues," and Collingwood's constant theme was "Do we earn that $10,000?"

But if Burbank was prepared to bet that it wasn't nightshade, neither could he easily prove what it *was.* His chaotic system of record-keeping provided little assistance, and his lack of precautions in hybridizing meant that there was always the possibility that his experimental specimens (or perhaps Childs' nursery-lot multiplications) *had* been fertilized by nightshade pollen from wild plants growing in the vicinity. The common reaction to Childs' product was so negative that it might just as well have been nightshade, however. As one Mississippi lawyer wrote Collingwood:

> Everybody in this section that bit at the fraud, has had the same experience with it—they got nothing but a black nightshade utterly unfit for man or beast to eat, altho they carefully matured it, and not only tried to use the "berry" when it first turned purple, but waited until it was thoroughly ripe, and never were they fit for a duck to eat, either raw or cooked.*

He offered the editor "the thanks of a grateful people" for exposing "Burbank's and Childs' fraud in this matter."[3]

---

*Though the unripe berries of the nightshade are definitely poisonous, the ripe berries are considered safe to eat when cooked. The nightshade family—or *Solanaceae*—to which the Wonderberry belongs includes the potato, *Solanum tuberosum,* and the tomato, both of which plants contain toxic solanum alkaloids (solanine) in their green parts and were once rejected as food partly because of their botanical associations.

Collingwood, in the upshot, thought that though "no one in the country ever expected Mr. Burbank would pay any $10,000 . . . it struck me at the time as it has struck most of the people who have heard about it as a very foolish proposition for a man like Mr. Burbank to make." A responsible horticulturist, in other words, ought not to throw the onus of botanical proof onto his customers when one of his products failed to live up to its advertising. "I don't know," the editor observed,

> of anything in recent years that has stirred up quite such a controversy as this "Wonderberry" proposition, but it is my judgement that Mr. Burbank has made a great mistake in letting the matter go as he has done. He has given the impression, to use a common expression, "That he bluffed without being able to make good."[4]

What was the Wonderberry? Charles B. Heiser, Jr., Professor of Botany at Indiana University, and an expert on the nightshade family, made every effort to find out, and concluded in the end that it was probably identical with a berry called *msoba*, which he obtained from South Africa. He tried some in a pie. "While they don't quite measure up to Childs' claims," he observes, "they are certainly not as bad as the *Rural New Yorker* would have had us believe."[5]

In August 1909, Burbank suffered another assault. A resolution passed by a meeting of the Pasadena Gardeners' Association condemned "the nature-faking methods and exploitations of alleged but false creations by Luther Burbank," deploring the fact that "a false impression has been given the public concerning plant breeding by Burbank." Defending himself in an interview with the San Francisco *Chronicle* shortly after this condemnation, Burbank protested,

> The extravagant estimates of my work have been the bane of my existence. There has been much written about me by sensational writers who know nothing either of me or my work. I am not responsible for all these things and anyone with any knowledge of

horticulture could discern at once that much of the stuff sent out is nothing but the space-writer's chaff.[6]

But there was no getting away from the fact that he had encouraged those sensational writers, and he would continue to encourage them. For what, after all, were the grumblers in Southern California to him? That year he was complimented by the publication of *The Scientific Aspects of Luther Burbank's Work,* a book by his Stanford friends, David Starr Jordan and Vernon Kellogg, that took him very seriously indeed, spoke of his genius, his ability to do things that few other men were capable of, and his extraordinary keenness of perception.[7] The authors were both prominent as scientists (Kellogg, then in his early forties, would later become permanent secretary of the National Research Council), and Burbank must have felt vindicated despite the carping in the trade. At home in Santa Rosa he was elected park commissioner, found it necessary to open an information bureau to deal with the ever-increasing volume of inquiries from the public, and allowed the local ladies to persuade him to ride in the annual rose carnival parade. The latter performance disgusted him to the point of nausea. Though he now was among the most famous men in America, he still found meeting people a painfully distasteful process.

And what of Shull? On August 26, 1909, "a very hot day," he married his second wife, Mary Julia Nicholl, in Brooklyn, New York. They had met on shipboard, returning from Europe, where she had been traveling with her mother. But duty soon called, and by November 1909 he was back in Santa Rosa, writing Davenport that

> Mr. Burbank has practically recovered from his long illness and has been able to finish up to the letter Z, but did not find time to go back over the earlier letters as we had hoped to do. He has asked me to leave with him the records I have of those earlier conferences and he will try to find some time to improve them this winter.

That winter, however, in mid-December, Burbank's mother died, aged ninety-six. Considering her advanced age, it can hardly have been unexpected, but they had shared the same roof for almost sixty years, and few, if any, relationships had been more important to him. Scarcely had he recovered from this blow when he received news that the Carnegie Institution was canceling his grant. In a letter dated December 27, 1909, President Woodward wrote:

> I regret to inform you that the Board of Trustees of the Institution, at their annual meeting, determined to discontinue subsidies in aid of your horticultural work.
>
> It is unnecessary here to set forth the reasons which have led to this action. The possibilities of such a determination were contemplated in drawing up the letter sent you under date of December 29, 1904 . . . The probability of such action was also indicated to you in the summer of 1908 on the occasion of my last visit to you.

Woodward concluded by hoping "that we may be able to complete for publication at no distant date the record of your work drawn up by Dr. Shull."

When Shull returned in May 1910, he found Burbank falling back on his earlier plea: he had no time to give him more help. "He says he has no income now, and that his time is worth $500-$600 an hour," he reported. Though Burbank was friendly enough to him personally and showed him his newer cultures and results (among them a Chinese climbing plum called "Mao-Li-Dzi" which Burbank thought might be a new species), Shull decided that he could expect little or nothing more from him in the preparation of his report.

He now submitted the first completed section of this—dealing with the subject of rhubarb—to President Woodward, with copies to his colleagues Davenport and MacDougal for their criticisms. Since this was the only section he ever did complete, it is perhaps worth looking at in some detail.

Rhubarb seems to have originated in central Asia and was

first cultivated there for medicinal purposes—the roots being used as a drug. By the latter part of the sixteenth century the plant itself had been introduced to Italy, and is known to have been grown near Padua. It reached England early in the seventeenth century, and as one of the earliest of fresh spring vegetables, and the only one which is a dietary substitute for fruit, it came to be prized as a culinary herb in private kitchen gardens. During the nineteenth and early twentieth centuries, Shull notes, there was a considerable demand for it, in supplying which a number of fortunes were made. Later, with the increasing availability of fresh fruit, the demand slackened off, and today it is comparatively little eaten, though a good source of vitamins A and C, as well as of iron and calcium.

Like all economic plants in long cultivation, it had given rise to numerous varieties, and when Burbank began to study it he found that the seedlings differed greatly in earliness, in thickness, length and color of the stalks, compactness of growth and cooking quality. He crossed a number of species but found that the hybrids did not compare with the best varieties already in existence, all of which apparently derived from *Rheum rhaponticum*, and perhaps also from *Rheum undulatum*, two of the species he was experimenting with.

Though it could be forced in greenhouses and cellars, the normal rhubarb season was then limited to a period of from four to six weeks in early spring. About 1890 Burbank heard of a new variety introduced in Australia and New Zealand, called Topp's Winter Rhubarb, which produced stalks during the winter as well as in spring. Practically an everbearing variety, it originated, apparently, from a seedling raised by a market gardener named Topp at Buninyong, Victoria. It had a better flavor and a finer crimson color than the old varieties, but the stalks were small, and it quickly ran to seed.

Burbank immediately saw the importance of obtaining a winter-bearing variety and ordered some of the plants. The first two or three consignments failed, as they died aboard ship, but eventually about 1892 he obtained about half a dozen small roots from D. Hay & Son, nurserymen of Auckland, New Zealand.

He multiplied his stock, and the seed was carefully harvested and planted over several years. All the plants raised reproduced true to their habit of winter bearing, though differing widely in other respects. The best individuals were selected each season, and by November 1, 1900, he was ready to offer these as "a new vegetable—the Australian Crimson Winter Rhubarb," in a circular which, to emphasize its winter growth, had a photograph on the cover of a one-year-old plant of the new variety taken on Christmas day.

Coincidentally, the same variety was imported into England from Australia about the same time, improved in much the same way by English seedsmen, and exhibited there at the Drill Hall Exhibition in London in 1903, as "Sutton's Crimson Rhubarb" and "Topp's Winter Rhubarb."

In 1902 Burbank turned over his stock to John Lewis Childs for distribution, and Childs, as usual, lavished on it a too-glowing description—particularly with regard to its being "robust and perfectly hardy anywhere." Burbank was ultimately forced to correct this impression in a circular dated June 1909, declaring that "Unfortunately I have not so far succeeded in producing a perpetual rhubarb which can profitably be grown in the cold Northern States . . . *These new rhubarbs will not be profitable out of doors where the Eucalyptus, the Orange, and the Fig can not be grown.*" In Southern California, particularly, however, the Crimson Winter Rhubarb did wonderfully. One grower reported harvesting seven tons of stems from three-quarters of an acre set out the previous year. Results were so good that a grower at Whittier nicknamed it "The California mortgage-lifter," and this sobriquet seems to have stuck.

Burbank went on with his work with rhubarbs, and by seedling selection alone produced several other varieties. "Burbank's Giant Winter Rhubarb" was sold to Childs in 1905 for $1500, and another variety, called "Burbank's Wonder Winter," was released in 1906.

When Shull was writing, Burbank was still at work in a small way, "having at the present time several dozen varieties of large-growing plants which are in the process of being tested and which were offered for sale as 'Select Improved Giant Varieties Mixed' in a circular issued in June, 1909."

It is a success story, and if not a very spectacular one, is enhanced by the fact that this was only one of numerous varieties he was improving at the time. This must always be borne in mind. While other breeders attacked the isolated salients that took their particular fancy, Burbank advanced over the broadest possible front.

One thing that clearly emerges from the rhubarb report, however, is that no magical abilities were involved: it was what anyone might have done—what Sutton & Sons did do almost simultaneously in England—given native wit and enterprise.

Toward the end of 1910, Shull wrote Davenport, "I am not complaining about the Burbank work. It has been exceedingly trying at times, but it has also been very pleasant in many ways and I am sure that the experience and knowledge gained will always be useful to me, as well as a source of satisfaction." Burbank had been kind to him from first to last, he felt, though rather free in his expression of disapproval of his treatment by the institution. As to the report, Shull hoped "to have it finished before next spring." But that was not to be.

Meanwhile work on the rival publication was also somewhat bogged down. The Cree Publishing Company had initially planned for the publication of a monumental account of the man and his work, to be written by Burbank himself, with editorial supervision by the Reverend Dr. William Mayo Martin and scientific advice from Dr. Leroy Abrams of Stanford. Abrams was in the field as early as 1907, and Martin set up shop in the old preearthquake Burbank cottage with a stenographer to tackle the editorial work.

Progress was slow, for Burbank was tugged two ways. On the one hand, he wanted very much to have the books, on the other

he could not easily provide his editor with the necessary material. Records were wanting, for a start. But the main problem was
that the projected work was to glorify him in exactly the way
Harwood had done—or rather more so. And he had scruples.
Besides, he knew very well that the people whose opinions he
most valued were not to be impressed with that kind of thing.

Charisma is a double-edged instrument. He was trapped by
his admirers. Reflected in their eyes was the image of himself
that they wanted to see. But he knew, at the same time, that it
was not a true image. All his training was for honesty: being
true to oneself. Anything less made the whole enterprise mean-
ingless. But he had this power—and it had nothing to do with
horticulture—of making other people see him larger than life.
And he had this weakness: he enjoyed their praise far too
much.

Now as to the books, only he could really write them, and if
he wrote honestly they must deflate the legend. He could not lie
and tell the public he was a wizard. Neither, however, could he
tell the strict truth and disabuse them. So he vacillated, as he
had vacillated in telling Shull his story. The Reverend Dr. Mayo
Martin and Dr. Leroy Abrams struggled with the vast mass of
what *seemed* like material: the catalogs, circulars and bro-
chures—over seventy of them by 1910, the books of clippings,
the thousands upon thousands of scribbled notes. Somehow,
when looked at more closely, the clouds of evidence on which
their ten volumes were to be based dissipated into thin air, leaving behind only the mute proofs on the ground—impossible
now to decipher with any degree of accuracy—and the man
himself, who would not be pinned down.

After a while Dr. Leroy Abrams and the Reverend Dr. Mayo
Martin gave up. Their places were filled by Oscar Binner, now
operating as a company, "Luther Burbank's Publishers," at
Santa Rosa, and by Wickson, who still cared and believed that
this story should be told. As for Burbank—the "Boss" they
called him—he was endlessly busy, especially with cactus.

In the end he would introduce thirty-four forage varieties.

There were critics to be answered and the struggle to obtain for his opuntias the fair trial they had never had. He was increasingly bitter.

> Nearly two hundred and forty thousand dollars of my own private earnings in other lines have been used in this work, not one-tenth of which has ever been received in return, nor was it expected, as few originators of new plants have ever made it pay themselves no matter how many untold millions their work may have been of benefit to others, . . .

he wrote in a pamphlet entitled *How to Judge Novelties,* issued in January 1911.

> No patent can be obtained on any improvement of plants, and for one I am glad that it is so. The reward is in the joy of having done good work, and the impotent envy and jealousy of those who know nothing of the labor and sacrifices necessary, and who are by nature and cultivation, kickers rather than lifters.
>
> Happening however to be endowed wth a fair business capacity I have so far never been stranded as have most others who have attempted similar work, even on an almost infinitely smaller scale.

In any case, we would be mistaken in thinking that his critics were ubiquitous. There were many in the trade who had no ax to grind, and a real sense besides of what he had achieved. As the introducer of so many invaluable varieties of plum, he was the star attraction at the Fruit Grower's Convention held in December of that year. A large portrait of him, appropriately draped, hung over the president's chair. Burbank modestly took the last chair in the last row, flanked by George Roeding, the "father of Smyrna fig culture in California," and the faithful Oscar Binner. "When Mr. Burbank was finally called upon by the Chair and he stepped up to the platform," Binner noted, "I had my doubts as to his talk being a success, but, after the first question had been fired at him, and I saw with what ease he

answered it and how he kept this up from Cactus to fodder, alfalfa to plums, from berries to apples and so on, it was a revelation to me."[8]

Binner was hard at work putting together and classifying the
illustrations for the books now. He thought that the project was
progressing well, but was anxious "that what is being done is
done *right*." In a letter dated January 21, 1912, Wickson
warned him:

> You must always be looking out for "bearings." I will fix the
> spots you indicate and the author may pass it without your rais-
> ing an issue. As you indicate he is really in conflict with himself
> and unconsciously with the history of plant breeding also. I
> think I can bring out his real meaning better than he does him-
> self for I think I know what he means. He naturally does not
> wish people to get the idea that such plant breeding as he has
> done is easy and so uses some phrases to which the general read-
> er would give too much technical significance. I am sure I can fix
> it. Keep on the line you are following. Shoot the thing all full of
> holes if you can!

Burbank, Binner reported back on February 5, was now
"ripe" for pushing the books to completion. Usually it was the
other way around, but now he was "itching" to hurry them
along. Since he could not be pushed or driven, he observed, it
was essential to cash in on this frame of mind. He asked Wickson to come up to Santa Rosa for a few days to go over the work
in detail with Burbank. "He feels that he is in the dark—grop-
ing about in a mass of stuff, some of which may be good; some
he feels would not do. He is uncertain and wants to know *definitely*, and I know that *you* can give him the desired information."

Evidently, however, the work was not being accomplished
speedily enough to satisfy the Cree Publishing Company. Early
in 1912 the project changed hands. A new firm, the Luther

Burbank Press,* was organized by John Whitson and Robert John, with the latter as president. The Cree people bowed out of the picture—handsomely compensated for a company that was over $30,000 in the red.

Even before this, however, Whitson and John had set up the Luther Burbank Society (incorporated on April 3, 1912) with a view to promoting the forthcoming books. Membership of the society was to be limited to five hundred, with the first hundred to be regarded as "charter members." Invitations to prospective members were sent out, a subscription of $1 being requested, and the publishers promised to send proofs of the forthcoming multivolume work to the members to criticize and help edit! The procedure was to be thoroughly democratic, but the ten volumes would cost the subscribers $15 each. It was a not untypical scheme, bearing all the marks of the most unscrupulous type of exploitation. "My own invitation," says Howard, then a young instructor in horticulture at the University of Missouri,

> stressed the importance of quick acceptance as it was pointed out that only a few of the most important people of the United States were being invited and that I had the honor of being one of the number. To emphasize this point the invitations bore serial numbers. Mine was somewhere in the seventies. With the feeling that an obscure instructor had been mis-catalogued, I dropped the invitation in the waste basket. In a month or two a second invitation came along, this time bearing a much lower number—thirty-five or forty or thereabouts. This went the way of the first.

These invitations evidently went out to horticulturists and botanists at institutions throughout the country. If a plan had especially been devised to prejudice them against the very name of Burbank, it could scarcely have been more effective.

In terms of the original arrangement with Whitson and John,

---

*Incorporated under the laws of the State of Maine on May 23, 1912.

Burbank was to have received an advance of $30,000 and additional royalties on books sold. Apparently, however, he was paid only a small part of this, perhaps waiving the balance for the moment in view of the financial exigencies of the operation as a whole. Meanwhile a bond issue of $300,000 to finance the work was advertised in the Santa Rosa *Press-Democrat,* commencing on November 3, 1912. The Luther Burbank Press, according to the full-page advertisement, "was originally set up by a group of prominent people from all over the United States who subscribed a total of $600,000 worth of stock—fully paid up, $480,000 preferred and $120,000 common . . ." It was, they claimed,

> the biggest business undertaking of its kind not only in Santa Rosa but anywhere west of New York and will turn over several million dollars a year at a profit of nearly half the turnover . . . The Company's securities have not been offered to the general public heretofore, and the present offer is confined to Sonoma County for special reasons, namely: the company will need the cooperation of Sonoma County residents in securing larger postal facilities from the Post Office Department, in petitioning the Interstate Commerce Commission for more equitable freight and express rates (since, when the delivery of the books commences, the company's freight and express bills will exceed $100,000 a year), in securing from the Department of Agriculture unpublished or private statistics or information, and from the Panama Pacific Exposition better than ordinary concessions.

The literature of the society contained explicit criticisms of the "other report"—which, it implied, had been dropped. "The Carnegie Institution of Washington appropriated a large sum of money for the promulgation of Mr. Burbank's discoveries," read an invitation to life membership issued in 1912. "But after several years of effort, this project was abandoned, because it was the purpose of the Carnegie Institution to limit the field of writing to pure science, whereas Mr. Burbank's steadfast ambition was to give the benefits of his life struggle to the many instead of the few." This by means of books priced at $150 a set—an amount which, *mutatis mutandis,* should be considered the equivalent of rather more than $750 in our own terms. "It is the *clear, practical* exposition of *everyday* methods which the Carnegie Institution would have made secondary to theories and science," the invitation adds, in a further appeal to populist sentiment.

On September 1, 1913, a professional writer, Henry Smith Williams, was hired to produce the clear, practical exposition, replacing John Beaty, who himself had succeeded the Reverend Dr. Mayo Martin, Dr. Leroy Abrams, Wickson and Binner on the job. Williams was an experienced compiler of semi-scientific books, including several encyclopedias. He now set to work to pull together the material accumulated by his predecessors (said to amount to some one and a half million words) with all due speed. This he did so efficiently that by November 25 the first volume was at long last ready for the printers. By this time over $236,000 had apparently been spent on "educational propaganda, materials and publications to date."

Already the promoters were eagerly anticipating the expansion of their scheme. In a brochure directed at potential investors, they looked forward to five special editions in addition to the first. These were to be:

1. Popular edition in 8 volumes to be sold to 7,000,000 farmers and 4,000,000 rural and suburban people—50,000 sets at a net profit of $10 a set.
2. The text book edition, consisting of a series of 8 books, 2 for primary, 2 for grammar, 2 for high school, and 2 for college grades—17,000,000 copies annually, $1,200,000 at a profit of $200,000.
3. Special reinforced library edition, 8 volumes, same as popular edition except bound especially strong for frequent handling—15,000 copies. The Burbank books are a necessity to the libraries and their entire demand can be supplied within two years at a profit of $300,000.

4. The special Monograph Edition, consisting of a series of approximately 3,000 bound bulletins and booklets to sell at 10 to 50 cents, each dealing with one specific subject, to solve the soil tiller's specific problems and to give him precise information on specific subjects, the information to be collected from reports of the United States Department of Agriculture and of the various states. An estimated business of $250,000 a year can be developed at a profit of about $50,000 a year.

5. Foreign edition, of 8 volumes, same as American Popular Edition but translated into French, German, Italian, Spanish, Japanese, and Russian, and adapted for sale in England, Australia, South Africa, and Canada. Total market as great as for the United States.

It is hard to believe that anyone at all could have been taken in by this amazing farrago of rapaciousness and optimism. Howard has pointed out that edition number four, the so-called "Monograph Edition," amounted to nothing less than a proposal to cash in on the agricultural publications and bulletins issued *free* by Federal and state governments, the presumption being that, with Burbank's name attached to them, people could be persuaded to pay for what they could otherwise obtain gratis from the Department of Agriculture and the experiment stations. But evidently many people were sufficiently impressed. The mail-order business was booming, so much so that the Santa Rosa post office had to be reclassified upward more than once to cope with the volume generated by the activities of the society.

As it happened, the Carnegie Institution had by no means abandoned the idea of producing its own report. Shull was busy on work of his own during most of 1912. In a letter to President Woodward, dated August 20 of that year, he observed that he had always felt it better that "the Burbank book should be backed by a scientific reputation made by original research than that my research should be estimated on the basis of a reputation created by the Burbank book." In September 1913, however, he felt ready to resume writing up his findings. He had other reasons for wanting to spend some time in Germany, and on September 10 he sailed for Europe with the intention of settling down in Berlin to finish the job.

THIRTEEN

The Luther Burbank Company

JUST HOW MUCH Burbank himself had to do with the Luther Burbank Society and Press is a matter of conjecture. Presumably he was not at all involved in their promotional activities, which clearly bear the stamp of different hands. He doubtless gave Williams what help he could and perhaps dictated some new material. But the new editor was not afflicted with the hesitations and scruples of his predecessors. He had before him the material already assembled by Wickson, Binner and the Reverend Mayo Martin and his helpers, as well as some which had originally been given to Shull. His instructions were to get on with the job and produce a readable—and salable—account. Where expansion became necessary, he found it easy enough simply to fill up the gaps, not hesitating to put his own words into Burbank's mouth, if needs be, and occasionally emerging into the text himself (it was supposedly written by Burbank) and referring to the subject in the third person.

245

That Burbank—who had always resented interlopers on his property and the interference of outsiders in general—was prepared to put up with this is evidence of his state of mind at the time. Williams left him alone, and attended to his business, and was not always after him to supply answers to unresolved difficulties. For the moment he was satisfied with that. He badly wanted to be free of the secondary entanglements that took him away from his *real* work. Business—and that apparently included literary business—was no pleasure to him. It was this desire to be free that now led him into a second debacle, that in damage to his reputation even outdid the John-Whitson scheme.

This was a new version of the project originally mooted by the Law brothers: a company that would assume responsibility for the marketing of all Burbank's products—past, present and future—and free him to get on with the great, perhaps divinely appointed, work that it was his to do.

The Luther Burbank Company—no connection with the society and press being simultaneously promoted—was incorporated in California on April 22, 1912, by Rollo J. Hough and W. Garner Smith. (Smith, a young San Francisco stockbroker and insurance salesman, was brought in by Hough, an Oakland banker, who was the main motivating force behind the scheme, to be secretary-treasurer of the organization.) The company agreed to pay Burbank $300,000 for exclusive rights to sell all his products, $30,000 in cash and the balance at $15,000 a year. It was provided that he should have the right to name the president of the company and that his attorney, through whom he would be able to approve the other members of the board, be made a director. The lawyer in question, F. S. Wythe of San Francisco, apparently found nothing wrong with the proposal. The contract was accordingly signed, James F. Edwards, a past mayor of Santa Rosa, was named president, and Burbank received his $30,000 down. Stock sales commenced in what appeared to be a very attractive investment. Ultimately some $375,000 in stock was to be sold to the public at par, purchasers including a number of leading San Francisco bankers, merchants and investment brokers.

The main trouble with the scheme was that neither Hough nor Smith had any experience in the highly specialized nursery and seed business. It seemed to them, however, that given the overwhelming public enthusiasm for Burbank's products, and the great respect which his name still commanded, they could hardly go wrong.

Now Burbank seldom had more than a comparatively small stock of his new varieties ready for marketing. It had been his practice heretofore to sell these to established nurserymen, like Childs of New York, who would then propagate, advertise and distribute the product. Even here there were hazards, as the buyer might fail to maintain the integrity of the stock or indulge in unscrupulous advertising which brought the originator's name into disrepute, as had happened with the Wonderberry.

A corporation named the Universal Distributing Company was now established to take over this function. Nurseries and seed farms had to be set up to multiply the stock, if it was to be sold in large quantities, and this seems to have called for an expertise which, at least on the managerial level, the company lacked. To complicate matters, it started out with one of the most controversial of all Burbank's products, the spineless cactus, which was virtually the only thing offered for sale in 1913, the first year of actual operation. The first general catalog, issued in 1914, advertised about a hundred varieties of seed and bulbs as Burbank productions, and went on to list thirty pages of standard varieties. All but a few of the Burbank varieties had previously been offered in his own earlier catalogs. Seeds of the standard varieties were apparently purchased in bulk from an Eastern firm. The fact that these were listed in a catalog entitled *Burbank Seed Book* probably had the effect of persuading many buyers that they were the work of the master himself.

Sales policies were determined by a man named Hoffer, whose standing instructions were that all orders were to be

filled *regardless of whether or not they had the proper stock on hand.*
How this might be done was illustrated by Fred Suelberger, for
many years horticultural commissioner of Alameda County,
and in that capacity the man responsible for the inspection of
the shipments of plants that passed through the company's
warehouse in Oakland for disease and insect pests. Suelberger
noted that

> great quantities of so-called spineless cactus [were] brought in
> from cactus farms in Livermore and other places to be shipped
> out, presumably for filling orders. The cactus leaves or "slabs"
> were tied up in bales and I particularly recall that Company em-
> ployees were kept busy removing the spines with wire brushes,
> which seemed dishonest as the cactus was supposed to be free of
> spines.[1]

Needless to say, the fraud was detectable as soon as the plants
began to grow, and the indignant buyers invariably gave Burbank credit for having perpetrated it.

The buyers were not the only ones disillusioned. Early in
1914, Smith made a sales tour of the Eastern and Middlewest-
ern states in an attempt to drum up business for the company.
On his return most of the orders he had obtained were turned
down, as there had been a decision to raise prices in his
absence. Smith, at least, had started out with considerable faith
in his product, so much so that he made a collection of all the
Burbank novelties he could get and sent them to be planted on
his father's farm in Kentucky. Everything was planted carefully, but the results were highly disappointing. This is indicative
of the poor quality of the stock being multiplied on the company's farms, and also perhaps of the fact that Burbank himself
was no longer the reliable broker that he once had been. He
was surrounded by charlatans at Santa Rosa, and his dealings
were increasingly with men whose sole interest was to sell his
name and reputation for whatever they could get. Meanwhile

his true friends—Wickson in particular—were falling away in disillusion.

But his fame, increasingly souring to notoriety though it was, continued to spread. In 1912 he traveled to British Columbia with a party promoting the Panama-Pacific Exposition to be held in San Francisco in 1915. He was honored at every stop and was personally greeted at Victoria by the Canadian Minister of Agriculture, who had apparently come all the way from Ottawa specifically to do so. Earlier that year, on February 29, while the House of Representatives was considering the bill making appropriations for the Department of Agriculture for the fiscal year ending June 30, 1913, California Congressman Everis A. Hayes had introduced a bill authorizing the Department of the Interior to turn over twelve sections of desert or semidesert land—totaling 7680 acres—to him for further experiments with spineless cactus. Hayes noted that "in certain quarters there has lately been manifested a desire to belittle this great man and his work." He observed that "a man connected with the Department of Agriculture—I purposely forbear mentioning his name*—has seen fit recently to assail Mr. Burbank and to minimize, even to ridicule, his genius and the great work he has done and is still doing to increase the prosperity and happiness of his fellow men." Teddy Roosevelt was quoted for the defense as saying, "Mr. Burbank is a man who does things that are of much benefit to mankind, and we should do all in our power to help him." Attention was drawn to the fact that "99% of the plums shipped out of California are of varieties originated by Burbank and practically all the potatoes." The bill passed in the House, only to be defeated in the Senate.

That Burbank himself did not lose his sense of humor over this rancorous issue was testified to by Cecil Houdyshell, who spent some days with him in the spring of 1913 and noted, "I hung around all day. Personally I get rid of people who stick

*This enemy was undoubtedly Dr. David Griffiths, senior horticulturist of the U.S. Bureau of Plant Industry, one of the chief critics of the spineless cactus promotion.

around like I did. But Burbank was always affable, patient and very friendly. Never the unapproachable 'big' man." One afternoon after lunch, Houdyshell was roaming around the gardens at Santa Rosa while Burbank was taking his nap. He had been eating the spineless cactus fruits, which he liked very much, and when Burbank came over from his new house across the street, he was busy trying to remove the tiny spicules that had stuck in his hands. "Ah ha!" Burbank exclaimed. "I see you've been into my spineless cactus." And he laughed at his joke, as much at his own expense as at his visitor's.

Shull, meanwhile, was in Berlin, his energies variously absorbed by his own work and by the task of writing up his Burbank findings. The Carnegie Institution had subscribed to the Williams books on his behalf, though Davenport noted that "the whole thing impresses me as a fake, particularly the way they write those personal letters which are identical with the printed forms . . .

In February 1914 proofs of volume one arrived in Berlin, forwarded on from Cold Spring Harbor. Whether this was by special provision (Burbank being particularly interested to know Shull's opinion) or the normal course of procedure is hard to tell. Other subscribers do not seem to have received proofs and been allowed to participate in the editing of the text, as promised in the prospectuses. Judging by the proofs, Shull wrote Davenport,

> It appears to me a criminal waste of good paper, and the "science" involved in the text is certainly amusing. But it is not for me to criticize; it remains to be seen whether I can do any better. . . . The colored plates will prove both interesting and valuable. Aside from the financial considerations, it is chiefly for these plates that the book will exist.

When in June 1914 the first three completed volumes arrived, with the immediate discovery that "considerable sections are al-

most word for word the same as my manuscript," Shull wondered whether it might not be better for him to simply abandon
his own report. The Carnegie Institution might rest content
"with having supplied the incentive as well as collected the data
for so good an account of Mr. Burbank's work as this." If he
was understandably bitter, there are also clear indications that
he was having trouble with his own writing and would have
been happy to use this pretext as an excuse for dropping the
whole thing: "As you know," he wrote Davenport,

> Dr. Williams is a much more gifted writer than I am, so that it
> seems to me wasteful to spend more time on a work whose chief
> difference lies in a less elegant style of presentation and more
> meagre illustrations. I am quite convinced that most of the value
> of the work has been attained through the competition with the
> Carnegie Institution, and I am personally content with that re-
> sult if the Institution should decide to go no further with its re-
> port on Mr. Burbank's work—only, I think that in that case the
> sooner we decide to drop the matter the better.

Davenport, on the point of leaving for Australia, cabled a suc-
cinct reply: "Stop." On June 28, the day before Shull's letter,
the Austrian Archduke Franz Ferdinand had been assassinated
at Sarajevo. World War I was about to begin and would be
offered in the Carnegie Institution's annual report for 1914 as
the reason for not finishing the report.

But the excuse was a thin one. Even if all the facts included in
Shull's notes were contained in the Williams' books, they were
so embedded in boastful adulation as to be useless. As Burbank
had told Shull early in 1907, the ten volumes—now expanded
to twelve—would not contain as much "meat" as ten pages of
the Carnegie report. Shull had not merely accepted Burbank's
dictation. He had studied his work objectively with the trained
eye of a geneticist. He was, perhaps, the only fully qualified
person to have done so in detail, and had devoted perhaps half
his time in the preceding eight years to this report. Now he pro-

posed simply to abandon it on the pretext of the European conflict, which had small conceivable relevance.

He drafted a sarcastic letter to Burbank in Berlin on August
1, the day Germany declared war on Russia, in reply to one giving some information he had requested on plum names.

> I was very much pleased to hear that your new books are being
> so well received, and congratulate you on that. I too have read
> them with a great deal of interest of course, and appreciate very
> much the charming manner in which you illustrate the Mendeli-
> an principle. I have noted several slight oversights, which you
> will be glad perhaps to call to the attention of your publishers in
> order that they may be corrected in subsequent editions . . .

Here the draft breaks off. Was it ever sent? What were the cor-
rections? At this late date it is unlikely that we shall ever know.

In 1941 Shull elucidated the position, writing in response to
Howard's request for access to his Burbank notes. "It was a decision of the Carnegie Institution, not myself, that no report
should be made until after Mr. Burbank's demise, but I was in
entire accord with President Woodward on this point," he
wrote.

> With the passing of time the urgency for the publication of a
> report on my experiences has subsided and it has not seemed
> wise to divert my time from my own fundamental researches to
> reanalyze the material and decide how much of it is worthy of
> publication. This reanalysis can be satisfactorily done only by
> myself and must wait until the time when my time and energy
> are not more advantageously devoted to my own special re-
> search problems.

He still felt that he had "a large personal equity" in the accumulated material resulting from his years with Burbank, and
that he would rather make the final report himself than have it
made at second hand by Howard. The latter was, therefore, denied the opportunity of making use of this unrivaled source of

information in preparing his definitive monograph on *Luther Burbank's Plant Contributions* and was also prevented from clarifying the role of the Carnegie Institution, as he would have been able to do had he seen the Shull-Davenport-Woodward correspondence and the minutes of the Carnegie Committee on Burbank.

There remains another possibility, hinted at in volume XII of the Williams' books. This is that Burbank himself had the Shull report suppressed. How he might have done so is a matter of pure conjecture. He did have influential friends, and some sections of the Shull notes which he may have seen could well have been extremely displeasing to him. "Most great undertakings experience a number of false starts before they are finally launched on their way to accomplishment. And such was the case with the beginnings of this work," Williams observes portentously.

> Laboring alone, and many years in advance of his time, it was not to be expected that Luther Burbank could be interpreted in the language of contemporary science. And in fact, with true Yankee keenness, he much preferred that his benefits be reaped directly by those who practice agriculture, rather than by those who merely study agriculture. If both classes could be equally benefited, well and good; but if one had to be slighted, then let it be the studier and not the practicer.
>
> With a willing heart, the able men appointed by the Carnegie Institution co-operated with Mr. Burbank, and the magnitude of the task, whatever the viewpoint, became apparent as page after page of manuscript was boiled together into what promised to become an interminable record.
>
> After a number of years Mr. Burbank saw and keenly realized that the work which had been done fell far short of his ideals—whatever its scientific value, it failed utterly to be the crystal clear presentation for the benefit of the practical man, which had always been his guiding ideal. So the first step toward success ended in what, at the moment, appeared to be but an expensive failure.[2]

George Shull died at Princeton, where he was Professor Emeritus of Botany and Genetics, on September 28, 1954. His work in the development of the pure line method of corn breeding had resulted in increased yields of from 25 to 50 percent, adding more than half a billion dollars a year to the value of the American corn crop without increasing acreage. He received no material recompense for his discoveries. He was content, he said, with the knowledge that he had made an outstanding contribution to the welfare of mankind: a Burbankian sentiment if ever there was one. Though his home had been at Princeton for almost forty years, he chose to be buried at Santa Rosa. His wife, Mary, was buried there beside him on her death twelve years later.

The report on Burbank's work, begun so long ago, was never completed. Perhaps, as he observed, the reanalysis of his notes could only have been done satisfactorily by himself. When these notes were studied by a colleague, Dr. E. Carlton MacDowell, in the late 1950s, the latter concluded that "the real reason that one of the first major projects of the Institution bore almost no fruit, can only be suggested."

It may be that it was a comparatively simple one: Shull, with all his diligence and expertise, found it an impossible task. It is true that he had his own work to do, and by 1914 he was already aware of how important this was likely to be. In later years he suggested that this was the overriding reason, saying that he had

determined from the start and with the full understanding and consent of the administration of the Carnegie Institution, that there would be delay in publication of the results, certainly until after Mr. Burbank's death. My own insistence on delayed publication was for the somewhat selfish reason that I was unwilling to have my reputation as a scientist rest to so large extent as it would have done if early publication had been required, on a work which even under the best of circumstances could not have had the high scientific value of a piece of personal research of my own.[3]

But this smacks of a saving afterthought. During the time that he was at Santa Rosa there is no hint of a suggestion that there was to be a deliberate holding back of the report until after Burbank's death. It seems far more likely that he simply could not write it. Even he could not unscramble the true from the false, the achievements from the exaggerations.

In many ways the real Burbank remains an enigma, even now. Did he in fact have mysterious powers? Or was it rather as the Chicago seedsman, Ralph B. Howe, observed sardonically, "Yes, he was a great man, so was Barnum."[4] Inevitably readers will tend to decide in accordance with their own predilections. So it has always been with Burbank. The truth probably lies somewhere in the middle. He did possess extraordinary capabilities; at the same time he was prepared to exaggerate, sometimes to the brink of falsehood, where his reputation seemed to require it. Those who have studied parapsychological phenomena have not infrequently observed a similar contradiction in other "wild talents."

FOURTEEN

Second Marriage

THE TWELVE WEIGHTY volumes of *Luther Burbank, His Methods and Discoveries and Their Practical Application,* "prepared from his original field notes covering more than 100,000 experiments made during forty years devoted to plant improvement, with the assistance of the Luther Burbank Society and its entire membership, under the editorial direction of John Whitson and Robert John, and Henry Smith Williams, M.D., LL.D.," commenced to appear in 1914. Published by the "Luther Burbank Press, New York and London," and copiously illustrated with "direct color photograph prints produced by a new process devised and perfected for use in these volumes," they were undeniably handsome, with ornate leather bindings, deckle edges and heavy paper watermarked "Luther Burbank Press" in large Old English. The hundreds of color photographs were remarkable for their time, and if some were of such inconsequential subjects as the boxes used by Burbank as seed flats, others were frequently skillfully chosen and composed. If editor-ghost-writer Williams lapsed into the absurdity of attempting to prove that rhubarb introduced from the Southern Hemisphere henceforth followed the calendar rather thari the seasons, and vainly contended that Burbank had hit on Mendel's laws before the rediscovery, this probably went unnoticed, save by a handful of horticulturists. Elaborate descriptions of ordinary techniques of grafting and budding, which had nothing particularly Burbankian about them, were included, and doubtless made quite an impression on the lay reader, who might suppose that these were part of Burbank's contribution to horticultural science. Williams carried the technique of padding—more widely practiced in his day than in our own—to a high art. Even now, one cannot fail to be impressed by his skill. But that, of course, was precisely what he had been hired for.

In January 1915 it was announced that the twelve-volume set was complete, and that the headquarters of the press was being transferred to New York—despite earlier assurances that "the Santa Rosa office is, and will continue to be, the principal place of business." In addition to the elaborate subscribers edition, a somewhat more functional one was evidently brought out for library and institutional use, also in twelve volumes, and plans were underway for the promised popular edition, condensed into eight volumes.

The bubble burst abruptly. Perhaps demand (there seems to be no surviving record of how many sets were published and how many sold) did not meet expectation. At least $400,000 had been spent on the project, and the press was evidently financially overextended. The whole enterprise seems to have collapsed in a matter of months. The announced move to New York was perhaps a preliminary precaution on the part of Whitson and John who probably knew what was coming. Those who had bought stock lost their investments, and needless to say much of the blame was laid at Burbank's door, though he himself claimed that the company owed him $100,000 when it went out of business. On March 12, 1916, the press forfeited its charter to do business in California for nonpayment of taxes, and the promoters (if they had not already done so) went back into the woodwork. Burbank now had his books—he retained copyright—but closely examined they were a strange hotch-potch. Shull, for example, noted that on April 20, 1908, Burbank had told him:

> Now I have what I believe to be the best collection of Amaryllis on earth. At least all those that know the Amaryllis in Europe and America who have visited my grounds pronounce them far superior to any they have ever seen, not only in size, but rapid multiplication and general effectiveness.

While Volume IX, page 98, of the Williams books read:

> From a mere horticultural standpoint, it is considered by experts to be the best collection of Amaryllis in the world. Not only has this colony the greatest diversity of forms but the most extraordinary individual plants.
> Experts of both Europe and America who have visited my grounds are agreed in pronouncing my galaxies of Amaryllis far superior to any to be seen elsewhere, *not only in size but in rapid multiplication and general effectiveness.* [Italics added.]

It seemed obvious to Shull that his own notes had gone into the compilation of this text, and the community of horticultural and agricultural scientists—of which he was an increasingly prominent member—probably knew it too before very long.

From Burbank's point of view, one of the most grievous casualties was his friendship with Edward Wickson, who had put a good deal of work into preparing the earlier draft of the books and received no shape or form of acknowledgment. He, too, now joined the ranks of the disillusioned. That Burbank was painfully aware of this is testified to by a letter dated April 20, 1916, in protest. Formally beginning "Dear Sir" in place of the old "Dear Friend Wickson," he observes:

I used to feel that I had your sympathy and confidence, but of late I know that I have not—not from what you have written, but from the attitude you have taken. Frankly—I had given you credit for having discrimination enough to know that the treatment which you received from the pirate book publishers was not Luther Burbank and I judge that their treatment of *you* has changed your attitude towards *me*. Future events will prove or disprove this.

I have no possible feeling towards you otherwise than the kindest and have been surprised and hurt at the attitude which you have taken on several occasions during the last year or two.

But it seems to have been too late to mend this fence.

Meanwhile the Luther Burbank Company was also moving toward catastrophe. Early in 1914 dividends as high as 12 percent had been paid to stockholders. Heavy sales of cactus provided momentum, but these inevitably fell off when the company's sharp practices began to come to light. Financial difficulties commenced and that spring saw the resignations of James Edwards and Garner Smith, both of them presumably disgusted by sales policy. They did not relinquish their stock, however, as they would have been well advised to do, and are said to have ultimately lost some $100,000 between them when the crash came. Dividends soon dropped to 6 percent, and then ceased entirely, and Burbank himself was obliged to accept promissory notes instead of cash.

Finally, in December 1915 he brought suit in the Superior Court of San Francisco for recovery of $9775 owed him. He had long delayed action—some of the stockholders were, after all, close friends. "Burbank has been the victim of stock pirates," one of his attorneys now declared. "This Company was formed three years ago. He took no stock in it and no interest in it. Some of the best men in town have also been made victims . . . " The contract was declared void, further use of Burbank's name was forbidden and another suit for $15,000, also in arrearages, was threatened. On February 8, 1916, the company was declared bankrupt, stockholders receiving little or no compensation from remaining assets, and in July of that year Burbank gave notice in a leaflet that he was resuming full control of his nursery and seed business himself.

Pirate book publishers . . . stock pirates . . . he had been imposed on all around. One of his secretaries, Miss Pauline W. Olson, who worked for him on and off between 1905 and 1912 and subsequently, thought him to have been a poor businessman, "careless, sloppy and unsystematic in his business affairs," and despite Burbank's own assertions to the contrary ("Happening to be endowed with a fair business capacity . . . "), she was probably right. He was shrewd enough, but lacked sufficient interest to manage business affairs on this scale well.

Stockholders and scientists might be disillusioned, but there is no indication that the general public had fallen out of love with him. And 1915 provided him with a propaganda countercoup to match his defeats. That October, almost at the peak of his troubles, Henry Ford and Thomas Alva Edison, visiting the great Panama-Pacific Exposition in San Francisco, took time out to pay their respects, traveling to Santa Rosa in Ford's private railway car in order to do so, and bringing in their entourage a small party of notables, among them Harvey Firestone.

It was no impromptu call. Burbank had extended the invitation to them in San Francisco a few days before, and arrangements had been made to receive them in proper style. The local paper announced the event in banner headlines, and the newsreel cameramen had been forewarned and were there to report it. (Burbank seemed to enjoy the new medium, readily "performing" for the "moving photo operators" among his spineless cactus, film which had wide circulation on the Pathé news.) Massed school children—in those days few opportunities were lost of dragging them into the act—had been assembled to pay homage to the three famous men. Everything had been stage-managed to perfection.

Since late 1914, Burbank had had a new private secretary, Elizabeth Jane Waters, who was eventually to be his second wife. Though her people had originally come from Massachusetts, and there was some talk of her being distantly related to the Burbanks, she was a Michigan girl with a strict Seventh Day Adventist background. On coming to California, she first went to San Jose, where she had a sister. Later she moved to Santa Rosa, bringing with her a child, Betty Waters, who was a few years old at the time. She started work with the Luther Burbank Press, but presently transferred to Burbank's own office, displacing Miss Pauline Olson, a local woman who had worked for him for more than seven years. Now she was there to share the duties of entertaining Ford and Edison with Emma Beeson—who can scarcely have appreciated the division of honors.

Elizabeth Waters was henceforth increasingly to be found at Burbank's side, taking a prominent place again in April 1916 when he was a guest of honor at a local parade (he had evidently not entirely sickened of parades). It was probably no surprise when they were married on December 21, 1916, by the pastor of the First Unitarian Church of San Francisco. But, as such marriages do, it certainly set tongues wagging; she was then in her mid-twenties, he was sixty-seven. Their honeymoon, the first real holiday Burbank had had in a long time, was a week in San Diego at the home of a friend.

Meanwhile, despite all criticisms, the publicity mechanism rolled on: once started, perhaps, it could no longer be stopped. In 1917 the California State Board of Education published a booklet on *Conservation, Bird and Arbor Day* that might have been deliberately designed to idealize Burbank. It came into wide use in elementary schools all over the country, with predictable effects on the generation then attending them. There were many, even among his critics, who did not want to see him debunked. George Shull succinctly voiced this opinion:

> It is my impression . . . that he was a man of the finest, cleanest character of any person I have ever known. I always felt that he was the sort of man who *deserved* to be a popular hero . . . Because of his clean life and formally expressed high ideals I have always wished to avoid saying anything which would tend to take

Mr. Burbank off of his popular pedestal. The ideals expressed in his various writings on childhood, and the advertised motivation of his life work have a highly inspirational significance.[1]

He was above all a hero of his time, and only time itself would dethrone him.

In April 1917 the United States entered the war against Germany and her allies, and although Burbank was an ardent pacifist, his reaction was much that of his friend, David Starr Jordan, who told the San Francisco *Bulletin*:

> *Our country is now at war and the only way out is forward.* I would not change one word I have spoken against war. But that is no longer the issue. We must now stand together in the hope that our entrance into Europe may in some way advance the cause of Democracy and hasten the coming of lasting peace.

In 1918 Burbank was to be found listed as a member of a "National Emergency Food Garden Commission," aimed at inspiring the planting of a million home food gardens. On the business side, he introduced several new varieties of grain, promoted as the answer to the food shortage provoked by the European conflict.

One of these was a wheat he called "Quality," seed of which was sold for $5 a pound, or $300 a bushel. After it had been grown for several years, it was found to be identical with an Australian wheat called "Florence," which had actually been tested at experiment stations in the Western states as early as 1914, but not released. It evidently did have commercial potential (some six thousand acres were still listed as being planted to Florence, or Burbank's Quality, as late as 1949 in Montana, Idaho, South Dakota and Oregon), but he was inevitably accused of sharp practice. How he came to reintroduce Florence in this fashion is a matter of conjecture, and it may simply have been an accident. He could conceivably have produced an identical hybrid, or Florence seed could have found its way into

wheat he had obtained for experimental purposes, been selected out and innocently renamed as a new variety. But many experts thought not, and the fact that the same thing occurred
with another Burbank wheat, named "Super," released the
same year, which was identified as Jones Fife, a variety introduced by the U.S.D.A. in 1893, did nothing to improve his
credibility as a cereal breeder, particularly with the experiment
stations.

As long ago as the 1880s, he had imported seed of quinoa, an
important food crop in pre-Columbian America, from Brazil,
and it had been offered for sale in a descriptive circular of 1897
as, "A new vegetable from Brazil which is easily grown and
promises to be the most valuable of any which has been introduced for years. The seed is the principal food of thousands of
people in Brazil, Peru and Bolivia. It is a delicious vegetable if
cooked like Spinach." This attempt to introduce it as a green
vegetable was a failure, but now, in 1918, he once again endeav-
ored to promote it, this time as "a new breakfast food, a forgotten cereal of the ancient Aztecs." It did not catch on in that capacity either, but this may well be one of Burbank's ideas that is
worthy of further consideration. In the high altitudes of the
Andes, where the tiny seeds are ground up for flour or por-
ridge, quinoa is said to produce more bushels per acre than
perhaps any other crop.

That Burbank's business had recovered after the twin debacles
of the Luther Burbank Press and the Luther Burbank Company, or that he was at any rate prospering, is indicated by his gift
in 1921 of $5000 to the development of Doyle Park, which was
presented to the city of Santa Rosa by the banker F. P. Doyle in
memorial to his only son, who had died at the age of fourteen.
Doyle afterward remarked that Burbank had had "a very sentimental interest in the park tract for the reason that when a
young man and new to Santa Rosa . . . he did not attend
church because he considered his clothes to be too shabby, so

instead he spent many Sundays communing with Nature under the trees of what is now Doyle Park."

The torrent of words flowed on. In 1921 an eight-volume condensation of the earlier Williams' books, put together by Burbank and his helpers and entitled *How Plants Are Trained to Work for Man*, was issued by F. P. Collier. It was around this time, too, that Wilbur Hall, the writer who was to ghost Burbank's autobiography, *The Harvest of the Years*, appeared on the scene, and began gathering material. Hall, a hard-drinking atheist, was an unlikely amanuensis for Burbank, but he was a ready flatterer, and the collaboration seemed to work.

Little noticed was the most remarkable visitor he had that year, the great Russian scientist, Nikolai Ivanovich Vavilov (1887–1942), whose work was to be of enormous importance in tracing the origins of cultivated plants and improving Soviet agriculture. (Paradoxically, Burbank's belief in the inheritance of acquired characteristics was later to be adduced in support of the theories of Stalin's protege, T. D. Lysenko, whose baleful influence dominated Soviet plant breeding during the period 1937–1964, and whose supporters hounded Vavilov and many other Soviet geneticsts to their deaths as "Mendelist-Morganist" heretics. Lysenko is on record as referring to Burbank as one of "the best biologists."[2])

What transpired at their meeting is unfortunately not recorded. Famine conditions prevailed in Russia—it was the period of "war communism" and the *cordon sanitaire*—and 1920 and 1921 were years of drought into the bargain. Soviet agricultural scientists were searching for new varieties, new strains of wheat, rye and barley in particular, to alleviate the hunger of their people. Vavilov was well aware that much of Burbank's own success lay in his canny importations of breeding stock. He later noted that the success of breeders "such as I. V. Michurin, Burbank, and Hansen, is chiefly based upon their use, in crossing, of extensive varietal materials from foreign countries."[3] Among the material he obtained from Burbank may have been seed of a new variety of sunflower the latter had recently introduced. Improvement in this plant would have been of considerable interest to Russian growers, in whose country sunflowers are extensively raised for the oil from their seeds.

Vavilov, who would later forfeit his life for his Mendelism, would undoubtedly have disagreed with his host's theoretical conclusions, were such matters discussed. Burbank's point of view had much in common with the Michurin-Lysenko theories he was subsequently obliged to do battle with. Lysenko's proposition that "Heredity is the concentrate, as it were, of the environmental conditions assimilated by plant organisms in a series of preceding generations," sounds almost like a paraphrase of Burbank's dictum that "Heredity is the sum of all past environments." Both in implication reject the genetic interpretation now almost universally current. Though true enough, and sounding profound, they are half-truths, .oversimplifications that contribute little to the understanding of the nature of descent and variation.

In December 1924 Burbank had a visitor of a very different stamp. Paramahansa Yogananda had arrived in America in September 1920 as a delegate to the International Congress of Religious Liberals, held that year in Boston under the auspices of the American Unitarian Association. Remaining after the congress was over, he visited Santa Rosa in the course of a transcontinental lecture tour in 1924. (This seems to have been a great success, inasmuch as Yogananda was able to found his Self-Realization Fellowship in Los Angeles the following year.) He and Burbank apparently hit it off wonderfully together. Yogananda tells in his autobiography of Burbank's remarking that in working with spineless cactus he had often talked to the plants "to create a vibration of love," saying, "You don't need your defensive thorns. I will protect you."[4] Evidently he also told Yogananda that his mother had appeared to him in visions and spoken to him many times since her death. For his part the Swami dubbed Burbank "an American saint," and dedicated his own *Autobiography of a Yogi* to him as such. When Burbank died, he informs us, he conducted a Vedic memorial rite in New York before a large picture of him.

He had apparently initiated Burbank into his technique of Kriya Yoga—described as a "simple, psychophysiological method by which human blood is decarbonated and recharged with oxygen" with "nothing in common with the unscientific breathing exercises taught by a number of misguided zealots"—and Burbank is quoted as saying, "I practice the technique devoutly, Swamiji." Yogananda also obtained an endorsement from him, reproduced in facsimile in the *Autobiography of a Yogi*. In a letter dated December 22, 1924, Burbank declares that

I have examined the Yogoda system of Swami Yogananda and in my opinion it is ideal for training and harmonizing man's physical, mental, and spiritual natures. Swami's aim is to establish 'How-to-Live' schools throughout the world, wherein education will not confine itself to intellectual development alone, but also training of the body, will, and feelings.

Through the Yogoda system of physical, mental, and spiritual unfoldment by simple and scientific methods of concentration and meditation, most of the complex problems of life may be solved, and peace and good-will come upon earth. The Swami's idea of right education is plain commonsense, free from all mysticism and non-practicality; otherwise it would not have my approval.

I am glad to have this opportunity of heartily joining with the Swami in his appeal for international schools on the art of living which, if established, will come as near to bringing the millennium as anything with which I am acquainted.[5]

FIFTEEN

"I Love Everything!"

THE YEARS HAD taken their toll. Despite Yogananda's Kriya
Yoga, despite the outdoor life and the temperance he so vigor-
ously championed,[1] despite his own protective hypochondria,
he was an old, unwell man. The best years of his work were
long behind him in the 1890s. In the eyes of those whose opinions he most valued he was at no very great remove from being
a fraud. He was too hardheaded to have much respect for the
legions of his admirers. How much enthusiasm could he, for
example, have had for the birthday pageant concocted in his
honor by the egregious Ada Kyle Lynch? Commencing and
ending with a special "Burbank March," it assembled a troupe
of unfortunate schoolchildren, costumed as "flowers, fruits,
buds or blossoms," or allegorically got up as Father Time, the
Seasons, America, Other Nations and what not, chanting the
authoress's "descriptive poem," "Luther Burbank," and singing
her unmelodious "Birthday Song" and "All Hail to Luther Bur-

269

bank." Four were selected to read his life story, dressed as roses, white, red, yellow and pink. The "Birthday Song" followed, with one member of the cast carrying a large banner with a "picture of Mr. Burbank in the center, bordered with a large heart of red. Above the heart in large green letters and figures is the date of Mr. Burbank's birth, and just below the apex of the heart the number of years of the birthday being celebrated." The whole farrago took three-quarters of an hour, concluding with a Yell. It was the sort of thing to make any genuine child lover cringe; and Burbank was undoubtedly a genuine child lover.[2]

Who was to carry on his work after his death? This nagging question had by no means been decided. Various plans that were mooted to convert his gardens into an experiment station to be operated by the two universities, Stanford and Berkeley, had come to naught—largely for want of adequate financial support, but also in large measure as a result of departmental opposition. His reputation with academic horticulture, particularly with the younger generation of scientists, was by now hopelessly muddied. In 1922 he hired Will Henderson, an assistant who turned out to be especially promising and who was gradually given an unprecedented degree of responsibility. But he never committed himself to naming Henderson his successor, and the latter being very young—still in his early twenties when Burbank died—no transfer of authority ever took place.

The newspapers, dubbing him "the Wise Man of the West," continued to seek his opinions on everything under the sun, and he could never resist giving them. An interview with the San Francisco *Examiner* in 1925 elicited pronouncements on subjects ranging from current homicides to jazz. With crime he could apply his theories of hybrid nature, declaring, "We have more geniuses and more criminals than any other nation." Jazz, about which he knew nothing, he simply denounced: "I hate the very word and as for the thing itself and all it stands for, I can't bear even to think of it." SPIRIT OF JAZZ WILL DRAG RACE TO LEVEL OF SAVAGES, SAYS SAGE ran the headline.[3]

In January of 1926, Edgar Waite, a young reporter for the San Francisco *Bulletin* visited him to ask for an interview. Casting about for some suitable subject for "copy," he asked Burbank for his views on the question of immortality. In trying to answer him, Burbank chanced to refer to himself as an "infidel."[4] This casual remark instantly impressed the reporter as front-page material, and so—given Burbank's status as hero of the Sunday schools—it was. The Scopes trial was only a few months in the past, and victory, however wretched, in Tennessee, had perked up fundamentalist courage. "Infidel" was translated to agnostic and atheist, and the news flashed around the world, linking his name with those of Bob Ingersoll, Tom Paine and Bolshevism. It is difficult now to conceive of the furor it created. Fifty years have all but obliterated the America that was then so incensed. In Santa Rosa itself women of the evangelical churches formed prayer groups to beseech God that Burbank be enabled to see the light. The Sonoma County Women's Christian Temperance Union—of which he was an honorary life member—slightingly invited him to a mass meeting organized to pray for his soul. (He communicated his regrets, and reportedly only ten of the ladies turned up for this pious occasion.) Letters poured in abusing him as an atheist, and he was besieged by demands that he recant his statement. His friends sought to find an opportunity for him to answer his critics, and he finally accepted an invitation from Dr. James L. Gordon, pastor of the First Congregational Church in San Francisco.

He spoke on the last Sunday in January, and more than twenty-five hundred people crammed into a church with a seating capacity of two thousand in order to hear him. Hundreds of them, his friend Frederick Clampett remarked, had perhaps not attended a church service for years. Burbank was under a considerable nervous strain. "There was something strangely fascinating about the man as he stood there," Clampett wrote afterward. "His clear, thin voice filled that vast auditorium. Frail in form, with pale face and classic head, no man, I will venture to say, ever stood on that spot whose personality suggested such startling contrasts. It seemed to me as if a prophet had sprung to life out of the ages. Knowing his dread of public functions, his shyness and reserve, I followed his opening sentences, my own throat tight with misgiving. But I was soon made to realize that he more than measured up to the requirements of the occasion. As he went on with slow, almost hesitating speech, a stillness like unto death came over the great audience, and men and women hung upon every word he uttered in a kind of spell."[5]

"I love everybody! I love everything!" Burbank began. "Some people seem to make mistakes, but everything and everybody has something of value to contribute or they would not be here.

"I love humanity, which has been a constant delight to me during all my seventy-seven years of life; and I love flowers, trees, animals and all the works of Nature as they pass before us in time and space. What a joy life is when you have made a close working partnership with Nature, helping her to produce for the benefit of mankind new forms, colors and perfumes in flowers which were never known before; fruits in form, size, color and flavor never before seen on this globe; and grains of enormously increased productiveness, whose fat kernels are filled with more and better nourishment, a veritable storehouse of perfect food—new food for all the world's untold millions for all time to come.

"All things—plants, animals and men—are already in eternity traveling across the face of time, whence we know not, whither who is able to say. Let us have one world at a time and let us make the journey one of joy to our fellow passengers and just as convenient and happy for them as we can, and trust the rest as we trust life.

"Let us read the Bible without the ill-fitting colored spectacles of theology, just as we read other books, using our own judgment and reason, listening to the voice, not to the noisy babble without. Most of us possess discriminating reasoning powers. Can we use them or must we be fed by others like babes?

"I love especially to look into the deep, worshipful, liquid eyes of Bonita, my dog, whose devotion is as profound and lasting as life itself. But better yet, I love to look into the fearless, honest, trusting eyes of a child who so long has been said by theologians to be conceived and born in sin and pre-damned at birth. Do you believe all our teachers without question? I cannot. We must 'prove all things' and 'hold fast that which is good.'

"What does the Bible mean when it distinctly says, 'By their fruits ye shall know them'? Works count far more than words with those who think clearly.

"Euripides long ago said, 'Who dares not speak his free thought is a slave.' I nominated myself as an 'infidel' as a challenge to thought for those who are asleep. The word is harmless if properly used. Its stigma has been heaped upon it by unthinking people who associate it with the bogie devil and his malicious works. The devil has never concerned me, as I have always used my conscience, not the dictum of any cult.

"If my words have awakened thought in narrow bigots and petrified hypocrites, they will have done their appointed work. The universal voice of science tells us that the consequences fall upon ourselves here and now, if we misuse this wonderful body, or mind, or the all-pervading spirit of good. Why not accept these plain facts and guide our lives accordingly? We must not be deceived by blind leaders of the blind, calmly expecting to be 'saved' by anyone except by the Kingdom within ourselves. The truly honest and brave ones know that if they are to be saved it must be by their own efforts. The truth hurts for a while as do the forceps that remove an old, useless tooth, but health and happiness may be restored by the painful removal of the disturbing member.

"My mother, who lived to the ripe old age of ninety-seven years, used very often in my boyhood and youthful days to say, 'Luther, I wish you to make this world a better place to live in than it was before you lived.' I have unfailingly tried all of my own long life to live up to this standard. I was not told to believe this or that or be damned.

"I reiterate: The religion of most people is what they would like to believe, not what they do believe, and very few stop to examine its foundation underneath. The idea that a good God would send people to a burning hell is utterly damnable to me—the ravings of insanity, superstition gone to seed! I don't want to have anything to do with such a God. I am a lover of man and of Christ as a man and his work, and all things that help humanity; but nevertheless, just as he was an infidel then, I am an infidel to-day. I prefer and claim the right to worship the infinite, everlasting, almighty God of this vast universe as revealed to us gradually, step by step, by the demonstrable truths of our savior, science.

"Do you think Christ or Mohammed, Confucius, Baal or even the gods of ancient mythology are dead? Not so. Do you think Pericles, Marcus Aurelius, Moses, Shakespeare, Spinoza, Aristotle, Tolstoi, Franklin, Emerson are dead? No. Their very personality lives and will live forever in our lives and in the lives of all those who will follow us. All of them are with us to-day. No one lives who is not influenced, more or less, by these great ones according to the capacity of the cup of knowledge which they bring to these ever-flowing fountains to be filled.

"Olive Schreiner says: 'Holiness is an infinite compassion for others; greatness is to take the common things of life, and walk truly among them.

"'All things on earth have their price; and for truth we pay the dearest. We barter it for love and sympathy. The road to honor is paved with thorns; but on the path to truth at every step you set your foot down on your own heart.

"'For the little soul that cries aloud for continued personal existence for itself and its beloved, there is no help. For the soul which knows itself no more as a unit, but as a part of the Universal Unity of which the beloved also is a part, which feels within itself the throb of the Universal Life—for that soul there is no death.'"[6]

His sermon—it was nothing else—received a maximum of publicity. It was published in the press, broadcast over the radio and cited from the pulpits of innumerable churches. Letters and telegrams by the thousand poured in. Some were abusive. "One Bryan is worth a million Burbanks to any world, and the Bible will be doing business when you and your flowers are blowing down the years," wrote an outraged fundamentalist from Abilene, Kansas. "You will be held responsible for your statement. You have set aside the Bible, made the God of the Bible a liar, made Jesus Christ an imposter. Thus you declare yourself to be a heathen. It is too bad you have so little sense," brayed another in Keokuk, Iowa. "Isn't it just splendid to get at the exact truth?" asked a New Yorker. "The physical strength of a healthy ape is three times that of a human being, and the mental strength three times that of an evolutionist." (We may, perhaps, imagine Burbank wryly remembering a remark he had made in a lecture many years before: "Yes! It is too true all men have not arrived from Monkeydom; they were consigned as freight and will be found sidetracked at some waystation.") A minister in Pasadena dismissed the horticulturist's unprofessional pronouncements on the subject of theology as "not even as valuable as John D. Rockefeller on 'How to Play Football,'" adding that he had "gathered to his banner hundreds of Christ's enemies, some of whom had been afraid to come out in the open. Unitarians, scientists, etc., who have always belittled Christ, are with him. But God is not mocked, and I tremble for them at the result, while I pity and pray for the man who is closing a great career as a poor, deluded dupe of the Devil."

On the other hand, a Baptist minister of Kansas City, who had been expelled from his church for endorsing Burbank's statement, wrote to say how he rejoiced at his new freedom of conscience, and a miner sturdily wished "Good luck to you, dear friend Burbank," saying, "let's have the truth at all costs. Self and family has quit church going till a man comes along who will give us a god of love and forget about hell fire."

Burbank had anticipated that 1926 would be a good year. Among other things he had perfected a number of new gladioli and a new strain of Shasta daisy. He was also at work on some new roses. In an interview with *Popular Science Monthly* shortly before his last birthday, he said that he looked forward to at least five more years of productive life. The work of the horticulturist is a long-term affair. One of the new flowers he hoped to send out that season, he remarked to a reporter in March, had been under development for almost twenty years.

Then, on the evening of March 24, 1926, he suffered a severe heart attack. The doctors ordered rest and quiet, and it seemed for a while that he was on the road to recovery. On March 30, however, he began to suffer spasmodic hiccoughs as a result of a gastrointestinal irritation, with resultant insomnia. During the week that followed, he rallied again, but the medical reports indicated "an exhausted nervous system . . . Prognosis is guarded, somewhat grave." The slow decline continued. He was worn out, unable to eat, wracked by ceaseless hiccoughing. By Saturday, April 10, he had fallen into a coma. He died, without waking, at thirteen minutes after midnight that Sunday morning.

He was buried on the afternoon of Wednesday, April 14, under a cedar of Lebanon near the old house. By his own choice, the tree was his only monument. Judge B. B. Lindsey delivered a funeral oration, and Wilbur Hall read the eulogy that Robert Ingersoll, the great agnostic, had spoken at the grave of his brother almost fifty years before.

The decision to read the Ingersoll eulogy seems to have been made by Hall—a militant atheist himself—and Mrs. Burbank. Lindsey's address was afterward published in a pamphlet, together with an article by Maynard Shipley, entitled "Luther Burbank's Last Rites," and a statement by Walter L. Liggett, another free-thinker, captioned "Baptists Lie About Luther Burbank," intended to refute the charge made in a journal called *The Crusader's Champion* that Burbank had recanted his unorthodox beliefs on his deathbed. Thus, even in dying, he became an instrument of propaganda. The socialist *New Masses* of June 1926 bore on its rear cover a lurid drawing of him, threatened by the forces of superstition and reaction, with the caption, "Old pious ladies railed at him—Ministers preached against him—The Ku Klux Klan threatened him—Because he tried to make a heaven on earth."

But Burbank was now beyond caring.

When his will was filed on April 15, the estate was appraised at $168,624.22. Elizabeth Waters Burbank was named as the sole divisee, inheriting the equivalent of almost half a million dollars in present-day terms.

Burbank's last catalog, put together with the assistance of Wilbur Hall, was issued later that year, and a "Final new fruits bulletin," eight pages long, came out in 1927. Will Henderson, the only person who knew much about Burbank's ongoing experiments, was discharged after a disagreement with his widow, and Stark Brothers Nurseries and Orchards Company of Louisiana, Missouri, purchased the rights to the uncompleted work.

John T. Bregger, a horticulturist brought in by Stark's for the purpose, made an extensive study of the hybrid fruits being tested in the Sebastopol orchards, and in the ensuing years numerous new varieties were introduced by the company. At the time of writing Stark still markets eight Burbank varieties, the July Elberta Peach,[7] the Flaming Gold Nectarine, the Grand Prize Prune, the Elephant Heart Plum, the Red Ace Plum, the Santa Rosa Plum, the Purple Flame Plum and the Van Deman Quince that Clarence Stark had bought from Burbank for $800 in 1893. A company spokesman notes that

> We certainly feel that our association with Burbank, the use of his name, and the varieties play an important part in our marketing efforts. A very high percentage of our customers are serious backyard gardeners who are quite knowledgable about Burbank's accomplishments.
>
> We continue to keep the trademark Luther Burbank registered. In fact, we pay Mrs. Burbank a royalty each year for the use of the name as well as for other considerations.[8]

It is a curious fact that Burbank's most important single introduction remains his first. The Russet Burbank potato, a presumed sport of Burbank's seedling, is the most widely grown potato in the United States, as indicated by the acreage of certified seed—61,709 acres in 1972, ranking first out of approximately one hundred varieties certified that year. One of its descendants, the Norgold Russett, released in 1964, ranked eighth by 1972 with 8060 acres of certified seed.

In California, the leading plum-producing state, the old Burbank varieties continue to lead. Plums account for some 20 percent of the fresh deciduous tree fruits shipped from the state year round, rising to 40 percent of shipments during May–July. Among early plums, three of the four main varieties are Burbank's, namely Beauty, Formosa and Santa Rosa. A fourth, Climax, held its own till 1959. Midseason plums fall into nine main varieties, and five Burbank introductions, Burbank, Duarte, Wickson, Gaviota and Sugar, are among them. Among late plums we find Giant, Ace, Late Santa Rosa and Late Duarte in the leading group. As recently as 1954, the three main California shipping plums were Beauty, Duarte and Santa Rosa, the latter with 36 percent of the overall total. By 1965–67, Santa Rosa had declined to 30 percent of the total, though still the leader, and Beauty and Duarte had been edged out by newer varieties.[9]

In other countries, too, the Burbank plums maintain their lead. In South Africa, for example, Santa Rosa and Gaviota are the main varieties grown for export (1974), and Satsuma is still grown for the processing industry. There can be no doubt that for his plums and his potato alone, Burbank must be ranked among the most successful breeders in horticultural history. Beside them we may place the Shasta daisy, his most successful flower, whose popularity needs no embellishing statistics. Most of his other introductions have been superseded, as was almost inevitable. Tastes change, and breeders are always at work trying to produce something better. Only the rare exception remains in the seed catalogs for more than five or ten years. But Burbank's plants are themselves numbered among the ancestors of many of today's vegetables and flowers: in that sense, at least, the work of the horticulturist is immortal.

SIXTEEN

Burbank's Heritage

EXPERIMENTATION, BURBANK ONCE stated in no equivocal terms, was "the sole object and purpose of my life." Yet it would be untrue to say that it is solely by his achievements as a breeder that he deserves to be remembered. The sum total was more than that. Like Henry Ford or Thomas Alva Edison, he was, in a sense, inevitable. If he had not existed, it might have been necessary to invent him.

There was a kind of interaction between these men and their age. Solitary individuals, working largely alone, they unlocked the gates of change and revolutionized society by sheer force of example. They became symbolic figures in terms of whom the public at large could identify and understand their areas of work. There were other car builders besides Ford, other inventors besides Edison, other plant breeders besides Burbank. But in the popular mind, Burbank was *the* plant man, just as Ford was *the* car man and Edison *the* inventor. The revolutions they wrought were two-edged, embracing both the worst and best of what is known as progress. Pandora's box is not to be opened lightly.

Burbank's influence is effectively summed up by Orland E. White, Professor of Agricultural Biology and director of the University of Virginia's Blandy Experimental Farm. In his youth, White confessed, Burbank had been one of his heroes, but as he progressed in the study of horticulture he found himself increasingly disillusioned. After he graduated he was asked by the editor of a botanical magazine to write a review of a new edition of Harwood's *New Creations in Plant Life*. He tackled the book in an ironical vein, "but it so happened that John Burroughs saw this review and took me seriously, writing me to the effect that as an honest scientist, which he had always thought I was, I ought to know better than to help propagandize such works and such men." Burroughs had known Burbank, and had once been something of an admirer himself. His name had appeared in the advertised list of life members of the Luther Burbank Society (others were Edison, Phoebe A. Hearst, John Muir and Hugo de Vries.) But by this time—around 1918—he had, like most scientists, come to associate the name of Burbank with the worst kind of horticultural quackery.

Even so, assessing Burbank more than a decade after his death, White felt that

> Because of his notoriety or fame it has been possible to secure a favorable and special consideration for many scientific projects that otherwise would have had a deaf ear turned toward them because of ignorance in regard to the possibilities of what they might attain. . . . He aroused the imagination of many unimaginative and ignorant people so that they became interested in a subject that otherwise they probably never would have heard of.
>
> When I explain to people that I am a geneticist, it means nothing to most of them outside of a very small scientific group. If I tell them I am a follower of Mendel, the group is only slightly increased. But if I explain to them that I am crossing plants such as

Burbank did, their faces light up, and many of them begin to feel quite at home and in a position to talk intelligently about a world that they know very little concerning.[1]

This was probably the feeling of most fair-minded horticultural scientists of his generation. The practical effects of Burbank's influence can be seen in the founding of the Eddy Tree Breeding Station, later the Institute of Forest Genetics, at Placerville, California. James G. Eddy, a lumberman of Port Blakely Mill on Puget Sound, Washington, had heard of Burbank's work in breeding the Paradox and Royal walnut hybrids, and his imagination was fired by the idea of producing hybrid forest trees for timber. In 1918 he visited Burbank, and asked him if he would be prepared to head a tree-breeding project. Burbank declined, pointing out that he was an old man, and that the work could not come to fruition for many years. Instead he recommended Lloyd Austin, a twenty-six year-old pomologist with the College of Agriculture of the University of California at Davis, for the job. When Eddy set up his tree-breeding station at Placerville, Austin was appointed to take charge of it, and from this research program sprang a worldwide interest in the improvement of forest trees. The project was taken over by the Forest Service of the United States Department of Agriculture in 1935, and since then scientists from all over the world have come to Placerville to work with the staff of the institute. Techniques for controlled pollination in pines developed here are now employed in many countries, and a number of highly successful hybrids have been developed.[2]

Another illustration of Burbank's far-reaching influence is to be found in the events surrounding the passage of the first Plant Patent Law in 1930. For many years legislation of this kind had been sought to protect the work of plant breeders from unscrupulous exploitation in the same way that the work of other inventors is safeguarded. Little was achieved, because of the ignorance of the average Congressman on the subject, until Paul Stark, of Stark Brothers Nurseries, who was then chairman of the National Committee for Plant Patents, and Archibald Augustine, president of the American Association of Nurserymen, who was himself a longtime member of the Plant Patent committee, took up the struggle in Washington.

Stark's committee argued before Congress that lack of patent protection was bound to have a negative effect on experimentation precisely when new vistas were opening up in the field. Among those who supported the measure was Edison, who sent a telegram urging that the existing patent law be amended to include the plant breeder. But adoption of the proposal was very much in doubt, and it was feared that if it failed to pass in the current session, legislation might not be forthcoming for many years, with disastrous results for American horticulture.

One of the main opponents of the Plant Patent Bill was Congressman Fiorello La Guardia, later famous as mayor of New York. Acting apparently on misunderstood protests he had received, La Guardia successfully blocked passage, until the sponsoring Congressman, Fred S. Purnell of Indiana, inquired what he thought of Luther Burbank. "I think he is one of the greatest Americans that ever lived," the New Yorker replied flamboyantly. Purnell then proceeded to read into the record a letter written by Burbank to Paul Stark shortly before his death. "I have been for years in correspondence with leading breeders, nurserymen, and Federal officials and I despair of anything being done at present to secure to the plant breeder any adequate returns for his enormous outlays of energy and money," Burbank had written.

A man can patent a mouse trap or copyright a nasty song, but if he gives to the world a new fruit that will add millions to the value of earth's annual harvests he will be fortunate if he is rewarded by so much as having his name connected with the result. Though the surface of plant experimentation has thus far been only scratched and there is so much immeasurably important work waiting to be done in this line I would hesitate to advise a young man, no matter how gifted or devoted, to adopt plant breeding as a life work until America takes some action to protect his unquestioned rights to some benefit from his achievements.

La Guardia thereupon took the floor again, announcing, "I withdraw my objection to this bill and move its adoption." This hurdle surmounted, the House of Representatives passed the measure, and the Senate followed suit soon afterward.[3] Burbank's posthumous authority had secured for plant breeders the protection he himself had always so grievously lacked. Henceforth the originator of new and distinctly different trees or plants could rely on patent protection for seventeen years (after which they passed into the public domain). The "Little Flower"—as La Guardia was called by his supporters—might not have known much about horticulture, but he knew and honored the name of Luther Burbank.

In evaluating scientific hostility to Burbank, it is worth remembering that the age was one of conflict for workers in the field of biology. In the public arena scientists fought the larger battle with the forces of ignorance and bigotry assembled under the fundamentalist interpretation of the Old Testament. Internal to biology itself was the protracted struggle between "Mendelian-mutationalists" and "Darwinian-biometricians." It was not until the 1930s that these factions were reconciled, with Darwin's original idea of slowly cumulative variation subsuming and modifying the radical mutationalist views of De Vries and Bateson, and Mendel's work coming into full acceptance with the biometricians who had previously adhered to Galton's law of ancestral inheritance.

Of the public struggle we might simply note that at the Scopes trial in Tennessee, which took place in 1925, William Jennings Bryan, popular hero, several times nominee for the Presidency and sometime Secretary of State, had gone so far as to deny that man was a mammal. Fundamentalism was alive and kicking in the twenties, and Bryan was not the only public man to try to make a virtue out of ignorance. Edgar Anderson recalls that after Vavilov's Soviet expedition to South America had discovered polyploid complexes of wild and semiwild potatoes, the Department of Agriculture was stimulated to propose sending a plant explorer to obtain a collection of these for American potato breeders. But the budget for the project was ridiculed in Congress by a demogogic legislator for the simple reason that it contained the word "polyploid," and the expedition, which was of great potential importance, never took place.[4] The currents of anti-intellectualism, never far from the surface in American life, ran strong in those years. The scientists were often on the defensive, and, in defending, they sometimes overstepped the bounds of purely scientific objectivity.

And Burbank's champions somehow arose in the most unacceptable quarters. In Russia, for instance, where as early as 1905 Mendelism had been branded as "clerical Anti-Darwinism" by Timiriazev, a prominent plant physiologist who also happened to be a Marxist, Burbank's name was appropriated by T. D. Lysenko and his followers, then engaged in ruthlessly dismantling the entire structure of Soviet genetics in favor of their own neo-Lamarckian views. "Marx had spoken well of Darwin so that Darwinism was sacred. Lenin had spoken well of Timiriazev, so that his views were sacred in the second order. Timiriazev had spoken well of the American commercial plant breeder, Burbank, so that he enjoyed third-order sanctity," Professor C. D. Darlington, one of the foremost contemporary geneticists, wrote in 1949. Lysenkoist doctrine held sacred the work of the Russian breeder, Michurin, whose American counterpart Burbank was represented as being. "Roosevelt honoured Burbank with a purple postage stamp," Darlington adds.

Stalin paid his homage to Michurin with a small town, Michurinsk. In both countries societies were formed to advance their work or reputation. Both men had worked for their private profit, collecting useful plants from other countries and breeding from them. Their methods did not include such precautions as are taken by scientific plant breeders, but sometimes, as in all botanical collections, useful seedlings turned up by chance from the seed set by open pollination. In these cases both Michurin and Burbank felt able (as commercial breeders usually do) to attribute the results to "scientific" crossing with particular, and often surprising, parents that happened to be growing nearby . . . In order to support their prodigious and, by scientific standards, fraudulent claims as creators of new plants, both Burbank and Michurin revived the good old Lamarckian theory of the direct action of a changed environment in changing heredity. They put the theory into a new dress and each probably thought he had invented it.[5]

This, as any reader of the present book will be aware, is blatantly unfair to Burbank (and it is perhaps unjust to Michurin as well). But Darlington was writing in the heat of combat: Western scientists were doing their best to aid their Soviet colleagues, who were literally in danger of their lives. Arrests of Russian geneticists had begun as early as 1932. The first death sentences came in 1935, and in 1937 S. G. Levit, head of the medical genetic research institute in Moscow, was executed. In 1940, Vavilov, the outstanding scientist in his field, and the man responsibile for the introduction of some twenty-five thousand experimental samples of wheat in his country, was arrested and condemned to death as a British spy. (It is believed that he died of illness and privation in a Siberian concentration camp near Saratov in 1942.) Lysenko thereupon assumed his position as president of the Lenin Academy of Agricultural Sciences and director of the Laboratory of Genetics of the Academy of Sciences.

Lest it be doubted that Western scientists themselves felt threatened by the political climate of the times, we might quote the embattled declaration of Professor H. J. Muller of Indiana University in his presidential address to the Eighth International Congress of Genetics in 1948:

. . . I believe that genetics has *not yet* [italics added] in Western countries, gone so far toward becoming an underground movement as to make . . . an eclipse necessary. Let us struggle to keep our science, in all its ramifications, connections, extensions, and even speculations, in the light of day.[6]

None of this had anything to do with Burbank. But he had been branded "unscientific" and adopted into the bargain as a Lysenkoist totem to set beside the canonized Michurin. Accordingly, in Western scientific eyes, he became a kind of Lysenkoist by posthumous association. Darlington does admit, in a rather curious paragraph that

When Roosevelt made the mistake over Burbank, the United States Department of Agriculture, the National Research Council, and the Carnegie Institution of Washington did not dismiss their very able staffs of geneticists. In Russia, however, Stalin's mistake was part of a plan which included the dismissal of the geneticists and a great deal more besides.[7]

But odd, indeed, to equate the honoring of Burbank on a three-cent postage stamp (one of a "Famous Americans" series commemorating intellectual leaders—artists, authors, composers, poets, inventors and scientists—the choice was not Roosevelt's personal decision in any case) with Stalin's "mistake" in permitting the ignorant and malevolent Lysenko to obliterate Soviet genetics and hound its leading representatives to death! When they turn to polemics, scientists, it seems, are no more objective than the rest of us.

Had Burbank lived fifty years earlier, there can be small doubt that he would be universally regarded as the father of American horticulture. As it was his working career too closely preceded the rise of plant genetics and scientific breeding. He was rejected as a reactionary rival by younger men whose paths he had done a good deal to ease. They did not hesitate to judge him by the most rigorous contemporary standards, forgetting that these had scarcely been established when he was doing his best work. Those who knew him well, like Shull, gave him his due. But the great majority simply took their cues from afar: after all, one had only to glance at the Burbank literature of the day to know what one was dealing with.

A hundred years ago the need to apply scientific methods to agriculture was far from recognized. In 1874 Eugene Woldemar Hilgard started the California Agricultural Experiment Station with a pitiful $250 allotted for the purpose. Another pioneer experiment station was opened in Connecticut in 1875—the very year Burbank set out hopefully for California with his ten seed potatoes. Although funds from the sale of government-owned land had been set aside to support agricultural and mechanical colleges in every state by the Morrill Land Grant Act of July 1862, and the Department of Agriculture established as an independent agency the same year, progress was slow. The system of agricultural experiment stations was not formally set up until the passage of the Hatch Act in 1887, and the head of the Department of Agriculture did not obtain cabinet rank until two years later. Once underway, however, the experiment stations, in combination with the land-grant colleges, provided a formidable nationwide basis for research and experimentation. This Federal support reflected the growth of the United States as an agricultural nation. In the last quarter of the nineteenth century the number of farms in the country more than doubled, with vast tracts of virgin land being brought under the plow. During Burbank's working life, the farm population reached its alltime peak of over twenty-eight million.

The same period corresponded with the phenomenal growth of California agriculture. And in California, where physical circumstances tended to dictate large single-crop farming operations, rather than small diversified holdings, the applications of agricultural science and engineering were particularly obvious. The development of scientific irrigation analysis and soil study under Hilgard's guidance, the increasing mechanization of farms and the introduction of new varieties of cultivar by Burbank and other breeders laid the basis for the California agribusiness empire of today.

Burbank accurately perceived the immense possibilities of the state for fruit and vegetable growing long before most people did. When he arrived in Santa Rosa, California was the site of the world's largest wheat field, an eighty-mile-wide strip along the banks of the San Joaquin River that produced more than a hundred thousand tons annually so economically that it could profitably be shipped fourteen thousands miles out of San Francisco to British markets. Wheat was a bonanza far bigger than gold. The venerable Don Luis Peralta (whose rancho of five leagues in the East Bay extended over much of the future sites of the cities of Berkeley and Oakland) had spoken with remarkable foresight when he told his sons, who were eager to seek their fortunes in the gold country, "Go to your ranch and raise grain, and that will be your best gold field, because we all must eat while we live." But by 1900 wheat production had declined dramatically, as a consequence of overcropping and increased surpluses on world markets, and other crops were coming in: grapes, citrus, olives, tree nuts and deciduous fruit in particular.

One concept that evolved side by side with California agribusiness was that of the crop tailored to suit market tastes, mechanical picking and whatever other requirements might be thought desirable. Burbank must be regarded as a central innovator of these techniques. In 1905, for example, he received an order from J. H. Empson, a Colorado canner, for a pea resembling the French *petits pois,* which would develop and ripen uniformly and be capable of mechanical harvesting. Empson had initially believed that an entirely different variety of pea was being packed in France, and ordered seed of several kinds grown there. When it was planted, however, he discovered that they were precisely the same as the varieties in cultivation in America, and did not actually grow any smaller. The tender little French peas that were so sought after were made possible by the cheaper labor available in Europe: peas were picked by hand there when they were half grown, and could be harvested in this way several times during the season off the same vines. The French canners also artificially sweetened their peas and used copper sulfate to give them their characteristically bright green color. These latter expedients Empson laudably sought to avoid, and he applied instead to Burbank to produce a variety that would duplicate the desired qualities naturally.

When he took on the job, Burbank contracted to produce a suitable pea in six years. He tackled it solely by selection, growing two crops a year, and by February 1908 was able to deliver the result, a pea that was uniformly 15 percent smaller than average, sweeter than before, matured earlier and produced up to twice as many pounds per acre into the bargain. These derived entirely from "Admiral" seed initially supplied by Empson, reselected through six generations.[8] It was a remarkable demonstration of the possibilities of simple selection—performed by a master selector like Burbank. Jones remarks that

> To any one who has worked with naturally self-fertilized plants like peas, it seems incredible that a marked improvement could be made in such a short time with the limited amount of material that Burbank could have grown along with his many other undertakings. Breeding projects with these plants usually involve the selection of many hundreds of individuals and the testing of them in progeny plots over a period of several years under the same conditions as the plants are to be grown ultimately. When superior selections are finally found and proven it takes several years to multiply seed in sufficient quantities to make a thorough test.[9]

In this case, however, the final testing was evidently left to the canners themselves, and that they were satisfied with what they had got is apparent from the fact that they commenced to raise and market the new pea—named the Burbank Admiral—in quantity.[10]

Today there is something of a rebellion against standardization as manifested in perfectly uniform produce, identical heaps of beautiful but tasteless tomatoes, glistening apples whose superb appearance belies an indifferent flavor and texture. In the interests of mass production, numerous varieties have literally vanished from the marketplace: and of the best among them. Those who have spent time in parts of the world where fruit and vegetables have been less completely tamed are not infrequently heard to complain about American produce, in which eating quality seems to have been the last consideration served. But it would be unfair to blame Burbank for the "plastic" products in the supermarkets. His own criteria were exacting, and high on the list were flavor, scent and beauty. He went so far as to forbid his helpers to smoke or drink, not so much for reasons of morality (though his well-advertised prejudices were certainly involved), as because it would dull their senses of taste and smell to do so.

Burbank was once dubbed "the only living incarnation of Emerson's philosophy," and like the sage of Concord, he was a product of the Unitarian tradition, and hence ultimately of the Enlightenment. But, like Emerson, he paradoxically favored intuition over law. If he was outside the scientific tradition, it was almost by choice. "Although he professes to prefer not to know the names of his species, *lest that knowledge should limit him in his efforts at hybridization* [italics added], he does know by their scientific names the thousands of plants with which he has worked," Shull noted. "This became very apparent when we ran rapidly through Vilmorin's catalog checking those species which they and Mr. Burbank had in common . . . Very often when I would mention the name of a genus he would immediately give all the species he has without the slightest hesitancy. This was something of a surprise to me because Bailey has represented Mr. Burbank as being almost wholly ignorant of the species upon which he has worked."

He shaped his flowers and fruit much as an artist works up his material, using methods he and he alone had evolved and was capable of applying, because they resided, finally, not in any procedure or technique, but in his own personal aesthetics. He tuned in to the "vibrations" that he identified as "the cause of all manifestation" and proceeded accordingly. He himself believed that this was more than what was ordinarily known as intuition, that there was something of a sixth sense to it. Even those who had worked with him longest and been closest to him, he said, had been unable to duplicate what he did as a mere matter of routine without thinking how he did it. He envisaged, too, that talents like his own would one day come to be better understood, and looked forward to a time when science would "concentrate on the wonders of the mind of man and on the subjects that we now consider mystical and psychic." There is no doubt that he believed himself to be psychic: he claimed as much in an article he wrote for *Hearst's International Magazine* in 1923, averring that both he, his mother and his sister Emma possessed telepathic powers. He also insisted that he possessed the ability to heal by a laying on of hands, citing several cases in which he had employed it.

These are matters which are beyond proving. All we can say is that he would not consciously have lied (though he might well have exaggerated). Moreover, science is beginning to look into the wonders of the human mind, and serious attention is being paid to subjects that were once dismissed as mystical. According to a recent newspaper poll, no less than 53 percent of the American public believe in psychic phenomena, and the percentage is strikingly higher among affluent, well-educated people.

This belief is finding support, astonishingly enough, in the very sciences that were once the bulwark of materialism. In a recent paper in the *American Journal of Physics*, Enos E. Witmer of the University of Pennsylvania observes that "It should be that a definition of the quantum-mechanical state of a microphysical system must include not only the microphysical system but also the *entire physical environment*."[11] In this he sees a similarity to the behavior of biological systems, going on to cite the view of G. G. Simpson of Harvard University, expressed in an article in *Science,* that physics may someday be merely a special case of a comprehensive biological theory, in the same sense that classical mechanics is a special case of the theory of relativity. Biological phenomena may, therefore, be thought of as being of a "higher type" than physical phenomena. "It is no doubt true that to assert that micro-objects have volition is too strong a statement," Witmer says, but, in his interpretation of quantum mechanics,

> they have attributes that are the vague beginning of volition and self-activity. Thus, just as the research on viruses demonstrated that there is no sharp line of demarcation between the living and the nonliving, so the development of quantum mechanics may be demonstrating that freedom is not something that is limited to man and the higher animals according to some conceptions of biological phenomena, but rather extends down in some measure to molecules, atoms, electrons, and all the elementary particles.[12]

Perhaps the idea of Burbank "teaching" his plants may yet turn out not to have been so absurd after all. If elementary particles adapt their behavior to the entire physical environment, and may be thought of as having "attributes that are the vague beginning of volition and self-activity," what price vegetables?

Our dependence on the skills of the horticulturist is increasing rather than decreasing. Among those who believe that we are on the brink of a worldwide food crisis is the agronomist Norman Borlaug, father of the "green revolution," and winner of the 1970 Nobel Peace Prize. Only North America and Australia are currently in a position to export grain in any quantity, and a major crop failure in these areas could bring starvation to hundreds of millions. As it is, millions of human beings still die of starvation and malnutrition every year. Better grain varieties developed by Borlaug and others have done a great deal to improve the world's food supply. But, he says, "I hear the dreadful ticking of the biological clock. Five births every two seconds. That means 70 million new mouths to feed every year."[13]

Unfortunately most of us are willfully deaf to that ticking. We shall not be able to remain so for long. The whole nature of our relationship with the world we live on, and with the plant kingdom on which we depend for life itself, will have to change in the not too distant future. It is safe to say that if it does not change for the better, it will change drastically for the worse.

The confident scientific predictions of yesteryear have turned out to be all too fallible. There is no particular reason to believe that today's dogmas are any more certain. Science and reason remain our best guides: but it is not unreasonable to require that they be tempered by a proper humility and caution in the face of what we do not, after all, really understand. In the case of Luther Burbank, we have come to a point where we may at last concede that his way was not all wrong, and the scientists who dismissed him were certainly not all right. The experimenter himself, the quantum physicists have admitted, is inevitably part of the experiment. The same may be true of plant breeding. Burbank, who placed his reliance on feeling rather than technique, always thought so. He may, even now, have something to teach us.

Appendix

The credit for recognizing Burbank's priority in reporting species hybrids that bred true belongs to Donald F. Jones. In a review in the *Journal of the New York Botanical Garden,* December 1943, Jones observed that, "Burbank's most valuable contribution to science, his *Rubus* hybrids that bred true, have been largely overlooked by geneticists. When these were first announced, Mendelian segregation was expected in all hybrids and his statements were not accepted. Now that amphidiploids are known to transmit without segregation, Burbank is not given the priority that he deserves for producing and putting these on record." Polyploidy, since understood to be one of the most important processes in the evolution of cultivated plants, seems to have been first reported in bryophytes (mosses and liverworts) in 1906, but it was not until 1914 that Ø. Winge began to speculate about the significance of chromosome numbers. Somatic doubling in an F hybrid was reported by R. E. Clausen

295

and T. H. Goodspeed in 1925, and the term amphidiploid (of which allotetraploid is a synonym) was introduced in 1927 by S. G. Navashin to describe tetraploid species hybrids whose somatic cells contain the diploid chromosome complements of both parent species.

While true-breeding species hybrids may have been observed earlier—the loganberry, which originated in the garden of Judge Logan at Santa Cruz, for example—Burbank's priority lies in having both produced such hybrids and clearly distinguished them as "Another Mode of Species Forming," which he did in a short paper delivered to the American Breeders' Association in January 1909. At the time, as Jones has pointed out, nobody believed him, and he got no credit for it. Here is his report:

[Reprinted from THE POPULAR SCIENCE MONTHLY, September, 1909.]

ANOTHER MODE OF SPECIES FORMING[1]

By LUTHER BURBANK,
SANTA ROSA, CAL.

THE MORE USUAL concept of the formation of species is by slow variations so well known as the Darwinian theory, which though attacked from every point, still is and must always in the main be accepted, for without question it gives the fundamental principles of evolution as had never been done before. Yet the boundless amount of research along these lines during the last half century has developed strong new sidelights which illuminate, and in some cases compel a slightly different view of, some of the suggestions of *the master, Darwin.*

During the period of forty years that I have been experimenting with plant life both in bleak New England and in sunny California, extensively operating on much more than four

---

[1]Read at the annual meeting of the American Breeders' Association, at Columbia, Mo., January 5 to 8, 1909.

thousand five hundred distinct species of plants, including all known economic and ornamental plant forms which are grown in the open air in temperate and semi-tropic climates, as well as many of those commonly grown in greenhouses and numerous absolutely new ones not before domesticated and on a scale never before attempted by any individual or body of individuals, numerous general principles have pressed themselves forward for discussion and observation. Only one of these can be discussed at this time, and this briefly, more as a text for further observations and experiments than as anything like a full view of this highly interesting mode of species formation.

In the first place, let me say that our so-called species are only tentative bundles of plants, no two individuals of which are exactly alike, but nearly all of which quite closely resemble each other in general outside appearances and in hereditary tendencies. Yet no one can tell just what the result will be when combinations of these inherent tendencies are crossed or subjected to any other disturbing factor or factors. Like the chemist who has new elements to work with, we may predict with some degree of accuracy what the general results will be, but any definite knowledge of the results of these combinations is far more difficult, even impossible, as the life forces of plants and animals act in infinitely more new directions than can any ordinary number of combinations of chemicals.

Only a few years ago, it was generally supposed that by crossing two somewhat different species or varieties a mongrel might be produced which might, or more likely might not, surpass its parents.

The fact that crossing was *only the first step* and *that selection from the numerous variations secured in the second and a few succeeding generations was the real work* of new plant creation *had never been appreciated;* and to-day its significance is not fully understood either by breeders or even by many scientific investigators along these very lines. Old tailings are constantly being worked over at great expense of time and with small profit, while the mother lode is repudiated and neglected.

Plant breeding to be successful must be conducted like architecture. Definite plans must be carefully laid for the proposed creation; suitable materials selected with judgment, and these must be securely placed in their proper order and position. No occupation requires more accuracy, foresight and skill than does scientific plant or animal breeding.

As before noted, the first generation after a cross has been made is *usually* a more or less complete blend of all the characteristics of both parents; not only the visible characters, but *an infinite number of invisible ones* are inherent and will shape the future character and destiny of the descendants, often producing otherwise unaccountable so-called mutations, saltations or sports, the selection and perpetuation of which give to new plant creations their unique forms and often priceless values, like the Burbank potato produced thirty-six years ago and which is now grown on this western coast almost to the exclusion of all others (fourteen millions of bushels per annum, besides the vast amount grown in the eastern United States and other countries), or the Bartlett pear, Baldwin apple and navel oranges, all of which are variations selected by some keen observer. Millions of others are forever buried in oblivion for the lack of such an observer.

But in this paper I wish to call attention to a not unusual result of crossing quite distinct wild species which deserves the most careful analysis, as it seems to promise a new text for scientific investigation, especially on biometric lines. The subject was most forcibly brought to my attention twenty years ago by the singular behavior of the second-generation seedlings of raspberry-blackberry hybrids. By crossing the Siberian raspberry *(Rubus crataegifolius)* with our native trailing blackberry (*Rubus vitifolius*), a thoroughly fixed new species was summarily produced. The seedlings of this composite *Rubus* (named *Primus*), though a most perfect blend of both parents but resembling neither, never reverted either way; all the seedlings coming much more exactly like the new type than do the seedlings of any ordinary wild rubus. Many thousand plants have been raised generation after generation, all repeating themselves af-

ter the new and unique type. No botanist on earth could do otherwise than classify it if found wild as a valid new species, which
it truly is, though so summarily produced by crossing.

Since the *Primus* species was originated, numerous similar
cases have attracted attention, such as my now popular Phenomenal produced by crossing the Cuthbert raspberry with our
native Pacific coast blackberry, and the Logan berry, both of
which, though a complete blend of two such distinct species, yet
reproduce from seed as truly as any wild rubus species.

I have had also growing on my grounds for some fifteen
years or more hybrids of *Rubus idaeus* and *Rubus villosus,* both
red and yellow varieties. All are exactly intermediate between
these two very widely different species, yet both always come
true intermediates from seed, generation after generation, never reverting either way.

By crossing the great African "stubble berry" (*Solanum gui-
ne[e]nse*) our Pacific coast "rabbit weed"(*Solanum villosum*) an absolutely new species has also been produced, the fruit of which
resembles in almost every particular the common blueberry
(*Vaccinium Pennsylvanicum*), and while the *fruit of neither parent
species is edible,* the fruit of the *newly created one is most delicious*
and most abundantly produced, and the seedlings, generation
after generation though produced by the million, still, all come
as true to the new type as do either parents species to *their* normal type.

Still another example of this mode may be found in my experiments with opuntias. By crossing *O. tuna* with *O. vulgaris,*
thousands of seedlings have been produced, all of which, in the
first, second and third generations, though a well-balanced
blend of the two natural species, still come as true to the newly
created species as do either parent species to their own natural
types.

Not only does this new mode hold true under cultivation but
species are also summarily produced in a wild state by natural
crossing.

The western blackcap (*Rubus occidentalis*) and the eastern red raspberry *(Rubus strigosus)* when growing contiguous, as they very commonly do in Central British America, often cross, forming an intermediate new species which sometimes sorely crowds both of the parent species, and when brought under cultivation still firmly maintains its intermediate characters, no matter how often reproduced from seed. And still further, our common "tarweed" *(Madia elegans)* with its beautiful large blossoms often crosses with *M. saliva* with its insignificant pale yellow flowers, producing a complete intermediate. I have not yet determined whether the intermediate will reproduce true from seed, but confidently expect it to do so. Similar results among wild evergreens and deciduous trees and shrubs and herbaceous plants have been frequently and forcefully brought to my attention, leaving little doubt in my own mind that the evolution of species is by more modes than some are inclined to admit.

Notes & Sources

Preface

1. Professor Walter E. Howard, personal communication to the author, January 6, 1975.

2. Donald F. Jones, "Destroyed by His Friends," *The Scientific Monthly* 63 (1946): 238–39.

3. Walter L. Howard, *Luther Burbank: A Victim of Hero Worship*, in *Chronica Botanica* 9, no. 5/6 (Winter 1945–1946): 448. A part of Jones's manuscript was eventually published in the Spragg Memorial Lectures on Plant Breeding, Michigan State College, East Lansing, 1937, pp. 57–76.

Chapter One

1. Hugo de Vries, *Intracellular Pangenesis*, trans. C. S. Gager (Chicago: Open Court, 1910), Introduction.

2. L. C. Dunn, *A Short History of Genetics* (New York: McGraw-Hill, 1965), p. 44.

3. Hugo de Vries, "A Visit to Luther Burbank," *Popular Science Monthly*, August 1905, pp. 329–347. See also *Plant-breeding; Comments on the Experiments of Nilsson and Burbank* (Chicago: Open Court, 1907), and "Luther Burbank's Ideas on Scientific Horticulture," *Century* 73 (March 1907): 674–681, by the same author. De Vries appears to have visited Burbank at least three times, in 1904, 1906 and again in 1909. The description of his visit is a composite, based primarily on the 1904 visit, but also on elements of the other two.

4. E. J. Wickson, *Luther Burbank, Man, Methods and Achievements: An Appreciation*, a series of four articles reprinted from *Sunset* magazine. (San Francisco: Southern Pacific Company, 1902).

5. *Luther Burbank, His Methods and Discoveries and Their Practical Application*, ed. Henry Smith Williams and others, (Santa

Rosa: Luther Burbank Press, 1915): 270–71.

6. C. D. Darlington, "Purpose and Particles in the Study of Heredity," in *Science, Medicine and History,* ed. E. A. Underwood (New York: Oxford University Press, 1953), 2:474.

7. Michael T. Ghiselin, *The Triumph of the Darwinian Method* (Berkeley: University of California Press, 1969), pp. 167–85.

8. *Luther Burbank, His Methods and Discoveries,* 2:96–98.

9. C. D. Darlington, and K. Mather, *The Elements of Genetics* (New York: Schocken Books, 1969), p. 263.

10. D. Briggs and S. M. Walters, *Plant Variation and Evolution* (London: World University Library, 1969), pp. 222–23.

11. Walter L. Howard, *Luther Burbank: A Victim of Hero Worship,* in *Chronica Botanica* 9, no. 5/6 (Winter 1945–1946): 327.

12. *Ibid.,* p. 328.

Chapter Two

1. Carl O. Sauer, *Seeds, Spades, Hearths and Herds: The Domestication of Animals and Foodstuffs,* 2nd ed. (Cambridge, Mass.: The MIT Press, 1969), p. 104.

2. Sir Gavin de Beer, *Charles Darwin: A Scientific Biography* (Garden City, N.Y.: Doubleday & Company, 1965), p. 177.

3. Quoted by Eric F. Goldman in *Rendezvous with Destiny* (New York: Alfred A. Knopf, 1958), p. 92.

4. Henry Adams, *The Education of Henry Adams* (Boston: Houghton Mifflin, 1918), pp. 225–26.

5. Sauer, *Seeds, Spades,* p. 27.

6. Sauer, *Seeds, Spades,* pp. 99–100.

7. See K. D. White's *Roman Farming* (London: Thames & Hudson, 1970).

8. Lynn White, Jr., makes this point very convincingly in *Medieval Technology and Social Change* (New York: Oxford University Press, 1962).

9. B. H. Slicher van Bath, quoted by Fernand Braudel in *Capitalism and Material Life 1400–1800,* trans. Miriam Kochan (New York: Harper & Row, 1973), p. 81.

10. U. P. Hedrick, *A History of Horticulture in America to 1860* (New York: Oxford University Press, 1950), p. 24. '

11. Quoted by Daniel J. Boorstin in *The Americans: The Colonial Experience* (New York: Vintage Books, 1958), p. 260.

12. A. W. Livingston, *Livingston and the Tomato* (Columbus, Ohio: A. W. Livingston's Sons, 1893).

13. Thomas Andrew Knight, "Introductory Remarks Relative to the Objects Which the Horticultural Society Have in View," *Transactions of the Horticultural Society* (London, April 2, 1805), quoted by Walter L. Howard, *Luther Burbank: A Victim of Hero Worship,* in *Chronica Botanica,* 9, no. 5/6 (Winter 1945–1946): 351.

14. Charles Darwin, *The Autobiography of Charles Darwin 1809–1882,* ed. Nora Barlow, (New York: W. W. Norton & Co., 1969), p. 120.

15. Jacques Barzun, *Darwin, Marx, Wagner* (Garden City, N.Y.: Doubleday & Co., 1958), p. 30.

16. Luther Burbank, with Wilbur Hall, *The Harvest of the Years* (Boston: Houghton Mifflin, 1927), p. 22.

Chapter Three

1. Henry Adams, *The Education of Henry Adams* (Boston: Houghton Mifflin, 1918), p. 53.

2. *Ibid.* In his introduction (p. viii) D. W. Brogan points out that "there were no legitimate descendants in the male line of Washington, Franklin, Jefferson, the only founders of the Republic to be compared with John Adams."

3. The hour of Burbank's birth is given by the astrologer, Marc Edmund Jones. There is no indication as to how he came by it and no independent corroboration, but my presumption is that it was obtained from Burbank during his lifetime, either by Jones or by some other astrologer.

4. Emma Burbank Beeson, *The Early Life and Letters of Luther Burbank* (San Francisco: Harr Wagner, 1927). This book was originally published in May

1926 under the title *The Harvest of the Years: Early Life and Letters of Luther Burbank,* according to the Library of Congress, Copyright Office. Presumably the title was changed because Wilbur Hall wanted to use "The Harvest of the Years" for his "autobiography" of Burbank. All quotations attributed to Emma are from the 1927 edition.

5. Luther Burbank, with Wilbur Hall, *The Harvest of the Years* (Boston: Houghton Mifflin, 1927), p. 2.

6. John Tebbel, *The Media in America* (New York: Thomas Y. Crowell, 1975), *passim.*

7. Luther Burbank, letter to E. J. Wickson dated November 8, 1907, in the Library of the University of California at Davis.

8. Burbank, *Harvest of the Years,* p. 7.

9. Luther Burbank, *The Training of the Human Plant* (New York: Century Co., 1907).

10. Burbank, *Harvest of the Years,* pp. 5–6.

11. Frederick W. Clampett, *Luther Burbank, "Our Beloved Infidel"* (New York: Macmillan, 1926), pp. 19–20.

Chapter Four

1. Luther Burbank, with Wilbur Hall, *The Harvest of the Years* (Boston: Houghton Mifflin, 1927), p. 10.

2. *Ibid.,* p. 11.

3. *Ibid.,* p. 12.

4. Donald F. Jones, "The Life and Work of Luther Burbank," unpublished manuscript, quoted by permission of the Connecticut Agricultural Experiment Station, p. 24.

5. H. G. Baker, *Plants and Civilization,* 2nd ed. (Belmont, Calif.: Wadsworth Publishing Co., 1970). See also Redcliffe N. Salaman, *The History and Social Influence of the Potato* (New York: Cambridge University Press), 1949. Salaman devotes almost 700 pages to the history of what he calls "this enigmatical root."

6. J. C. Walker, "Genetics and Plant Pathology," in *Genetics in the 20th Century,*

ed. L. C. Dunn, (New York: Macmillan, 1951).

7. U. P. Hedrick, *A History of Horticulture in America to 1860* (New York: Oxford University Press, 1950), p. 44.

8. Walter L. Howard, *Luther Burbank: A Victim of Hero Worship,* in *Chronica Botanica* 9, no. 5/6 (Winter 1945–1946): 477.

9. Information supplied by the U.S. Department of Agriculture, Agricultural Research Service, Beltsville, Maryland.

10. Vernon L. Parrington, *Main Currents in American Thought* (New York: Harcourt, Brace, 1930), 3:8.

11. *Luther Burbank, His Methods and Discoveries and Their Practical Application,* ed. Henry Smith Williams (Santa Rosa: Luther Burbank Press, 1915), 12:61.

12. Howard, *Luther Burbank: A Victim,* p. 322.

13. Henry James, *The Bostonians* (New York: The Modern Library, 1956), p. 343.

14. Parrington, *Main Currents,* 3:11.

Chapter Five

1. Ralston bank failure: The leading financial organization on the Pacific Coast, the Bank of California, of which William Chapman Ralston was a founder, failed in August, 1875, with substantial losses to depositors. See also *Ralston's Ring* by George D. Lyman (New York: Charles Scribner's Sons, 1937).

2. Luther Burbank, with Wilbur Hall, *The Harvest of the Years* (Boston: Houghton Mifflin, 1927), p. 31.

Chapter Six

1. *Luther Burbank, His Methods and Discoveries and Their Practical Application,* ed. Henry Smith Williams and others (Santa Rosa: Luther Burbank Press, 1915), 12:72–74.

2. Luther Burbank, with Wilbur Hall, *The Harvest of the Years* (Boston: Houghton Mifflin, 1927), p. 39.

3. Walter L. Howard, *Luther Burbank: A Victim of Hero Worship,* in *Chronica Bo-*

tanica 9, no. 5/6 (Winter 1945–1946), p. 336.

4. *Ibid.,* p. 339.

5. *Luther Burbank, His Methods and Discoveries,* quoted by Howard in *Luther Burbank: A Victim of Hero Worship,* p. 340. Howard's italics.

6. Luther Burbank, unpublished letter to Professor H. E. Van Deman, August 22, 1888, from a copy in the Bancroft Library, University of California, Berkeley.

7. H. M. Butterfield, "History of California Plum and Prune Production," the third article in a series on the deciduous fruit industry in California published in *The Blue Anchor,* the official publication of the California Fruit Exchange, vols. 14 and 15, Sacramento, August 1937 to April 1938. Most of the details on the early history of plums and prunes in California are from this source. Butterfield apparently had access to certain notes on the subject kept by Burbank, supplied to him by John T. Bregger, a horticulturist employed by Stark Brothers to make a study of the Sebastopol experimental orchard after Burbank's death, but his dating of Burbank's introductions often seems faulty and at odds with the latter's own catalogs.

8. *Luther Burbank, His Methods and Discoveries,* 12: 108.

Chapter Seven

1. It must be admitted that his meeting with Helen cannot be precisely dated. Howard states that it took place "on one of his transcontinental trips," and this seems to be the only one in the years in question.

2. William Allen White, *The Autobiography of William Allen White* (New York: Macmillan, 1946), p. 176.

3. George H. Shull, unpublished letter to W. L. Howard dated February 22, 1940, in the Bancroft Library, University of California, Berkeley.

4. Walter L. Howard, *Luther Burbank: A Victim of Hero Worship,* in *Chronica Bo-*

tanica 9, no. 5/6 (Winter 1945–1946), p. 377.

5. *Ibid.,* pp. 322, 375.

6. Donald F. Jones, "The Life and Work of Luther Burbank," unpublished manuscript, quoted by permission of the Connecticut Agricultural Experiment Station, p. 178.

7. *Luther Burbank, His Methods and Discoveries and Their Practical Application,* ed. Henry Smith Williams and others (Luther Burbank Press, 1915), 2:138–43.

8. Jones, "Life and Work of Luther Burbank," p. 117.

9. Edwin G. Conklin, "A Generation's Progress in the Study of Evolution," *Science* 80, no. 2068 (August 17, 1934).

10. A. H. Sturtevant, *A History of Genetics* (New York: Harper & Row, 1965), pp. 22–24.

11. E. D. Cope, *The Primary Factors of Organic Evolution* (Chicago: Open Court, 1896), cited by Conklin (See note 9 above)

12. Dickson Terry, *The Stark Story* (St. Louis: Missouri Historical Society, 1966), p. 32.

Chapter Eight

1. E. J. Wickson, *California Nurserymen and the Plant Industry: 1850–1910* (Los Angeles: The California Association of Nurserymen, 1921).

2. Donald F. Jones, "The Life and Work of Luther Burbank," unpublished manuscript, quoted by permission of the Connecticut Agricultural Experiment Station, p. 63.

3. *Ibid.,* p. 113.

4. W. L. Howard, *Luther Burbank's Plant Contributions,* University of California College of Agriculture, Agricultural Experiment Station, Berkeley, Bulletin no. 691, March 1945.

5. Walter L. Howard, *Luther Burbank: A Victim of Hero Worship,* in *Chronica Botanica* 9, no. 5/6 (Winter 1945–1946): 319.

6. Luther Burbank, *Partner of Nature,* Ed. Wilbur Hall (New York: D. Appleton-Century Co., 1939), p. 169.

7. John Tebbel, *The Media in America* (New York: Thomas Y. Crowell, 1975), p. 265.

Chapter Nine

1. Donald F. Jones, *"The Life and Work of Luther Burbank,"* unpublished manuscript quoted by permission of the Connecticut Agricultural Experiment Station, p. 27.

2. Walter L. Howard, *Luther Burbank's Plant Contributions,* University of California College of Agriculture, Agricultural Experiment Station, Berkeley, Bulletin no. 691, March 1945.

3. Burbank to E. J. Wickson, unpublished letter dated August 20, 1901. This letter and other Wickson correspondence cited in this chapter is to be found in the Wickson papers in the custody of the Library of the University of California at Davis.

4. Edwin G. Conklin, "A Generation's Progress in the Study of Evolution," *Science* 80, no. 2068 (August 17, 1934).

5. Judge S. F. Lieb to E. J. Wickson, October 11, 1901.

6. E. J. Wickson, *Luther Burbank, Man, Methods and Achievements: An Appreciation* (San Francisco: Southern Pacific Company, 1902), pp. 9–11.

7. Jones, *"Life and Work of Luther Burbank,"* p. 29.

8. Burbank to E. J. Wickson, February 14, 1902.

9. *Pacific Rural Press,* July 6, 1901.

10. H. E. V. Pickstone to W. L. Howard, May 18, 1938. In the Bancroft Library, University of California, Berkeley.

11. In early 1942, a friend of Howard's found May Maye living in Santa Barbara "down by the beach in a little shack, desperately poor, half blind" in a room so full of books she could scarcely get the door open. "Despite all the squalor & confusion," he noted, "her head is as clear as a bell." Howard wrote to her, inquiring about the doings of the "Luther Burbank Company" and the "Luther Burbank So-

ciety," and she replied, "I was working for Luther Burbank while he was engaged in his plant experiments, and left there before they had merely begun to talk about them; and so never met the 'Burbank Company,' or the 'Luther Burbank Society' to which you refer. Luther Burbank was an honest man, and any frauds that they got up were not of his doing, and he was more of a victim to them than any of the patrons who lost money, for he lost much more, the work of a lifetime, his faith in the honesty of those who came pretending to help him; and he died a broken hearted man. If you write of Luther Burbank's *work,* there are many places prior to the forming of this dishonest Company where you will find about it; and if you write an authentic life of the man, you will find that too, before he was old, and easily imposed on. His life work was too wonderful to have one in your position put into print these sad things not really Burbank, but the gossip of those who did not understand . . . I return the dollar you enclosed." (March 12, 1942.) Evidently he had sent her the money to pay for her answer.

12. These opinions were offered in response to questionnaires sent out by Howard. As with other Howard correspondence cited, they are to be found in the box of papers he deposited with the Bancroft Library, University of California at Berkeley.

13. Carnegie Institution of Washington, Year Book No. 4, 1905, p. 22.

14. David Fairchild, *The World Was My Garden* (New York: Charles Scribner's Sons, 1939), pp. 264–265. The remark concerning Harwood's book is from a letter to Howard dated January 21, 1938.

Chapter Ten

1. E. J. Wickson, *California Nurserymen and the Plant Industry: 1850–1910* (Los Angeles: The California Association of Nurserymen, 1921).

2. Harry M. Butterfield, *A History of*

Subtropical Fruits and Nuts in California (Berkeley: University of California, Division of Agricultural Sciences, 1963).

3. Henry W. Kruckeberg, *George Christian Roeding 1868–1928: A Tribute* (Los Angeles: The California Association of Nurserymen, 1921).

4. Harwood says $3500, but this conflicts with a memorandum, typed apparently by Burbank himself, a copy of which is in the author's possession.

5. Carnegie Institution of Washington, Year Book No. 5, 1906, p. 24.

6. Paul C. Mangelsdorf, "Hybrid Corn: Its Genetic Basis and Its Significance in Human Affairs," in *Genetics in the 20th Century*, ed. L. C. Dunn, (New York: Macmillan, 1951).

7. Luther Burbank, *Partner of Nature*, ed. Wilbur Hall (New York: D. Appleton-Century Co., 1939), p. 194.

8. George Shull, letter to W. L. Howard, dated February 22, 1940. Other quotations are from the papers of George Harrison Shull in the custody of the American Philosophical Society in Philadelphia and from the records of the Carnegie Institution of Washington, used with permission from those bodies.

9. *Ibid.*

10. W. C. Williams, manuscript reminiscence of Luther Burbank, quoted by permission of the director, the Bancroft Library, University of California, Berkeley.

Chapter Eleven

1. Richard Hofstadter, *Social Darwinism in American Thought* (Boston: Beacon Press, 1944), p. 161.

2. David Starr Jordan, *The Days of a Man,* (Yonkers-on-Hudson: World Book Co., 1922), 2:296.

3. These figures are quoted in a letter dated June 20, 1940, from Dr. F. O. Butler, medical director and superintendent of the Sonoma State Home, who was a prominent spokesman for sterilization, to Walter L. Howard. The sterilization program has technically speaking never been terminated, though sterilization is now controlled by numerous procedural forms, and performed on individual rather than eugenic considerations. The total number of sterilizations in California, performed in state hospitals on the mentally ill and retarded, to date approaches 20,000, but less than 200 of these have been done in the last fifteen years.

4. Hofstadter, *Social Darwinism*, p. 185.

5. *Ibid.*, p. 165.

6. Luther Burbank, *The Training of the Human Plant* (New York: The Century Co., 1907). First published in *Century* 72, no. 1 (May 1906): 127–38.

7. Ernest Braunton, letter to E. J. Wickson, August 28, 1906, in the Library of the University of California at Davis.

8. E. J. Wickson, letter to Ernest Braunton, September 9, 1906, in the Library of the University of California at Davis.

9. E. J. Wickson, *Luther Burbank, Man, Methods and Achievements: An Appreciation,* (San Francisco: Southern Pacific Company, 1902), p. 15.

10. Patrick O'Mara, "Luther Burbank, A Short Review of His Work in Plant Hybridization and Brief Comparison with Other Hybridizers," *Florist's Exchange*, October 20, 1906.

Chapter Twelve

1. W. E. Castle, "The Beginnings of Mendelism in America," in *Genetics in the 20th Century*, ed. L. C. Dunn (New York: Macmillan, 1951), p. 65.

2. Charles B. Heiser, Jr., *Nightshades: The Paradoxical Plants* (San Francisco: W. H. Freeman & Co., 1969), pp. 62–105.

3. Van B. Boddie of Greenville, Mississippi, letter to the *Rural New Yorker* dated September 9, 1909, in the Wickson papers, Library of the University of California at Davis.

4. H. W. Collingwood, letter to Professor E. J. Wickson dated September 14, 1909, in the Wickson papers, Library of the University of California at Davis.

5. Heiser, *Nightshades*, p. 105.

6. San Francisco *Chronicle,* August 10, 1909.

7. David Starr Jordan and Vernon Kellogg, *The Scientific Aspects of Luther Burbank's Work,* (San Francisco: A. M. Robertson, 1909).

8. Oscar E. Binner, letter to Professor E. J. Wickson dated December 21, 1911, in the Wickson papers, Library of the University of California at Davis, along with other related correspondence referred to in this chapter.

Chapter Thirteen

1. W. L. Howard, interview with Fred Suelberger, June 10, 1941.

2. *Luther Burbank, His Methods and Discoveries and Their Practical Application,* ed. Henry Smith Williams (Santa Rosa: Luther Burbank Press, 1915), 12:254.

3. George Shull, letter to W. L. Howard, November 25, 1939.

4. Ralph B. Howe, letter to W. L. Howard, March 2, 1938.

Chapter Fourteen

1. George Shull, letter to W. L. Howard, November 25, 1939.

2. T. D. Lysenko, *Heredity and Its Variability* (Moscow: Foreign Languages Publishing House, 1953), p. 94.

3. N. I. Vavilov, *The Origin, Variation, Immunity and Breeding of Cultivated Plants* (New York: The Ronald Press, 1951).

4. Paramahansa Yogananda, *Autobiography of a Yogi* (Los Angeles: Self-Realization Fellowship, 1973), p. 411.

5. *Ibid.,* p. 415.

Chapter Fifteen

1. Burbank's lifelong temperance was a byword. Frank P. Doyle, the Santa Rosa banker, recalled a trial in which Burbank was called for jury duty. "The case lasted for several days. Out of hours the jurors were allowed considerable freedom. For convenience in eating, sleeping, and walk-

ing for exercise, the men were paired off. Burbank's partner liked his drink, so when out walking they were apt to stop at a saloon. Burbank always refused to take anything except on one occasion when he swallowed a thimbleful or two. They then returned to their rooms where Luther proceeded to turn handsprings in his pajamas. His companions wondered what he would have done if he had had a real drink." (Interview with W. L. Howard, August 7, 1940.)

2. Ada Kyle Lynch, *Luther Burbank, Plant Lover and Citizen; with Musical Numbers,* (San Francisco: Harr Wagner Publishing Co., 1924).

3. San Francisco *Examiner,* January 27, 1925.

4. An alternative version of this incident was given by Frank Piazzi, writing in *Coronet* in May 1937 (pp. 170–72). According to Piazzi *he* was the reporter who asked the fatal question on behalf of the Oakland *Post-Enquirer.* His account of the matter, titled "Murder by Print," is in the nature of a confessional and seems to me a little suspect.

5. Frederick W. Clampett, *Luther Burbank, "Our Beloved Infidel"* (New York: Macmillan, 1926), p. 36.

6. Olive Schreiner, *The Story of an African Farm* (London: Chapman & Hall, 1883).

7. The Elberta peach was originated by Samuel H. Rumph of Marshallville, Georgia, around 1870. It was a seedling of a Chinese cling peach, the pollen parent being presumed to be an Early Crawford. This July Elberta was introduced by Stark Brothers after Burbank's death, and was apparently a selected seedling from the Sebastopol orchard.

8. Thomas G. Sexton, national sales manager, Stark Brothers Nurseries & Orchards Co., letter to the author, October 16, 1974.

9. Jerry Foytik, *California Plums: Economic Situation, 1968,* California Agricultural Experiment Station, Giannini Foundation Research Report no. 295, April 1968, pp. 5–6, *passim.*

Chapter Sixteen

1. Orland E. White, letter to W. L. Howard, December 21, 1938.

2. *The Eddy Tree Breeding Station: Institute of Forest Genetics.* Interviews conducted by Lois C. Stone, sponsored by the Forest History Society, Regional Oral History Office, University of California, Berkeley, 1974.

3. Dickson Terry, *The Stark Story* (St. Louis: Missouri Historical Society, 1966), pp. 84–87.

4. Edgar Anderson, *Plants, Man & Life* (Berkeley: University of California Press, 1971), p. 81.

5. C. D. Darlington, "The Retreat from Science in Soviet Russia," in *Death of a Science in Russia,* ed. Conway Zirkle (Philadelphia: University of Pennsylvania Press, 1949), pp. 70–71.

6. H. J. Muller, "Genetics in Relation to Modern Science," in *Death of a Science in Russia,* p. 93.

7. Darlington, "The Retreat from Science in Soviet Russia,"p. 74.

8. Luther Burbank to J. H. Empson, letter dated February 29, 1908; J. H. Empson to George Shull, letters dated September 21 and 27, 1910, and April 16, 1914.

9. Donald F. Jones, *"The Life and Work of Luther Burbank,"* unpublished manuscript, quoted by permission of the Connecticut Agricultural Experiment Station, pp. 51–52.

10. Walter L. Howard, *Luther Burbank: A Victim of Hero Worship* in *Chronica Botanica* 9, no. 5/6 (Winter 1945–1946): p. 476. This author states that "A letter from the company, dated March 31, 1943, verifies the foregoing statements and adds that they have grown from 1,500 to 2,000 acres of the peas, annually, since 1908." Jones, on the other hand, refers to a letter from the Kuner-Empson Company of Brighton, Colorado, dated February 28, 1928, saying, "The Empson Packing Company, which this company succeeded, formerly used a Burbank type of pea seed, but discontinued its use a number of years ago, having found it unsatisfactory for canning purposes." The internal evidence leads me to believe, on no very firm grounds, that Jones may have been more accurately informed here. In any case, however, the Burbank Admiral would appear to have been grown for at least a decade after its introduction.

11. Enos E. Witmer, "Interpretation of Quantum Mechanics and the Future of Physics," *American Journal of Physics* 35 (1967): 46.

12. *Ibid.,* pp. 49–50.

13. Lennard Bickel, *Facing Starvation: Norman Borlaug and the Fight Against Hunger* (New York: Reader's Digest Press, 1974), p. 10.

Index

Abrams, Dr. Leroy, 221, 222, 235–36, 241
Acquired characteristics, 30–32, 167, 209–10, 212, 265. *See also* Heredity
Adams, Henry, 39–40, 59, 60
Adlum, John, 50
African "stubble berry," 299
Agassiz, Louis, 71, 75 ff., 115
Agriculture, 35–36, 40–53, 286–87
Agriculture, Department of. *See* U.S. Department of Agriculture
Aiken, Charles Sedgwick, 170
Alcotts, the, 71
Alexander, W. B., 188
Allen, John Fisk, 51
Allometry, 31
Allotetraploid hybrid. *See* Amphidiploid hybrid
Almond, 22, 114–15, 139, 184
Amaryllis, 153, 259
American Association for the Advancement of Science, 71
American Association of Nurserymen, 282
American Breeders' Association, 175, 208–9, 296

American Journal of Physics, 291
American Pomological Society, 134, 152
Americas
  agriculture, 48–53
  plants of, 42, 48–49
Ames Plow Works, Worcester, 75, 80
Amoore, J. E., 120
Amphidiploid hybrid, 136–37, 137 ff., 171, 226, 295–96
Anderson, Dr. D. B., 128
Anderson, Edgar, 284
Animal domestication, 43, 45, 131
"Another Mode of Species Forming" (Burbank), 175, 225, 295–300
Apples, 18, 41, 73–74, 119; LB hybrids, 139, 140
Apricots, 139; Rutland plumcot, 179–80
Aristotle, 274
Arrhenius, Svante, 19
Artichokes, Jerusalem, 49
Atavism. *See* Mendelian principles of heredity
Augustine, Archibald, 282
Austin, Lloyd, 281
Austrian Natural History Society, 86

309